Spinoza and Other Heretics

THE ADVENTURES OF IMMANENCE

Spinoza and Other Heretics

THE ADVENTURES

OF IMMANENCE

★★

YIRMIYAHU YOVEL

PRINCETON UNIVERSITY PRESS

Published by Princeton University Press, 41 William Street,
Princeton, New Jersey 08540
In the United Kingdom: Princeton University Press,
Guildford, Surrey

Library of Congress Cataloging-in-Publication Data
Yovel, Yirmiahu.
Spinoza and other heretics.
Includes bibliographies and indexes.
Contents: v. 1. The Marrano of reason — v. 2 The adventures of immanence.
1. Spinoza, Benedictus de, 1632–1677. 2. Marranos. 3. Immanence (Philosophy)—
History—17th century.
I. Title.
B3998.Y67   1988   199'.492   88-28931
ISBN 0-691-07344-9 (v. 1 : alk. paper)
ISBN 0-691-07346-5 (v. 2 : alk. paper)

Publication of this book has been aided by a grant from the
Whitney Darrow Fund of Princeton University Press

This book has been composed in Linotron Bembo

Printed in the United States of America by
Princeton University Press,
Princeton, New Jersey

Acknowledgment is gratefully made to Dover Publications, Inc. for permission to
quote from *The Chief Works of Benedict de Spinoza*, tr. R.H.M. Elwes (1951); Random
House, Inc. for quotes from *Basic Writings of Nietzsche* (1968) and Nietzsche, *The Gay
Science* (1974), tr. Walter Kaufmann; The Viking Press for quotes from *The Portable
Nietzsche* (1965), tr. and ed. Walter Kaufmann and Nietzsche, *The Will to Power* (1967),
tr. and ed. Walter Kaufmann; Loyd D. Easton and Kurt H. Guddat (ed. and tr.) for
quotes from the *Writings of the Young Marx on Philosophy and Society* (New York:
Doubleday, 1967); Sigmund Freud Copyrights Ltd., The Institute of Psychoanalysis,
The Hogarth Press, and W. W. Norton & Co., Inc., for quotes from *The Standard
Edition of the Complete Psychological Works of Sigmund Freud*, tr. and ed. James Strachey;
Suhrkamp Publishers New York, Inc. for quotes from *Germany: A Winder's Tale* in
The Complete Poems of Heinrich Heine, tr. Hal Draper, copyright by Hal Draper (1982),
used with permission of Suhrkamp Publishers New York, Inc., Harper and Row,
Publishers, Inc. for quotes from Kant, *Religion Within the Limits of Reason Alone*, tr.
T.M. Greene and H. H. Hudson (1960). "Spinoza," by Jorges Luis Borges and
translated from the Spanish by Yirmiyahu Yovel, is published by arrangement with the
Estate of Jorge Luis Borges. All rights reserved.

For Ronny

Spinoza

The Jew's translucent hands
Shape the crystals in the twilight.
And the dying evening is all fear and chill.
(In the evenings, evenings are the same).
His hands and the hyacinth's space
Paling at the purview of the ghetto
Are almost inexistent for the quiet man
Dreaming a clear labyrinth.
Fame does not perturb him, that reflection
Of dreams in another kind of dream,
Nor the girls' fearful love.
Free of metaphor, free of myth
He shapes a rigid crystal: the infinite
Map of the One that is All Its stars.

—Jorge Luis Borges
translated by Yirmiyahu Yovel

Contents

(vii)

Preface

This book is the sequel to *Spinoza and Other Heretics: The Marrano of Reason*, and is also an independent work in itself. What connects the two volumes is the philosophical revolution generated by Baruch Spinoza and its underlying principle, which I call "the philosophy of immanence." This principle views this-worldly existence as the only actual being, and the unique source of ethical value and political authority. All being is this-worldly and there is nothing beyond it, neither a personal creator-God who imposes His divine will on man, nor supernatural powers or values of any kind. The laws of morality and politics, too, and even religion, stem from the this world by the natural power of reason; and recognizing this is the prelude and precondition for human emancipation.

As such, the idea of immanence challenges the major premise of Judaism and Christianity (and Islam), and is closely related to naturalism and secularization. Spinoza's philosophical revolution had given this idea its most powerful and systematic expression in the history of philosophy, whereby it served as a paradigm for its later modern varieties. But Spinoza did not draw this idea from the void. His being an ex-Marrano was an important factor.

The first book, *The Marrano of Reason*, identified the origins of the idea of immanence in the undercurrents of the Marrano culture, the group from which Spinoza sprang. Marranos were former Jews in Spain and Portugal who had been forcibly converted to Christianity. For generations, however, many of them maintained crypto-Jewish life in secret, an experience that produced many dualities, such as an opposition between the inner and outer life, and a mixture of the two religions that, in certain cases, led to the breakdown of both Christian and Jewish beliefs. It also made the mask, including *linguistic* masks—equivocation and dual language—into a life-necessity.

In *The Marrano of Reason*, I analyzed the Marrano experience and identified several characteristic patterns in it that also recur in Spinoza's case, although they are translated into a new, secular and rationalistic context. These Marrano patterns include a this-worldly disposition, a split religious identity, metaphysical skepticism, a quest for alternative ways to salvation that oppose the official doctrine, an opposition between inner belief and the outer world, and a gift for dual language and equivocation. By closely examining other cases of Marrano intellectuals—both among Spinoza's contemporaries and in the early phases of Marranism—I show the recurrent nature of these patterns and how they reappear in Spinoza as well, while they are being transformed from transcendent historical religion into the world of reason and immanence. Hence my calling Spinoza *The Marrano of Reason*.

The present book—*The Adventures of Immanence*—will take a different path and follow the adventures of the philosophy of immanence after Spinoza, in the work of later thinkers who helped shape the Western mind.

Spinoza's immanent revolution was as slow in leaving its mark on future thought as its principle was radical. For over a century after his death, Spinoza was excluded from respectable circles, either abhorred or ignored, and usually more gossiped about than read. His influence, though already penetrating, remained marginal and half-underground.[*] What made his case particularly embarrassing was the combination of an intolerably heretical philosophy and a virtuous, almost saintly life—as Spinoza's existence, with evident idealization, has often been perceived, even by many of his foes. To the conventional mind, the idea of a "virtuous atheist" was a shocking scandal and a contradiction in terms. A person with Spinoza's views could never lead a life of serene virtue, and yet this was reported to have been a fact—irksome, unsettling, and potentially subversive to the vested beliefs of Christian Europe.

It was only in late eighteenth century Germany that Spinoza emerged into prominence, both among poet-philosophers like Goethe, Lessing, and later, Heine, and within the major trends of post-Kantian philosophy from Fichte to Hegel and beyond. Today Spinoza is considered, and studied, as a classic of modern philosophy along with Descartes, Hume, and Kant. Yet even in recognition, Spinoza fundamentally remains an outsider; his theories have never become part of a philosophical establishment and have continued attracting

---

[*] For a thorough discussion of his impact in France, see P. Vernière, *Spinoza et la pensée française avant la Révolution* (Paris: PUF, 1954, 1982).

nonphilosophers. It is characteristic of Spinoza that he is as important in nonprofessional philosophizing as he is in academia. Equally, it is no accident that some of the most unorthodox and innovative minds in the last two centuries (Goethe, Marx, Nietzsche, Freud, Einstein, and others) have either been what we may call root-Spinozists, or operated, as Freud defined it, within Spinoza's "climate of ideas."

What they shared with Spinoza was more, however, than an intellectual climate. It was a common systematic context: (1) immanence is the only and overall horizon of being; (2) it is equally the only source of value and normativeness and (3) absorbing this recognition into one's life is a prelude—and precondition—for whatever liberation (or, emancipation) is in store for humans.

Within this nuclear context, one can still argue about the adequate way to construe the world of immanence. For example (1) Is it Nature, as in Spinoza, or rather Spirit, History, *Wille*, or any other such metaphysical construction? (2) Should it be individuated as a single, infinite totality? (3) Should it also be deified? (4) What *structure* applies to it: mechanical causality, organic purposiveness, dialectical logic—or a much more fluid and flexible model? (5) Does it have this structure eternally? Is our Spinozistic quest for fixed, eternal laws well-founded, or rather a prephilosophical bias, perhaps the vestige of theological thinking? (6) Should the human being (either as subject, or as a natural species) be assigned a special position within the world of immanence? If so, in what capacity? And how is the role of human history affected by answering the former question? Finally, (7) Should human liberation (which presupposes the immanent revolution) translate the religious view of salvation into an equally absolute secular eschatology, or should it (by its very secularity) be confined to a humbler vision, restrained by critical boundaries?

These questions and alternatives will emerge as we follow the adventures of the idea of immanence in some of the major thinkers who left their mark on modern culture. We shall see each of them evolving his own alternative version in response to the flaws he was bound to find either in Spinoza's original model or in rival varieties of it, thus taking part in a tacit multiple debate. In the end, *The Adventures of Immanence* tells a conceptual story, and thereby also draws a map of *logical possibilities* of construing a philosophy of immanence, as they have actually emerged in the course of history. In addition, I hope this approach can offer fresh views of the individual thinkers under discussion, as seen from the perspective of this common Spinozistic problem.

The Epilogue is a philosophical essay in which I use the contours of the preceding map to draw a distinction between a dogmatic and a critical philosophy of immanence, arguing that the latter must also be a philosophy of *finitude*. While my conclusion is frequently critical of Spinoza, I hope it will show that he can still be read as a vital and relevant intellectual challenge today, just as the preceding chapters show that his presence in modern thought is far more pervasive than most people suspect.

Selections are always somewhat arbitrary, and mine is no exception. I include Heine because he is simply irresistible, and prefer Hegel to Fichte and Schelling, and Nietzsche to Schopenhauer, because their impact on contemporary thought is greater and their models of immanence are more strongly defined. But I readily admit that the list can be expanded (and will only welcome such attempts).

A final word about my choice of terms. I think the concept of a philosophy of immanence is more fundamental, and therefore more apt to convey Spinoza's basic idea, than the more current terms "pantheism" or even "naturalism." Pantheism is but a specific variety of the philosophy of immanence. (Of the cases we shall discuss, only Hegel and Spinoza show pantheistic leanings, whereas all the others— notably Marx, Nietzsche and Freud—reject the deification of immanent being as an illusion). As for "naturalism," this term as currently used will hardly convey the complex view Spinoza has of nature as a mental and logical entity no less than a physical one. More important, "naturalism" is both too broad and too restrictive; it may well include the deist's belief in a transcendent God who had created nature and then let it run by its natural laws alone—a profoundly un-Spinozistic view; on the other hand, it will exclude such unmistakable Spinozistic disciples as Hegel and Marx: Hegel because he views immanent reality not as nature merely but as its *Aufhebung* by history and Spirit, and Marx because his concrete reality is *humanized* nature (history again) and not nature in a "raw" or physicalistic sense.

Using the concept of a philosophy of immanence will avoid such paradoxes and will be better suited, I think, to capture the *fundamental* Spinozistic idea that other philosophers have adapted or reinterpreted. As for the word "heretics," it should be taken with a grain of ironic salt. I use it to designate thinkers who, when properly understood, must be deemed heretical in terms of their *own* orthodox tradition. Almost every orthodoxy denounces heretics, which does not mean it has truth on its side. Denying superstition or false authorities is also often called heresy. The Marranos were considered heretics by the Inquisition, and the Protestants were considered heretics by the Pope.

Therefore, I use this term with no derogatory undertones; if anything, a reader discerning a shade of sympathy in the title will not be totally mistaken.

Earlier versions of some of the following chapters have appeared in print as follows: "Bible Interpretation as Philosophical Praxis: A Study of Spinoza and Kant," *Journal of the History of Philosophy* 11 (1973): 189–212; "Substance without Spirit: On Hegel's Critique of Spinoza," in *Spinoza–His Thought and Work*, ed. N. Rotenstreich and N. Schneider (Jerusalem: The Isreal Academy of Sciences and Humanities, 1983), pp. 71–84; "Heinrich Heine and the Message of Pantheism," *Jerusalem Quarterly* 35 (1985): 101–11; "Nietzsche and Spinoza: *amor fati* and *amor dei*," in *Nietzsche as Affirmative Thinker*, ed. Y. Yovel (Dordrecht: Nijhoff, 1986), pp. 183–203.

In the Preface to *The Marrano of Reason*, I thanked those who in various ways have helped with the two-volume work. Here I would like to mention (and thank) again, besides my students, friends and colleagues whose contribution related specifically to the present volume. They include my friends Alexandre Matheron, Sylvain Zac, Pierre Macheray, Pierre-François Moreau, Yvon Belaval, Jean Marie Beyssade, Etienne Balibar and many others in the *Association des Amis de Spinoza*. Raymond Polin, Janine Chanteur and Geneviève Rodis-Lewis have made my two-year visiting professorship at the Sorbonne even more worthwhile, as has Jean-Luc Marion. In the United States, Edwin Curley, Alan Donagan, Margaret Wilson and George Klein have made pertinent comments on my Spinoza interpretation, as have Emilia Giancotti and Filippo Mignini in Italy, Manfred Walther in Germany, Wim Klever and the late Hubertus Hubbeling in the Netherlands. In Israel, Elhanan Yakira, my former assistant and present colleague, provided much help in the early stages of this study. The text and notes were diligently typed by Florence Da Costa. Above all, I am thankful to my longtime collaborator and friend Eva Shorr, Managing Editor of the Philosophical Quarterly *Iyyun*, for investing as much of her competence and devotion in this work as she has in many of my earlier publications.

Last and dearly, my friend Yizhak Torchin, a physician-philosopher in the style of Spinoza's times, and his elegant wife Suzanne, have welcomed me to their country house in Barbizon, France, with its gracious surroundings and its library well stocked in Spinozana, where I worked my way through several chapters of this book. To both of them, *merci encore de tout mon cœur*.

Note on Sources

Bibliographical references are given in the endnotes to each chapter. When possible, the more accessible editions were used.

Translations from non-English documents, when not otherwise indicated, were made by the author.

The standard edition of Spinoza's work to date is *Spinoza Opera*, edited by Carl Gebhardt (Heidelberg: Carl Winter, 1925). For the English version I used *The Collected Works of Spinoza*, vol. 1, edited and translated by Edwin Curley (Princeton: Princeton University Press, 1985). To quote from the *Theologico-Political Treatise* (due to appear in Curley's vol. 2), I used the translation of R. H. Elwes in *The Chief Works of Benedict de Spinoza*, 2 vols. (New York: Dover, 1951), vol. 2.

Short titles and abbreviations used include:

Treatise on the Intellect	*Treatise on the Emendation of the Intellect* (quoted by section number).
Short Treatise	*Short Treatise on God, Man and His Well-Being* (quoted by part and chapter numbers).
TTP	*Theologico-Political Treatise* (quoted by Elwes's page numbers).
Metaphysical Thoughts	*Appendix Containing Metaphysical Thoughts* (quoted by Curley's page numbers).
Ethics	*Ethics Demonstrated in Geometrical Order*.

The following abbreviations apply to the *Ethics*: pt. = part; prop. = proposition; S = scholium; dem. = demonstration; exp. = explanation; ax. = axiom; def. = definition; C = corollary

Spinoza and Other Heretics

THE ADVENTURES OF IMMANENCE

Spinoza and Kant:
Critique of Religion and
Biblical Hermeneutics

BIBILICAL INTERPRETATION AS PREPARATION FOR PHILOSOPHY

Let us imagine that a religious fanatic had stolen Spinoza's post-humous papers before they were published, in order to save the world and posterity from a dangerous heretic. In this unfortunate case we would have lost the *Ethics*,[1] and Spinoza would have remained a marginal figure in the history of philosophy.

Still, Spinoza would even then have retained his absolutely central place in the history of another discipline—biblical criticism—for what he says on this subject in the *Theologico-Political Treatise* is sufficient to ensure that place. Spinoza's contribution to biblical criticism is thus independent of his contribution to general philosophy, and could be discussed with little regard to it.

And yet, from Spinoza's own viewpoint, the two are intimately connected. His biblical hermeneutics is not only an independent science in itself; it is also—and primarily—a weapon in combating historical religion and a vehicle in constructing a purified substitute for it.

For Spinoza, the historical religions (above all, Judaism and Christianity) are the greatest obstacles to clear philosophical knowledge and the emergence of the principle of immanence. The counter-rational force that Descartes attributed to "prejudice" and tradition in general, as the veil blurring the natural light of reason, Spinoza, in a more daring and radical move, attributes specifically to the historical religions, their dogmas, images, and entrenched beliefs. Therefore, prior to any positive philosophy of immanence, a critique of these religions must be undertaken, in order to clear the mind of transcendent images and to prepare the ground for its awakening (or enlightenment) to the call of immanent reason. In other words, confusion and skepticism about historical religion are necessary prerequisites for attaining true knowledge and, through it, a worthwhile life and even salvation.

Spinoza as an individual had the benefit of his Marrano background which helped him leap outside Judaism and Christianity alike and become what we called in volume 1 "a Marrano of reason." But this uncommon, special background cannot serve as a general paradigm—nor did Spinoza wish to remain secluded like a Marrano in his inner philosophy while the rest of the world opposed and even abhored it. Unlike former Marrano heretics described in volume 1, Spinoza did not regard his rationalist philosophy as a private affair. What makes him a thinker of modernity are not his views alone, but his desire to universalize his message and to make it the basis for a new cultural and social universe, based upon reason, secularization, mechanical science, social tolerance, and political freedom, and thus opposing the medieval world in its most essential aspects. For this purpose Spinoza needed a cultural power that would purge religious *superstitio* from the minds not of an esoteric minority but of the *multitude*—a category that gains in Spinoza philosophical status in and of itself. This power Spinoza finds in the critique of religion and its attending biblical hermeneutics.

Socrates had also sought a means by which to purify the soul of prejudice; he found it in a self-defeating sophistry, leading through paradoxes and *aporias* to fertile confusion. Descartes, two millenia later, in proclaiming a new philosophical beginning, sought to achieve this purification by a single, powerful act of the will, which turns against itself and abstains from all judgment where no rational certainty (based upon evident truths) is available. Descartes hoped thereby to sweep away the whole burden of tradition in a single stroke, preparing the mind, as a kind of tabula rasa, to experience the inner revelation of the "natural light" and its rationally clear and distinct ideas.

Whether Descartes was a thorough Cartesian himself, or whether he remained compromising and conventional on religious matters, is an open question. In any case, Spinoza must reject the Cartesian "preparation for philosophy" as inadequate, since the free act of will on which Descartes relies is to Spinoza a metaphysical illusion. There is no free will; nor is there a special faculty of judgment capable of denying or affirming our ideas as a separate act, or able to abstain from passing such judgment by its own choice. For Spinoza, judgment is an integral part of the act of ideation, not a second act added to it (*Ethics*, pt. 2, prop. 49s). We judge as we perceive (or conceive); more precisely, we cannot have an idea without automatically affirming the existence of its object and of the properties it represents as belonging to this object.

Negation, too, results from the affirmative power of a *new* idea that is incongruent with the first and thus replaces it. This occurs in every cognitive process: when a true idea corrects a false one; when a new superstition replaces an old one; and also when the mind vacillates back and forth in a state of doubt and confusion, which can help destroy entrenched beliefs and clear the way for philosophy. Whatever attitudes we have, whatever happens to us intellectually, does not depend on an illusory "will" but on causal chains of ideas that affect and modify our minds in a law-governed way.★

It is within this causal process that Spinoza wishes to interefere, using a proper dosage of truth and metaphor. His critique of religion is, as we shall see, a combination of philosophical knowledge and rhetoric. Based on clear and distinct ideas, it frequently couches them in metaphor, popular language, and dialectical strategems—and uses the idiom and authority of tradition as a lever to uproot this very authority. The role of the critique of religion and biblical hermeneutics is thus to perform in the multitude the same, or similar, effects that Spinoza drew from his former Marrano background and that Descartes sought in vain to produce by a one-time purifying act of the will.

CLEARING THE PATH OF THE "TRUE IDEA": THE PROBLEM OF METHOD

Spinoza at first tried to follow in Descartes' footsteps. In his first work, the *Treatise on the Intellect*, he set out to write his own "essay on method" that was to precede his substantive philosophy. But even as he wrote it he found that the project was impossible and self-defeating. Method, Spinoza discovered, is reflective knowledge: it is "the idea of an idea." As such, it presupposes a basic, substantive idea upon which to reflect. A theory of knowledge (or of method) cannot be formed purely a priori. To know what valid knowledge is, and to frame a strategy for gaining and expanding it, we must already have in our possession some true substantive knowledge, which we then investigate for its typical features and conditions. We must, in Spinoza's words, start already with an *idea vera* (true idea) in order to know what having such an idea entails.

To fulfill its role, moreover, the first *idea vera* cannot rely on an external sign of truth, but must contain its own justification within itself. This calls to mind the self-evidence of the Cartesian "clear and distinct

---

★ By "causal" Spinoza refers both to psychological causes and to logical reason; this pertains to his assimilation of causes and reasons generally.

ideas" (to which Spinoza also subscribes). But not any of them will do. The basic true idea of Spinoza makes sense only if its object is the ontic cause of itself, that is, the totality of the universe taken as God. We start with the recognition that God is identical with all there is, and is thus the single substance in existence—necessary, self-caused and eternal, encompassing all the aspects and dimensions of reality, including matter and mind, extension and thought, finite and infinite, and the like. From here the rest of the system, and all the specific ideas in the universe, are to follow as the *internal* explication of the comprehensive first idea.

That Spinoza's *idea vera* should be so novel and revolutionary presents a problem. If this idea is inherently self-evident, why was humanity so slow in recognizing it, and why does it continue to generate so much hostility? Spinoza, who unlike Kant or Hegel does not have a theory of the historical growth of rationality, and who unlike Freud lacks a theory of repression and resistance, again appeals to his pervasive category of religious *superstitio*. What stands in the way of the true idea—and makes it look revolutionary—is the enormous bulk of revealed religion with its false images of the deity, nurtured in the imagination by fear and ignorance of true causes, refined into theistic theology and transmitted through generations by education and language. Consequently, the inherent self-evidence of the *idea vera* cannot assert itself in actual consciousness unless a critique of religious superstition is first proffered, not only as a pure logical argument but as a social and cultural power as well.

KANT AND HUMANISTIC IMMANENCE

In this context, the name of Kant comes to mind as a companion and counterpart to Spinoza. Despite their otherwise great differences, here they meet on common ground. Both use the critique of religion to purify the mind of false images and to eliminate the social and institutional obstacles built upon them. Moreover, both use biblical hermeneutics to divert their audience's transcendent dispositions toward an immanent religion of reason.

Kant, however, in spite of his radical critique of religion, cannot be called a philosopher of immanence without qualification. In respect to knowledge Kant takes the position of *critical* immanence, and in ethics he ends up in a transcendent position that opposes an Is/Ought dualism to Spinoza's naturalism. Yet Kant remains attached to the principle of immanence in what counts most; for in establishing the *foundations* of the natural and the moral world he allows no appeal to a power or authority over and above man. No Creator-God is necessary to explain the work of nature, and no Divine Legislator is allowed to prescribe the laws of morality. Religion itself must exclude the idea of God from its foundations and be grounded exclusively in the autonomy of the rational human will. Nor is there room other than rhetorical (to educate the multitude) for revelation, the Law of Moses, or the love and passion of Christ. The human mind itself, when exercising its rationally structured spontaneity, prescribes the basic laws of morality and religion to itself, just as it legislates the universal and necessary lawlike patterns that nature itself obeys.

Kant's Copernican revolution establishes a humanistic philosophy of immanence. (Perceiving this, Heine, as we shall see, improperly called it "pantheism.") It places man at the center of being and grounds all significant domains of reality in his free rational powers. And it is equally a theory of emancipation, since it frees man from self-enslavement by false transcendent images, and puts him, as Kant says, under his own "tutelage," the judge, master, and educator of himself and the critical (hence limited) measure of all things around him.

At the same time, Kant conceives of reason as external to nature (including nature within man), a foreign power that has to impose its laws upon nature from without. Reason cannot be construed as part of the actual world but constitutes a second, separate world over and above it, with man participating as "citizen" in both. This is a vestige of the old Christian dualism, translating into secular terms the notion of man being endowed with a divine faculty emanating from heaven. It is also where Kant breaks with a strict philosophy of immanence, which requires that all normativity, all source of binding value be anchored within the actual world. This is an offshoot of the same dualism which, all along, has given Kant his gravest inner problems; its recurrence here is neither special nor particularly intentional.

Kant's qualified philosophy of immanence is thereby both human-centered and anti-naturalistic, two features Kant passed on to Hegel and which I shall discuss in the next chapter. Kant, too, seeks to destroy historical religion and to build his rational ethics and metaphysics upon its ruins. The critique of reason is also, for Kant, its declaration of independence. Despite its finitude—and also because of it—human reason takes over the role of God as legislator for both nature and morality. Unable to prove or disprove the existence of God (and other major theological claims), human reason assumes this finitude as a binding norm, forbidding itself to rely upon external authorities and reaffirming its power to produce of itself, as the explication of its own inherent structure, the metaphysical features of natural objects and the fundamental moral commands.

Kant views the *finitude* of human reason and its *autonomous* power as two complementary sides of the same critique of reason. It is as "transcendental Ego" that the human mind—not God—determines the metaphysical substrate of nature, that is, the system of categories and logical-synthetic laws that make its objects possible. And it is as rational will that, again, human reason (and not divine legislation) lays down the supreme laws of ethics as well as the ultimate goals of politics and of moral history. The entire domain of morality, with its absolute worth and awe-inspiring sublimity, is based not upon the will of a transcendent God whose existence cannot be known and must not be presupposed, but upon the will of man, expressed as universal practical reason whose inherent laws it explicates and obeys. Even religion— Kant's "religion of reason"—consists in viewing the inherrent commands of human reason as divine. Kant thereby secularizes the historical concept of divinity, and equally sacralizes his own humanistic morality. Throughout his book on religion, Kant reduces religious feelings, motifs, and symbols to a purely moral-secular context. Even his famous moral argument for God's existence has a purely humanistic function.[2] Not only is the concept of God derived from morality; it also tells us nothing about God, only about human powers and about a *moral teleology* underlying the universe. When the moral argument has been completed, all we are entitled to believe is that humans have the capacity to transform the existing world into the "highest good"— a moral-historical ideal projected as a duty by the rational will. But both the duty and the capacity are ours—and of God we know at the end just as much as we knew at the beginning, namely, nothing.

All this would not make of Kant the deicide Heine declared him to be (see chap. 3), but would surely place him among the religious heretics of the Enlightenment whom Spinoza foretold. Kant's attack on historical religion is, indeed, as fierce as Spinoza's in both content and style. Some of his derogatory expressions border on colloquialism (*Pfaffentum*), even vulgarity (*Afterdienst*, "bottom-worship"). His description of Judaism, Catholicism, the Byzantine Church, and the wars of religion following the Reformation are full of repudiation and moral indignation, sometimes injected with sarcastic venom. Kant's dual language and persuasive metaphors do not attenuate the feeling that, in addition to pure philosophy, the aging Kant is also getting even with the perpetrators of what he once called his "youthful slavery" in the pietist school he had attended as a child. In those early days, reading of the Romans, including Lucretius, was a consolation; and Lucretius was the great Epicurean critic of religion, setting a model for the tradition that reaches through Spinoza to Kant himself. Small wonder that, decades later, when writing his own critique of religion, Kant uses the old Lucretian exclamation *tantum religio potuit suadere malorum* (such evil deeds could religion prompt).[3]

It is doubtful whether Kant read Spinoza's *Theologico-Political Treatise*. But in all probability, as Julius Guttmann has shown, he was indirectly influenced by Spinoza's ideas—the mediating link being Moses Mendelssohn, Kant's Jewish friend and rival, and his book, *Jerusalem*.[4] Kant adopts and elaborates Spinoza's ideas about the Jews and their ancient state. He contends, like Spinoza (and, unknowingly, like many medieval Jewish rabbis) that the Bible makes no cognitive claims and supplies no knowledge, only a moral lesson; and requires a good deal of historical and philological scholarship in order to put this lesson to actual use. In contrast to Spinoza, Kant subordinates this biblical scholarship to extrinsic moral interests and thus runs into insoluble problems; but in invoking the need for this kind of historical learning, he echoes a revolutionary demand that Spinoza was the first to make.[5]

BIBLICAL HERMENEUTICS AS THE PHILOSOPHER'S MODE OF ACTION

Even assuming with Gebhardt[6] that it was Spinoza who laid the foundation for biblical criticism as an objective, immanent science, it does not follow that Spinoza's own biblical investigations were disinterested. Leo Strauss shows how Spinoza had turned to this particular branch of knowledge with the intent of propagating his new, subversive ideas and of fighting religious authority and practices. Yet Spinoza seems to have believed that, given the actual nature of the Bible and of prophetic inspiration, an objective, scientific approach would prove more detrimental to the Scripture's authority than any biased attack: as if here, too (as in the case of the supreme form of knowledge), rationality was a self-rewarding virtue. This view has inherent difficulties I shall address later; for now, we may conclude that Spinoza saw biblical interpretation also as a means for broader ends.

This conclusion is even clearer in Kant's case. The study of the Bible is for Kant antiquarian and devoid of value unless it serves moral ends and reinforces the will to realize them. As a purely scientific object the Bible is dead; its importance lies in its power to influence. But in its literal sense, the Bible's influence is in most cases perverse, both from the moral and the cognitive viewpoints. Therefore one should in most cases prefer an allegorical interpretation, even at the expense of consciously distorting the original intent of the author. Yet allegorical interpretation is not a rigid rule. In each case, the sole criterion by which to determine the proper interpretation is the moral interest. For Kant, then, biblical exegesis is *only* a means for other ends.

These broader ends concern, in both cases, the philosopher's critique of religion in its search to transform the existing reality. This critique is not a pure science of religion, but equally an instrument of change. The philosopher is not content with knowing, for himself, that miracles or personal providence are ontologically impossible, that *superstitio* is a kind of opiate for the masses, that religion is born from fear and the *imaginatio,* or that suprarational faculties (and their documented offsprings) are in fact inferior to reason. He wants to share this awareness with the multitude, thus purging their lives and institutions from the rule of irrational powers and preparing an emancipated mode of existence. Understanding religion, which is surely part of the process, is not merely academic but is ipso facto liberation from superstitious religion—in which its major purpose lies.

This democratization of reason, this ambition to extend its effects to the masses and to shape human history by it, marks a break with medieval attitudes—a clean break in Kant's case, while Spinoza maintains his reserve. Kant, more utopian, believes that the rational attitude itself can be propagated on a mass historical scale; he is committed to this belief by his view of reason as strictly universal, founded or constituted by human subjects, and by the dichotomy he draws between pure morality or none at all. Spinoza, more sober and spared the either/or Kantian alternative, wishes to propagate the products of rational enlightenment which in themselves are less than fully rational: a reformed popular religion, a more enlightened state, and the like. For Spinoza, pure rationality remains an affair for the minority and, at its height, even esoteric.

While Spinoza and Kant not only overestimated the power of reason, they also recognized the weight of psychological and institutional obstacles. Major obstacles in the way of the critique of religion are belief in the Bible's suprarational authority, in the literal truth of its stories, and in the sacred validity of the vast dogmatic, ritual, and institutional apparatus that grew up around it. To be effective, the critic must have an affinity with the mind of his audience. As long as the public is immersed in *vana religio* no meaningful dialogue is possible, much less a change in attitude, without taking their point of departure also into account. This is where biblical exegesis becomes instrumental, serving as a fictitious common ground between the critic and his audience. Since the believer in revealed religion cannot share the philosopher's first principles, the latter, by appealing to the Bible, must *appear* to share the first principles of the believer while actually turning them against themselves.

This is not to deny that Spinoza's appeal to the Bible had other motivations as well, such as the need for prudence and personal security. Spinoza's works are a masterly example of allusion and dual language, and what Strauss has called "the art of writing within persecution."[7]

Probably to a lesser degree, Kant was also in conflict with officialdom and mindful of his steps. His open conflict with the censorship of Friedrich-Wilhelm II is only one sign of this.[8] It is clear, then, that both Kant and Spinoza used biblical exegesis for personal security: It helps the philosopher delineate the delicate path between faithfulness to his own ideas and apparent faithfulness to the ruling tradition.[9] Yet this is neither the sole nor main function of using the Bible. Even if security considerations had not existed, it is safe to assert that both philosophers would have appealed to the Bible for another reason: reaching out to the masses and subverting their established attitudes. Moreover, prudence does not require (and sometimes should rather discourage) the formation of generalized hermeneutic methods—Kant's being an overt challenge to the pious mind. Even when Spinoza and Kant intend to diminish the unnecessary risks, their preoccupation with the Bible reflects a fundamental resolution to assume the necessary ones. Its defense value is a strategic corollary, coming from the same feature that initially recommended it as an offensive weapon. In this sense biblical hermeneutics is an aggressive activity, offering the philosopher a mode of involvement in the social and cultural processes of his time.

Kant considered the Enlightenment and the free dissemination of ideas as the genuine action of the philosopher, which can affect society and politics no less than the minds of the audience; and Spinoza argued in his *Theologico-Political Treatise* that free philosophical thought is necessary for the strength and stability of the state. Yet both estimated that the process of liberating thought, with its social and political offshoots, could not be historically effective unless it passed through a critique of revealed religion and looked for support in its sacred documents. Seen from this angle, biblical interpretation is not an incidental activity among many others, but a major avenue for the social and practical involvement of the philosopher.

The Aims of the Critique of Religion

No wonder, given this backdrop, that Spinoza and Kant share the fundamental interest of "rationalizing"* the historical religion—translating it out of itself into a rational substitute. But this aim must take a

---

* I use this term in the sense of "rational purification" or secular reform, not of an *ex post facto* justification.

different shape in each case, mainly because, as philosophers, Spinoza and Kant hold different views of rationality, its nature and task.

To grasp Spinoza's intent we must recognize that he speaks of religion in three different senses. In the first and supreme sense religion is identical with the state of existence attained through the "third kind of knowledge" and *amor dei intellectualis* (intellectual love of God), which means that one has achieved true religion.[10] This is the semireligious dimension in Spinoza's thought, the alternative way to salvation offered to the happy few. That Spinoza insists on the word *religion* in this context has the same fundamental reason as his keeping the word *God* (with its sublime and resounding connotations) to denote the totality of the universe. Spinoza indeed suggests a new religion, a supreme metaphysical and mental liberation, a semimystical reunion with God that realizes the infinite within the realm of finitude and, charged with powerful emotion and love, transforms the person as a whole and dominates a wholly new life-course. But this sublime stage is as difficult as it is rare and not a prospect for the multitude. Most men and women cannot be expected to reach true religion at all. For them a different sort of "religion"—a merely social one—must be devised.

Spinoza goes on to discuss a second kind of religion, then, the *religio catholica* ("universal religion," not to be confused with Catholicism though trying to usurp its claim to universality). This popular religion remains within the domain of the *imaginatio*, but tries to shape its effects as an external imitation of *ratio* (reason), using for that purpose the principle of obedience to God, itself a product of the imagination. Here, indeed, the term *God* has a different meaning altogether—a metaphoric, misleading meaning that is used deliberately as such. From the viewpoint of metaphysical truth there is no personal God at all, no divine entity endowed with will and prescribing commands. But the God of the Bible did pronounce commands, or people largely believe he did, and think that they should obey his will. The aim of *religio catholica* is to put these beliefs to good social use, assisted by a proper interpretation of the Bible. The latter is to reduce the imaginary "will of God" to a number of socially beneficial rules: justice, mutual help, and obedience to the laws of the state (which become the authoritative interpreters of the "will of God").

This popular type of religion is purely social and secular; and although it is based upon the lower powers of the *imaginatio*, they no longer produce wild and arbitrary conduct, but are so regulated as to make possible conduct resembling that which is produced by reason.[11]

In the third place there is crude historical religion (*vana religio*) based upon imaginary tales, sacred histories, rituals, and a predominantly political constitution. From ancient paganism to the contingent elements of Judaism and Christianity, all the manifestations of this third form of religion, stem from superstition and are grounded in human fears and passions. Its cognitive claims are explained by a lack of knowledge of true causes, which produce wonder and superstition in the masses and drive them to believe in miracles, final causes, and hidden forces operating in nature. The practical aspects of revealed religion have a basically political character; they are intended to exploit fear and ignorance in the service of the rulers—be they secular or theocratic. This form of religion is particularly repugnant to Spinoza who makes it the target of his severest attacks.

Given this triple distinction we can now define the aims of Spinoza's critique. It is clear he wished the spurious form of religion to be completely abolished. It is equally clear that Spinoza's ultimate wish, at least in theory, was to have all men attain religion in the philosophical sense. This would involve renouncing not only historical religion but also intermediary "universal religion." Yet elevating the masses from *vana religio* to philosophy was, as Spinoza realized, a remote if not hopeless task, so his major efforts were directed to a more realistic end: to neutralize the damaging effects of religion and, while leaving it in the inferior mental domain, to try and make it socially useful. The final outcome would be a religion that provides complete freedom in matters of belief and confines itself to the general (and vague) commands of social justice and mutual help.[12]

The "purification" of historical religion is to be accomplished by reshaping the effects of the imagination (the lower powers of the mind) as an external imitation of reason. There is no intention to pass from superstition to scientific knowledge; religion should rather have no cognitive role whatsoever. Nor is there an intention to pass from the passions and behavior arising from superstition to those actions and positive emotions (*actiones*) whose source is reason. Religion, even purified, remains in the realm of imagination and revelation, and all behavior which religion prompts is motivated not by reason or *scientia intuitiva* but by obedience.

Neither superstition nor philosophy, purified religion is thus a kind of universal popular morality. Historically the idea is not new, but its place in Spinoza's system is noteworthy. Judging by the epistemology of the *Ethics* there is no intermediary link between imagination and reason, or between the first and the second kinds of knowledge.[13] However, in the field of behavior Spinoza does suggest such a bridge. This topic is developed in full only in the *Theologico-Political Treatise*, but its principle can be traced in the *Ethics* as well (pt. 5, prop. 10):

The best thing, then, that we can do, so long as we do not have perfect knowledge of our affects, is to conceive a correct principle of living, or sure maxims of life, *to commit them to memory*, and to apply them constantly to the particular cases frequently encountered in life. *In this way our imagination will be extensively affected by them*, and we shall always have them ready [emphasis added].[14]

This is in essence the same program as that of the *Theologico-Political Treatise*, only without the large-scale historical ambition and, therefore, without having to rely upon the Bible and the power of obedience. In essence, Spinoza's idea here is reminiscent of the Aristotelian *hexis* and lays the ground for using the imagination as an imitation of reason.

Spinoza's program is worked out throughout the *Theologico-Political Treatise*; it provides the link between the "theological" and the "political parts," and gives them systematic continuity. The treatise as a whole deals with the multitude, not the philosopher, and treats it as a philosophical question in itself. What to do about the multitude is the general problem underlying the work and spelled out in both its parts. The general answer is to reshape the cognitive and emotive power governing the multitude—what Spinoza calls *imaginatio*—as an external imitation of *ratio*, using obedience to authority in order to enforce and institutionalize the results.

This program is carried out in two stages, theological and political. First, biblical interpretation reduces the message of Scripture to an embryonic doctrine of universal morality, denying the Bible any cognitive import. This minimal morality—justice and mutual help—is the content of the new "universal religion," which is destined for the multitude, and relies on its respect and obedience to "the Word of God" as incarnated in the Bible. Of course, this is no longer obedience to all the particular and changing demands of the prophets but only to their semi-national nucleus—their "true meaning" as defined by biblical interpretation. Yet the need to rely on a prophetic text produced by imagination, and on obedience to external authority, testify that the *imaginatio* is still in control, although its effects have been transformed: now they have turned against their usual aggressive and divisive nature, to produce socially beneficial results.

The "purified" Bible thus becomes the cornerstone in reshaping the imagination as an imitation of reason. But this also requires a political complement and institutionalization. In themselves, the principles of justice and mutual help are bare and abstract. How are they to be practiced under actual legislation? Who is to apply them to concrete social situations? Spinoza, who recognizes no other authority or normative power than the political, presents an unequivocal answer. The state, the political government, is to become the sole and true "interpreter" of the nuclear moral-religion, to which the message of Scripture has been reduced by biblical hermeneutics.

Kant, too, sought to rationally purify religion, to deny its cognitive import and reduce it to practical principles alone. But Kant's understanding of the nature of rationality is at variance with that of Spinoza.

First, in sharp contrast to Spinoza, Kant *is* interested in raising the purified version of religion to a genuine rational level. Like the rest of the practical sphere, religion is no longer grounded in the imagination but in pure reason, and even enjoys the primacy which Kant assigns to practical reason over the theoretical. In confining religion to the practical field Kant therefore assigns it a role that is rational par excellence. Within the sphere Kant calls "religion," all action is motivated by pure rational imperatives, mixed with no sensual or natural motive. Religion and morality are fundamentally the same, except that religion refers primarily to individuals, while religion links the individual agents into a moral totality (called the "ethical community" or "invisible church") and provides institutional aids ("the visible church") for moral education and the propagation of the ethical community.

Spinoza's use of the biblical hermeneutics as a means to create an external imitation of reason might count, in Kantian terms, as an answer to the problem of schematism (that is, of building a bridge between the rational and the empirical) in the field of action.[15] Spinoza's way also suggests another Kantian concept, "legality," signifying action that conforms externally to the moral law but originates in natural desires. The two ideas are clearly incompatible. Significantly, Kant avoided using legality to "schematize" rational action, but turned to more complicated mediators,[16] while insisting upon the uncompromising gap between morality and legality, a distinction without which his whole ethics would collapse. Thus, not only is Kant unable to find help in Spinoza's program but he must oppose it.

Unlike Kant, Spinoza neither builds his ethics as a doctrine of absolute imperatives nor makes morality depend on the subjective mode of decision. He therefore has room for an external resemblance between the sensual and rational motives and can place such semirational conduct on a higher level than mere caprice. Kant must reject this solution as "mere legality" and in order to purify religion, he must raise it to the highest—and only—level of rationality.

Legality does reign in Kant over politics and right, but these only provide an institutional framework to support and embody the truly moral community. Legality and internal morality complement each other in forming the final end of history; but they do not enjoy the same status: only the inner moral system is an end in itself, which bestows value and meaning to the rest of the system, including the legal and political institutions.

This leads to another significant difference. Kant and Spinoza agree that politics should be completely divorced from the historical form of religion, which is based on fear, superstition, and a clerical class. This type of religion must not intervene in the life of the polity in any form. But how should purified religion relate to politics? Here Kant and Spinoza are divided again. Kant, by reducing religion to inner morality, places it on a higher level than politics: the state itself must embody moral principles and serve the propagation of the ethical community. Spinoza, on the other hand, flatly subordinates purified religion to the secular authorities, whom he anoints as its true interpreters. Purified religion in both cases becomes a secular way of life, but in Kant it shares the independent and sublime status of morality, while Spinoza assimilates religion to the state and assigns a political role to it.

This reflects Spinoza's pessimism—or sense of realism—concerning the multitude. Had Spinoza believed that *vana religio* could be transformed into pure philosophical religion and prevail universally, he would free it of the state and even consider the state itself as superfluous.[17] But Spinoza holds that "human nature is different from this" and so he concentrates on the popular religion of obedience and gives the secular government the power to translate the principle of justice embedded in the Bible into concrete legislation.

THE METHODS OF BIBLICAL INTERPRETATION

Spinoza summarizes his method in the statement that "the knowledge of Scripture must be sought from Scripture alone, even as the knowledge of nature is sought from nature" (*Opera* 3: 99). But as a simple reexamination will prove, this hermeneutic slogan (which echoes the slogan *sola scriptura*, then fashionable in Protestant circles) does not adequately express Spinoza's intentions. The Bible itself does not supply us with all the relevant material for understanding it in Spinoza's way. Knowledge of its grammar and etymology, the history of each book, the circumstances of each epoch, and the like, are derived not just from the biblical documents but primarily from auxiliary sciences. One should, then, follow Strauss's advice and read Spinoza in about the same way he treats the Bible,[18] interpreting his slogan in terms of the comprehensive context of his arguments. Spinoza does not mean that the Bible should serve as the exclusive source of data, but that the methodological starting point should be in the biblical text alone. The actual content of the Bible is not to be determined by an a priori idea (theological or philosophical) to which the meaning of the text is then adjusted. Rather, the basis for research is the document itself, from whence one can proceed to discover a general pattern.

Oversimplified as it is, the comparison Spinoza draws between biblical criticism and natural science may help in understanding this point. As in the investigation of nature we must start from the simplest data, and proceed through enumeration and deduction to the definitions of all phenomena, so too in the study of the Bible, the difference being that there the data are physical or biological and here the data are biblical texts and the historical and philological facts that are relevant to their understanding as "natural" phenomena.

The rejection of preestablished schemes implies the rejection of an allegorical approach to the text and the primacy of a literal interpretation. Yet this is not a rigid rule. In fact, the literal meaning itself is not manifest but usually requires a complicated deciphering. Here lies the main difference between Spinoza's approach and other doctrines of literal interpretation. Spinoza insists there is a gap between the actual literal meaning and what it appears to be. The reader and the ancient author are both affected by cultural and personal associations and by contemporary beliefs and ways of speech. In order to understand the original meaning of the text we must discount the effect of these factors upon ourselves and consider how they worked on the biblical authors; and this requires a detailed investigation, based upon a great deal of extrabiblical material. Spinoza does not give a full account of these factors, much less of the rules by which they are to be knit together and reevaluate each other; but his general criteria are clear and his ample examples add much pertinent detail. In the *Theologico-Political Treatise* he succeeds in spelling out the principles of, and part of the detailed apparatus for, treating the Bible as a purely scientific object, whose sole norms are reason and experience.[19]

Spinoza's rejection of general schemes is not unqualified. It applies only to schemes that are imposed on the Bible from without, thus creating an a priori bias. But there are hermeneutic generalizations derived from the objective study of the Bible itself, and these are not only legitimate but indispensable for correct interpretation. This is because the texts as given are not self-explanatory and because a genuine method requires some degree of deduction and application. "As in the examination of natural phenomena we try first to investigate what is most universal and common to all nature . . . and then we proceed to what is less universal, so, too, in the history of Scripture, we seek first that which is most universal and serves for the basis and foundation of all Scripture" (*TTP*, p. 104, *Opera* 3: 102). The study of the Bible, like the study of nature, is based on two stages, which are (in Cartesian language) enumeration and deduction.[20] The first is a kind of induction, a "biblical history" (parallel to natural history, *historia naturalis*) whereby all relevant scientific material is gathered and catalogued. From these sets of data we have to extract: (1) permanent principles expressing the overall approach and spirit of the Bible; and (2) rules for interpreting specific types of problems. With these at hand, one can assess every story and verse in the Bible. If the literal meaning fits the basic principles of interpretation (even though it might conflict with religious dogma or philosophical truth), it should be accepted as such. Yet, if the literal meaning of a specific item is not compatible with the hermeneutic rules we have extracted, then even if by accident it fits the interest of reason or religion, we must reject it, and understand the story as an intended allegory and the words as metaphors (*TTP*, pp. 100, 103, *Opera* 3: 99, 102). This is the correct immanent method.

Did Spinoza follow his own method? One cannot answer with an unqualified "yes." His approach to the Bible was not free of a priori principles and presuppositions,[21] the most important of which was his very claim of an immanent approach. In opting for an objective scientific method, Spinoza presupposes a fundamental principle that negates the sanctity of the Bible and denies the authority of revelation, replacing it by reason. Here we have reached the inherent structural limit of an "immanent approach." Yet once this crucial presupposition has been admitted, Spinoza's method does not presuppose anything beyond it. The demand to learn "only from the Bible" is actually the demand to learn only from the *science* of the Bible, that is, from relevant scientific investigations. This involves the absolute rejection of any religious authority and its replacement by reason and science. Biblical hermeneutics, serving the critique of revelation and tacitly presupposing it, should thus help do for the masses what Spinoza's own Marrano background did for him.

It might be remarked, following P. F. Moreau, that Spinoza performed a second revolution in biblical reading (the first revolution was prompted in the sixteenth century by the humanists and their philological science).[22] The new Renaissance philology applied in the first place to the secular, even pagan ancients; Virgil, Terence, and Cicero were studied in new and different light. Spinoza applies this philological science to the Bible—demanding to see its authors as another group of secular ancients. To be sure, humanist philology has made remarkable progress in biblical research as well; and, rather ironically, it was the polyglot Bible of Cardinal Cisneros—a former Inquisitor General and persecutor of the Marranos, who capitalized on the scholarship of other Marranos—that gave the philological study of the Bible a significant push. This movement reached its apex with Richard Simon, the greatest biblical scholar of his age, and in many ways the "father" of modern biblical criticism together with Spinoza. Spinoza, though a great biblical scholar himself, could not rival Simon's immense knowledge; but in what concerns *method* he offered a more radical approach—the de-deification of the text.

Moreau suggests that the humanists had turned the Bible from mere story into a "text," while Spinoza's second revolution turned it into a "document." "Becoming a text" means that the reader pays attention to the material content and context, not only to the moral lesson; and "document" means that the text is made indicative of other, extratextual facts and processes (cultural, mental, intentional, etc.), in a way resembling the work of an archaeologist. But this is not the only novelty. The crucial point is that the Bible, as text and as document, had ceased to be a document of divine will—revelation—and became subject to the banal and secular authority of biblical sciences. In other words, with Spinoza the Bible has become a *secular* document.

Kant's Method of Interpretation

Kant did not elaborate his method of biblical interpretation as an explicit topic; but fragmentary remarks and, especially, dozens of instances in which Kant puts biblical verses into actual use, supply us with the required material. For example:

> What is written here must not be read as though intended for *Scriptural exegesis, which lies beyond the limits of the domain of bare reason.* It is possible to explain how a historical account is to be put to a moral use without deciding whether this is the intention of the author or merely our interpretation, provided this meaning is true in itself, apart from all historical proof, and is, moreover, the only one whereby we can derive something conducive to our betterment from a passage which otherwise would be only an unfruitful addition to our historical knowledge. (*Rel.*, p. 39 n., *Werke* 6: 41, emphasis added)

Here Kant advocates a method that is contrary to Spinoza. Renouncing a pure scientific approach to the Bible, he has little use for the authors' authentic intentions. At the same time Kant authorizes, and even recommends, attributing meanings to the text which are taken from external, a priori schemes—in this case from his own moral philosophy. And this leads him to argue that what deserves our attention is not the Bible as a whole, but only those selected passages which can, by allegory, be mobilized in the service of morality:

> We must not quarrel unnecessarily over a question or over its historical aspect when, however it is understood, it in no way helps us to be better men, and when that which can afford such help is discovered without historical proof, and indeed must be apprehended without it. (Ibid.)

Kant summarizes his rejection of the cognitive approach to the Bible by remarking,

> That historical knowledge which has no inner bearing valid for all men belongs to the class of *adiaphora*, which each man is free to hold as he finds edifying. (Ibid.)

In a passage entitled: "The Pure Religious [Philosophical] Faith is the Supreme Interpreter of the Ecclesiastical Faith,"[23] Kant later resumes the question from another angle. Moral progress on a large, historical scale requires a reciprocal relation between revealed religion and moral philosophy, to be established by biblical interpretation. The common man cannot attain a purely rational position in a single leap. He must instead go through a process in which the moral principles couched in the sensual stuff of biblical language are gradually brought to light through a proper (i.e., intentional) interpretation.[24]

Kant believes that a latent rational nucleus is couched in various shades of sensual cover in all historical faiths and hence also in the Bible. However, it cannot be present in *every* biblical verse or passage. Where this is lacking, and where the proper excuse can be found, Kant says we should engender the moral meaning even by departing from the literal sense.[25]

In an argument with the biblical scholar Johann D. Michaelis,[26] Kant asks rhetorically "whether morality should be expounded according to the Bible or whether the Bible should not rather be expounded according to morality?" (p. 101 n., *Werke* 6: 110 n.,). Evidently Kant accepts the second way. Autonomous, secular morality sets the norm, both for itself and for the Bible. And Kant's book on religion duly abounds with allegorical manipulations of biblical verses, some of them sharp and witty—and more than once he even takes the liberty of misquoting the text while using quotation marks.

In his *Contest of the Faculties*,[27] Kant continues the arguments of the

Religion. He denies the common claim that "the Bible, as revelation, must be interpreted out of itself and not through reason"—a variety of the Protestant slogan *sola scriptura* that Spinoza had turned against itself. Kant rejects the method of *sola scriptura* not because it discovers contradictions in the Bible (as the Catholic Counter-Reformer, Francisco Suarez, has argued against it), but because the Bible is morally useless without a proper rational interpretation. Precisely because it *is* [mere] revelation, Kant cryptically says, the Bible needs the guidance of moral reason which alone can bring out its divine nature.

Clearly, the divinity of Scripture is gauged here, as in the *Religion*, by its conformity with autonomous human ethics. "In religious matters," Kant concludes, "reason is the supreme interpreter of the Scripture" (p. 41). When a biblical sentence contradicts moral reason, it "must be interpreted to the latter's advantage" (p. 38); and this must be done "intentionally" (*absichtlich*), almost as an imperative.

The Justification of Kant's Method

What can justify this approach? Kant believes that rational religion is latent in the ancient text itself, since "earlier by far than this [popular] faith, the predisposition to moral religion lay hidden in human reason" (*Rel.*, p. 102, *Werke* 6: 111). But this vague and general implication cannot, of course, be found in any particular verse. The Kantian allegory relies on the inbred respect which its audience has for the Bible; but the allegorist himself does not share the same respect, and may well know that what he attributes to a given verse has never existed in it either explicitly or by implication.

Is not this, then, a violation of the principle of truth bordering on cynicism? Kant's answers in the *Religion* sound like excuses[28] and fail to give theoretical grounds for his methods of interpretation. But Kant's system recognizes another mode of justification, which yields the so-called "postulates" of pure practical reason. These are cognitive propositions (like "God exists" or "the will is free") which can neither be proved nor refuted by cognitive means. However, accepting them as true is a condition for fostering moral action. This, Kant holds, provides sufficient reason for accepting them and acting on their grounds, for, in the absence of possible proof, the moral interest of reason takes precedence over all the others.

So, I suggest the method of biblical interpretation may be construed as an extension of the doctrine of postulates, thus reflecting Kant's view that, Spinoza notwithstanding, the scientific study of the

Bible is on the whole impossible, and the original intentions of the authors must lie forever beyond our reach.

Kant makes room, however, for a special kind of biblical scholarship (*Schriftgelehrsamkeit*; *Rel.*, p. 103, *Werke* 6: 112), to mediate between rational religion and the masses. Where possible, the biblical scholar mobilizes his moral insight and encyclopedic knowledge to find a moral sense in the literal text or, where this is impossible, to offer an adequate allegory. In this way the moralizing biblical savant usurps the traditional role of the priest or the theologian to become the direct authority for the masses. Kant consoles himself that such use of authority, which "does not pay proper respect to human nature," will only be a passing historical stage.

How would Spinoza have answered Kant? We can guess the answer from Spinoza's critique of Maimonides, who also advocated a method of philosophical allegory. Violating the text in the name of reason, says Spinoza, makes reason contradict itself. Moreover, such biased interpretation would only establish "a new sort of priests or pontiffs, more likely to excite men's ridicule than their veneration" (*TTP*, p. 116, *Opera* 3: 114).

The opposition between the methods of Kant and Spinoza reflects to some extent a difference in philosophical temperament—especially if we juxtapose Kant's demanding moralism with Spinoza's objective comprehension of necessity. But even more important are their divergent interests in the critique of religion, and several specific views each of them held. To be faithful to his system of rational naturalism, Spinoza must make the Bible an object for scientific research, since this applies to every particular thing in the world without exception. Moreover, he actually believed that the Bible is a product of *imaginatio*, and thus could have expected that a disinterested study of the Bible, apart from its contribution to knowledge, would also yield the practical result of exposing the Bible's flaws and subverting its authority. Spinoza must be aware that scientific research cannot destroy the authority of the Bible unless this authority has already been rejected at the outset by accepting science as the supreme judge. So instead of starting with a person's arguments he uses interpretation as a rhetorical means to perplex and convert the nonphilosophers. Kant, on his part, believed that the human mind actually has the propensity to rational religion, and, therefore could expect his allegorical method to gradually develop and bring to light the moral potential of the human race.

This is related to Kant's view of history (to which I devoted a different book).[29] For Kant history is the process whereby reason brings its latent potential to light, gradually liberating itself from sensual cover and shaping the objective world in its image. Such a view of history is not merely evolutionary, but teleological. History is not simply a change from one state to another; it realizes an underlying human potential or essence: reason and autonomy. Reason has manifested itself since ancient times under the cover of myth and ritual of the various historical religions; they are all stages in an overall process and should be used to enhance its advance. Therefore, one must start from the Bible and the historical religions, but guide them out of their sensuousness, that is, out of their *literal form*. Kant's exegetical method thus reflects his historical outlook in a dual way. The Bible is an example of the rational essence that became embodied sensually, and it is also an instrument for pushing this essence toward further development and shedding its sensuous shell.

Spinoza and History

Does Spinoza have a historical perspective? Certainly not, if what we have in mind is the Kantian idea of a latent rationality governing history and asserting itself through its strifes and vicissitudes. This view (as we shall see in the chapter on Hegel) would be rejected by Spinoza as a teleological illusion and a residue of the notion of providence. Spinoza's rationalism—the view that everything in the universe, down to its minutest details, is inscribed and structured by reason (which expresses the immanent essence of God)—is fundamentally atemporal and ahistorical, construed *sub specia aeternitatis*. The rational laws and essences of nature translate the notions of divine presence into secular and scientific terms—but they are purely mechanical and deductive, lacking development or purpose.

Kant—and Hegel—extended the rational structure of the universe into history as a special, and even privileged domain, governed by purposive reason. But this view is utterly foreign to Spinoza. History has no special ontological status. It is but the way we humans cut out our experience of natural occurrences from a standpoint which interests us—that of our desires. Historical events are of the same kind as natural events and fall under the same eternal laws of nature. Hence, the study of history is but a branch of the study of nature, except that its data are usually more obscure because of the remoteness of time. This, precisely, is what Spinoza's biblical criticism brings to the forefront. It provides a paradigm case for the kind of natural science of history which alone is possible in Spinoza.

And yet, as Sylvain Zac points out, biblical interpretation does imply a historical consciousness in embryo on Spinoza's part.[30] Spinoza presupposes that culture, language, custom, and mentalities change and evolve, while leaving their decipherable marks; and they flow into the present, where they provide us with a tradition within which a new revolution can take place. Spinoza, furthermore, tries to extract from the Bible a nucleus of semirational morality, the basis for the universal religion he destines for the masses. This implies the reinterpretation of tradition as a means for historical advancement. Past and present are separated by a revolution but are also bridged by a hermeneutical enterprise. The Bible is even said to contain *in fact* the nucleus of popular morality, if we take this contention at face value (which perhaps we should not); and since Spinoza's method is supposed to unveil the original intention of the authors, it will follow that Spinoza, perhaps unwittingly, postulates a common moral insight that underlies centuries of biblical authorship and provides, under its various forms of the imagination, an element of continuity between past and present, between superstition and reason.

The same, on a broader scale, can be observed in Spinoza's pure philosophy. When Spinoza chooses to retain such words as *God, freedom, beatitude,* or *right*, or when he uses expressions like "God's intellect," "God's power," the "love of God," and the like, he is not merely practicing subtle camouflage. He employs the terms by which tradition correctly located and designated certain crucial problems and perennial philosophical tasks, though it was led astray in trying to identify the true objects of these terms; and Spinoza feels that, for the first time, his philosophy succeeds in doing so. Spinoza's *champs de chasse* contains the inadequate ideas of the past (along with their names, the words by which they are designated), as a necessary substrate within which his own conceptual and semantic revolution takes place. Behind the mantle of Spinoza's "geometrical order," a full-scale hermeneutial endeavor is pursued, not dissimilar to the one which his biblical interpretation implies (though addressed to a philosophical, not a popular audience), and likewise implying a nascent historical consciousness.

Spinoza, moreover, could have gained this consciousness by looking closely at himself. His life from early childhood was interwoven with a momentous historical adventure: the return of the Marranos from Catholicism to Judaism and their intensive effort to create an old-new culture. This was also a hermeneutic enterprise to a large extent. The Amsterdam Jews were working to reinterpret the past as a means for creating a new present and future; they struggled constantly to suppress former symbols and traditions and to reinterpret others, in order to overcome their former identity and create a new culture. Spinoza, in breaking from them, maintained a similar effort but went in the opposite direction; for they strove to resuscitate an even older religious tradition, while Spinoza tried to transcend the religious universe altogether. But this only highlights Spinoza's position as a Marrano of reason. Here, again, Spinoza stands one step ahead of the actual former Marranos, retaining a similar *pattern* of experience yet turning its *content* diametrically against them.

History was certainly stirring around Spinoza. The rise of the Dutch republic, the wars of religion, the revolution in England, the new sun in Versailles—and Descartes, Huygens, the Royal Society—might still pass, despite their weight, as historical routine, Not so the messianic fervor that circulated among Jews and Gentiles alike in Spinoza's neighborhood. Here was something absolute, the evidence of divine guidance. Already the return of the Marranos was perceived as a messianic redemption in minuscule, a fact that, as Gershom Scholem points out, added its peculiar Amsterdam flavor to the messianic uproar around Sabbetai Zevi, the most galvanizing false messiah in Jewish history, which erupted a few years after Spinoza's ban.[31] Spinoza was asked about it by Oldenburg, himself of chiliastic leanings, in a letter from London. Though no letter exists with Spinoza's response, we know his answer very well—it is given at the end of chapter 3 in the *Theologico-Political Treatise*. Spinoza holds that *historia sacra* is a myth and messianism a delusion. There is only nature with its uniform natural causes; history does not exist as a special domain and everything in it is the result of natural causes—even though these causes can bring about the most astonishing phenomena: for example, the persisting of the Jewish people, the liberation of the Marranos, possibly even the return of the Jews to political independence in their ancient land. By reflecting on his personal background and the fate of his former people, and especially on phenomena that usually call for providential explanations, Spinoza thus gained a sense of history which was utterly secular and naturalistic.

And this corresponds exactly to the approach he advocates in biblical interpretation.

Finally, a word about the inner limitations of the methods of Spinoza and Kant in biblical criticism. Spinoza's major problem is that his acceptance of the believers' principles is fictitious, and in fact he subordinates his opponents to his own rational criteria from the outset. His claim of ethical compatibility of reason and the Bible is misleading, for Spinoza does not mean to say that reason is compatible with the Bible as given, but only with the criticized Bible, namely, after it has been reduced and interpreted by this very same reason. The alleged autonomy of reason and revelation in Spinoza is rhetorical, a lip service paid and a bait extended to the religious and the faithful.[32]

Kant's major difficulty lies in the possible clash between two rational interests, truth and moral education. An exegetical method that is consciously ready to overlook historical truth is incompatible with Kant's own spirit of the Enlightenment and the autonomy of objective knowledge. To little avail is his doctrine of the moral postulates, since the principle is flawed in itself.[33]

In conclusion, the inner limitations of the methods of both Spinoza and Kant stem from their attempt to maintain a fictitious parallelism between the practical and the scholarly interest in biblical exegesis. Kant subordinated the one to the other, and Spinoza assumed (or pretended he did) a preestablished harmony between them. If there is a philosophical lesson to be drawn from these attempts, it is the need for a radical separation between the two interests. Turning one of them into a means for the other may produce theoretical contradictions and practical distortions, of which self-deception, censorship, and brainwashing are a few extreme examples. The lesson we are trying to draw is, in other words, a more rigorous Spinozism. If separation is declared, let there be separation.[34]

Spinoza and Hegel: The Immanent God— Substance or Spirit?

In the previous chapter we saw the prephilosophical work which the critique of religion is to perform in clearing the mind of transcendent images and religious superstition. Only after such obstacles have been removed, or at least seriously undermined, can the clear and distinct ideas of reason emerge and assert their self-evidence in the philosopher's mind.

The first and most important idea to emerge is the recognition of the absolute immanence of God and his identity with the whole of reality. This is Spinoza's supreme rational intuition, the very first and most comprehensive true idea (*idea vera*) from which his philosophy takes its departure (whatever its formal order in the *Ethics*, Spinoza's chief work). The rest of the system serves to explicate this idea and specify it in detail.

It is also a most daring and heterodox idea—not only for the theologians, Spinoza's usual opponents, but in the history of rational philosophy itself. Among the major philosophers, only Hegel, a century and a half later, adhered to a viewpoint similar to Spinoza's, while trying to transform it in a more coherent and, in Hegel's view, a more spiritual perspective. Hegel is also the only heterodox thinker we shall discuss who not only denies the idea of transcendence, but sees the realm of immanence as divine—a move which the others refused to make and which Nietzsche denounced as an illusion and aberration.

This provides Spinoza and Hegel with a common ground and a deep philosophical affinity, but it also serves as their major point of contention. For, once the immanence of God, as absolute totality, has been established, the question arises: What is the nature of this totality? Is it to be construed as substance, or as spirit? Should we understand it as an absolute beginning or as a result? And is the divine present and actual in physical nature, or perhaps only in human history, as a higher ontological domain?

A Paradigm of Dialectical Critique

Hegel's critique of Spinoza is a dialectical one, aiming to retain the essence of Spinoza's doctrine within a different and "higher" system. This critique may also serve as a paradigm for any dialectical refutation in philosophy.

It is, indeed, with regard to Spinoza that Hegel states his methodological principle in clear and vigorous terms:

> In refuting a philosophical system . . . one should exclude the wrong notion that the system must be exposed as being throughout *false*, and that the *true* system must be merely *opposed* to the false. . . . Rather, speculative thinking [= genuinely philosophical thinking] finds itself in its course of evolution necessarily taking the same standpoint [as the criticized system], and to that extent the system is perfectly true.
>
> Yet *it is not the highest standpoint*. On that count, however, the system cannot be seen as false, as calling for refutation and as lending itself to it. What should be regarded as false in this system is only the notion that it is the highest standpoint. Therefore, the *true* system cannot relate to it in the manner of mere opposition; for if it did, then the opposed system itself would be one-sided. But as the higher system it must rather contain the subordinate system within itself.[1]

Hegel recognizes two proper forms of dialectical refutation. One is historical and takes place in the succession of systems in time; the other is systematic refutation, inscribed within the simultaneous interrelations of the components within the final system of philosophy.

Historically, systems of philosophy are properly refuted by accepting the element of partial truth they contain while developing their logical implications to a point where the inconsistencies from which they suffer—because of their partiality and the one-sided nature of their governing principle—are brought to light. When we adopt and interiorize such a system, we also experience its deficiencies as our own, and this drives us to transcend the system and to take a more satisfactory position, one that will preserve the basic truth of the former in a more coherent form. According to Hegel, this process will go on until the final synthesis of philosophy—the system he calls "absolute knowledge"—has emerged.

When this occurs, a supratemporal perspective for refuting former philosophers becomes available. Within the final system we can now discern the whole history of philosophy sketched as in a shadow. Every great philosopher of the past now figures as a "moment" (or a logical ingredient) within the overall synthesis. His personal marks abolished, his historical particularity eliminated altogether, and his claim to express the total truth negated, he has been crystallized into a conceptual component within the totality of the final system.

In his critique of Spinoza, Hegel uses the same principle in an almost paradigmatic precision:

> The only refutation of Spinozism can therefore consist, first, in recognizing its standpoint to be essential and necessary, and then, however, in letting this standpoint elevate itself *of itself* into a higher one. The relation of substance [Spinoza's main category], when considered merely in and for itself, leads itself over to its opposite, the Concept [Hegel's main category]. Therefore, the exposition of substance as offered in the last book [of Hegel's Logic], which leads over into the Concept, is the sole and true refutation of Spinozism.[2]

Among the many forerunners Hegel wished to assimilate as "moments" into his new system, Spinoza occupies a privileged position, comparable only to that of Aristotle and Kant. Spinoza's absolute monism, reviving the early Greek philosophers, provides Hegel with the necessary substrate and beginning of *all* philosophy. More importantly, Spinoza marks for Hegel the culmination of traditional, object-oriented metaphysics, with its view that the object, the universe in itself, is inherently structured and governed by reason (*logos*). Hegel called this standpoint "Objective Logic,"* his own, somewhat odd re-naming of what Kant had termed "dogmatic metaphysics."

Whereas Kant saw his German predecessor, Christian Wolff, as "the greatest among all dogmatic philosophers,"[3] Hegel reserves this title for Spinoza. "When beginning to philosophize, one must first be a Spinozist," he says in one characteristic statement.[4] In Hegel's *Science of Logic*, it is Spinoza's system, duly modified, which brings to a climax the whole march of traditional philosophy, crystallized into "Ob-

---

* By "Logic," as the term appears in the title of his metaphysical work, *Science of Logic*, Hegel does not understand formal logic but the study of *logos* as it structures being, or reality itself. Hence "Objective Logic" signifies the one-sided recognition of *logos* as only embodied in external reality; "Subjective Logic" involves the recognition (of idealism in general) that the rational subject participates in determining the rationality and actuality of the object.

jective Logic." This purely objectivist doctrine has been superseded by Kant's idealistic revolution, according to which the structure of the object is identical with (and determined by) the structure of the rational subject. Hegel sees this as a momentous discovery which brought traditional metaphysics to its end; it established the standpoint of "Subjective Logic"—or modern idealism—which was then to take its adequate form in Hegel's own philosophy: his dialectical identification of object and subject, of actuality and its self-conceptualization through man.

For Hegel, the absolute is neither a thinglike substance (Spinoza) nor a merely subjective "I think" (Fichte, following Kant), but comprises them both as moments in a higher synthesis called the "Concept." Hegel thereby assigns to Spinoza a position analogous to his own: having brought to its apex the whole history of philosophy prior to the advent of idealism, Spinoza stands at a crucial turning point for metaphysics: from tradition to modernity, from dogmatic objectivism to (Hegel's own) dialectical idealism.

It is, as Hegel sees it, the dialectical marriage of Spinoza and Kant which makes his own synthesis possible. Just as Kant remedies the one-sided, thing-oriented metaphysics of Spinoza, so does Spinoza, with his concept of absolute totality, serve to redeem the major shortcomings that Hegel finds in Kant, especially his radical dualism and his view that human reason is finite and severed from actual reality (from the so-called "thing in itself"). The result is an idealistic version of Spinozisms—dialectical, dynamic, and—as we shall see—historicized.

Hegel attributes the same pivotal position to Spinoza in another major work, *The Phenomenology of Spirit* (1807). "According to my viewpoint," he declares in the preface, "everything depends on this, that we grasp and express the true not [only] as *substance*, but equally also as subject."[5] The allusion to Spinoza is obvious. Spinoza's substance must be taken as a basis, but given the features of a dialectical subject. This includes, as we shall see, the process of self-constitution, whereby the subject becomes other than itself and then, by a "second negation," recuperates and *actualizes* its true self in and through this other. Eventually, this also means that the absolute in Hegel cannot enjoy the status of eternity (supratemporality) *simpliciter*, but must rise to this status through a process in time and within human history—a novelty which, in its sheer heterodoxy, even surpasses Spinoza.

I shall now reconstruct the main points of Hegel's critique of Spinoza, avoiding lengthy exegesis and secondary points (which are, however, frequently relevant in Hegel). For the sake of clarity, I shall first present an analytic summary of Hegel's main claims as they emerge, connected, from all relevant sources.[6] Then, following the text of Hegel's *History of Philosophy* and *Logic*, I shall complement these points and spell them out in further detail.

From this logical and ontological analysis, I shall then develop its less abstract implications for religion and the philosophy of history. Then, in the last part of this chapter, I shall delve beneath the hard core of the Spinoza-Hegel controversy for a possible clash between a heterodox Lutheran philosopher and a former ex-Marrano Jewish heretic. Finally, commenting on Hegel's critique, I shall argue that Spinoza came closer to Hegel than the latter admitted, and yet the remaining differences are irreconcilable. Showing why Spinoza must refuse the dialectical (and teleological) *Aufhebung* by Hegel, I shall indicate how this leaves two other grand alternatives for carrying on a *nonteleological* philosophy of immanence—that of Marx and Nietzsche.

Overview of Hegel's Criticism

Generally speaking, Hegel views his critique of Spinoza as an attempt to specify the coherence conditions for maintaining Spinoza's principles, above all his idea of God as immanent totality. It is because Hegel accepts and wishes to maintain Spinoza's principle of absolute totality that he wants to remove other aspects of Spinoza's thought that make the coherent explication of his main idea impossible.

Analytic Summary of Hegel's Critique

Hegel, in particular, criticizes Spinoza for his one-sided view of negation; his non dialectical (and, therefore, incoherent) construal of the concept of totality; and—as a consequence—his view of the totality as an inert thing, a substance, rather than an organic and conscious subject. Most of Hegel's detailed criticisms are such that even non-Hegelians might (and often did) voice them. But Hegel tries to *systematize* the various difficulties found in Spinoza, by attributing them to a common root—Spinoza's one-sided view of negation, leading to his non-dialectical concept of totality. Hegel identifies the following major flaws in Spinoza's thought:

1. Substance qua substance is only pure being and simple identity, excluding all negation.
2. In that, the absolute must exclude all inner differences and particularization.
3. For this reason, Spinoza cannot show the necessity of there

being particular things at all; the finite aspect of the universe remains inexplicable and at best contingent.

4. Even as contingent, Spinoza cannot attribute reality to the finite modes. Although declared to be real, they must be considered the fruit of an "external reflection" or the *imaginatio*.

5. Similarly, the so-called attributes cannot count as self-specifications of the substance, but only as external and subjective projections of our minds.

6. The absolute is there as a beginning, not as a result; the modes depend upon the substance unilaterally, and do not condition, in turn, the possibility of the substance itself. The substance is *causa sui* in itself, prior to and independently of its being the cause of the particular modes. (This, to Hegel, is the single most important expression of a nondialectical, nonreciprocal system.)

7. The former points add up to a fundamental break between both aspects of the universe—the infinite and the finite, *natura naturans* and *natura naturata*. Spinoza's intended monism splits into an actual dualism—an adverse outcome from Spinoza's viewpoint and, again, the result of his lack of dialectical logic and its movement of dual negation.

8. Because the totality as such has no inner negativity, it also lacks development and life. There is movement *among* the particular modes (mechanical movement), but no movement as the inner development of their principle of unity; the totality qua this unity remains inert and static.

9. Finally (and partly as a result of the former), the absolute is perceived as a mere thing (*res*), an unconscious object, devoid of subjectivity, personality, and spirit.

Points 1 through 7 sum up the *lack of dialectical logic in Spinoza*. Point 9 indicates the *lack of subjectivity*, and point 8 serves as a link between them. Accordingly, Hegel would demand (and performs in the *Logic*) two dialectical corrections in order to overcome Spinoza's shortcomings.

First, the totality must be constituted and governed by the negation of negation (or dialectical reciprocity); in other words, the absolute must not be conceived as a ready-made beginning, but as a result.

Second, the totality must also be conceived as subject. The first dialectical correction takes place on the level of substance (or "Objective Logic"); the second correction completes the passage of substance into subject.

Atheism, Acosmism, and Pantheism   Spinoza was charged with atheism. Hegel reverses this charge, claiming that, on the contrary, the trouble with Spinoza is that "with him there is too much God."[7] In other words, it is not God, the infinite, but the finite and particular modes that are denied actual reality. This makes Spinoza's system a form not of atheism but—in Hegel's polemical phrase—of "acosmism" (denial of the reality of the world of finite things).

Hegel's critique is based upon the systematic implications of Spinoza's doctrine, not on his explicit position. Having started with absolute unity and identity—and lacking a dialectical logic—Spinoza, Hegel claims, is unable to maintain the actuality of particular and finite things. His totality becomes an overpowering principle in which all differences are obliterated. This boundless totality allows of no real distinctions in the universe—only of modal variations of the same. Whatever does appear to us as distinct and specific is such only because of the imagination—or, in Hegel's language, of an "external reflection"—and not by virtue of its objective ontological status. Only the substance existing *in se* (in itself) and conceivable *per se* (through itself) is an actual individual, whereas the finite modes are but passing and fluctuating "affections," or states, of this single substance. Spinoza's inability to do justice to the realm of the finite is what Hegel means by having "too much God."

At the same time Hegel praises Spinoza's achievement in grasping the structure of reality in terms of a single totality, in which the dualism of God and world, the Creator and the created, the transcendent and the immanent, is overcome. This pantheism will serve as the foundation of Hegel's own system; but in Hegel it will be given a processual and spiritual dimension. The absolute totality does not exist beforehand and eternally, as in Spinoza, but produces itself as absolute in the process of history; and, rather than being conceived as an inert and thinglike substance, the totality of God and world is viewed as a free subject.

Hegel's modified version of Spinoza's pantheism is not less but more "heretical" in terms of conventional theology. With all his daring ideas, Spinoza still maintained that God was eternal and not subject to becoming or change. In Hegel, God is not only deprived of his absolute transcendence, but is even made the product of a process in time (namely, of the self-actualization of spirit through human history). Rather than being absolute and eternal from the outset, God, the absolute unity of the immanent and the transcendent, emerges in Hegel as the outcome of a dialectical process of self-constitution and self-mediation. This view of the "becoming God" should have earned Hegel—from the viewpoint of traditional theology—an even greater crown of thorns than the one placed on Spinoza's head. Yet Hegel already wrote in a different *Zeitgeist*—and that makes a difference.

Deduction and Method   Hegel's second criticism concerns Spinoza's use of the geometrical—that is, formal-deductive—method. Hegel argues that this method should be banned from philosophy because philosophy must reflect the "inner movement" of its own subject matter. Already Kant distinguished the "mathematical" from the "philosophical" method. In philosophy (thus Kant), reason has only itself to build upon, working its way from the less clear and articulate to the more clear and articulate. Clarity and distinctness can be expected in philosophy only at the end and not, as in a deductive system, at the beginning. Accordingly, Kant concludes, the method of philosophy is the *gradual self-explication of reason*. In the "mathematical" method, on the contrary, full clarity and conclusive certainty are attained at any stage of the deduction; we do not move, as in philosophy, from lesser to greater clarity of whole contexts but proceed on the level of absolute clarity from one particular item to the next.[8]

Hegel accepts the thrust of this Kantian argument but adds to it specific reasons of his own. First, verification in philosophy depends on the complete systematic context and cannot be obtained prior to its full unfolding ("the true is the whole"). Second, the logical genesis of an idea in philosophy is an integral part of its meaning and truth; it cannot be communicated as a single "conclusion" and yet retain its meaning or truth value. In the same way, the "proof" is not an external ladder that can be disposed of once the ensuing "proposition" is reached. In the formal-deductive method, however, the process of demonstration is extraneous to the ensuing conclusion which has a truth value and meaning in itself, independently of its genesis. The logical equipment of "proofs," "propositions," and the like, indicates an external relation between process and consequent, and is therefore suitable only to the formal and the empirical sciences (mathematics, formal logic, physics, etc.), as well as in daily argumentation and ratiocination (including practical arguments and strategies), but not in philosophy. Third, philosophy is based on *Vernunft* (concrete reason), not on *Verstand* (formal understanding); its subject matter is actual reality, which can be expressed only in a logical form that has the characteristics of its object—namely, of organic totality, rather than a series of single propositions. Fourth, and more broadly speaking: in philosophy one cannot separate form from content, method from subject matter; the philosopher is supposed to follow the immanent movement of the subject matter itself (*die Sache selbst*) as it evolves through contradictions and their partial resolutions; and the "method" of philosophy is nothing but the structure of the finished process as it comes to light in retrospect. Philosophy thus has no a priori method at all; it lets its subject matter *structure itself* as it evolves—and the shape that results is called its "method."

As can be seen, all these specific arguments follow from one major source: Hegel's "organic" view of philosophical truth as a self-unfolding dialectical totality. Hegel thereby applies his ontological critique of Spinoza's "rigid" totality to the field of method as well. He fails, however to recognize that Spinoza (at least in his *Treatise on the Intellect*) was his major forerunner in rejecting an a priori method.

From Bacon and Galileo through Descartes to Locke and Kant, modern philosophers have given logical priority to the study of method—that is, more broadly, of epistemology, over the substantive sciences. In order to know, one was supposed to learn first what knowledge was and how it could be correctly obtained. Spinoza, in the fashion of the day, set out to write in the *Treatise on the Intellect* his own "essay on method" prior to writing his substantive system; but what happened to him was not dissimilar (in reverse) to the fate of the biblical Balaam, who intended to curse and ended up blessing. Starting with the program of investigating method prior to having substantive knowledge, Spinoza reverses his original position; method, as the form of true knowledge, can be known only in retrospect, by reflecting upon the structure and properties of some true knowledge that we already possess. Method is an idea of an idea (i.e., reflective knowledge); but in order to have this reflection we must first have the basic true idea. Method is better understood—and the capacity to obtain true knowledge is strengthened—the more substantive knowledge we in fact obtain.

Whether Spinoza was faithful to this conclusion is another question. But the literal text of the *Treatise on the Intellect*, at least, comes as close to Hegel's rejection of an a priori method in philosophy as any important predecessor or successor has ever come.

The Absolute as a Spiritless Substance   The third criticism Hegel makes in the *History of Philosophy* overlaps with his fuller discussion in the *Logic*, and I shall combine them.

In rejecting the formal-deductive method, Hegel also rejects the nondialectical view of negation it implies. This is the link between the flaws of method and the flaws of content that Hegel finds in Spinoza's metaphysics:

Because negation was thus conceived by Spinoza in one-sided fashion merely, there is, in the third place, in his system an utter blotting out of the principle of subjectivity, individuality, personality, the moment of self-consciousness in Being.[9]

This is the most important criticism Hegel voices, and it links together many of the specific points listed above. In particular, we see that, for Hegel, the lack of a negation and dialectical logic is also responsible for the lack of subjectivity in the absolute. This one sided view of negation seems to lie at the root of Spinoza's problems, and therefore it is worthwhile to begin with it.

Spinoza conceives of the absolute substance in terms of pure being and simple identity. Its agreement with itself is not based upon a primordial self-differentiation; it is not construed—as in a dialectical system—as a return to self or as a process of self-*identification* on the basis of previous self-separation. Rather, the identity of the substance is given beforehand, simply and immediately, in a way that makes any further differentiation logically impossible.

This situation is due primarily to the fact that Spinoza defined the absolute, God, as pure being that involves no negation. The totality is absolute affirmation, with no inherent principle of negativity. But this, Hegel claims, makes it impossible for it to have inner differences, to particularize itself, and to give rise to finite modes or to any other form of limitation, and also to movement, change, or life. In other words, the exclusion of negativity from the substance qua substance must lead to a Parmenidean kind of unity, wiping out all distinctions and making all finite entities, all change and dynamism, ontologically impossible.

Hegel understands this criticism to be immanent. It is based upon Spinoza's own principle, which Hegel extolls beyond limit, that *determinatio negatio est*, and on the traditional logic of particularization, as established ever since the Pre-Socratics, according to which all differentiation and movement in the "one" presuppose the work of a negative principle in being (Parmenides' "that which is not").

If the negation is external to the substance, finite things cannot have ontological reality but must—again in the fashion of Parmenides—be considered the products of a lesser degree of knowledge, the *imaginatio* (or, as Hegel says, an "external reflection"). This, at least in part, is admitted by Spinoza himself when he claims that no real distinction exists in the universe—either between the substance and its attributes or modes, or between any two modes. In other words, there are no real individuals in the world except the world as a single totality; and all differences must be dismissed as superficial fluctuations or passing states of the same entity. (In claiming that modes are unreal, Hegel does not represent Spinoza's official doctrine, but takes sides in a well-known interpretive debate.)

Even assuming, for the sake of the argument, that the modes can be construed as real, they are still merely contingent, in the sense that there is no necessity for the substance to produce them. In fact, Spinoza is unable to show the necessity of there being particular things at all, and the finite aspect of reality (his *natura naturata*) remains inexplicable and at best contingent. Not only is every particular mode contingent in itself—namely, there is nothing inconceivable in its not having been—but the very existence of a *natura naturata* must count as contingent; given the lack of negativity in the absolute, it is perfectly conceivable that there would be no finite things at all. Thus, contrary to Hegel's dialectical conception of a totality (in which the contingent aspect of being is itself logically necessary), in Spinoza there is no logical necessity in there being contingent entities at all; contingency itself is contingent.

This criticism could be made also by a non-Hegelian, when closely examining one of the most crucial propositions in the *Ethics*: "From the necessity of the divine nature there must follow infinitely many things in infinitely many modes (i.e., everything which can fall under an infinite intellect" (pt. 1, prop. 16). This proposition introduces for the first time the plurality of modes that are supposed to flow "necessarily" from the substance. Yet proposition 16 itself has a somewhat contingent (or arbitrary) status, for it is not deduced from the foregoing propositions or axioms, but is rather defended in isolation, as if it represented a new axiom.

The so-called "attributes," too, cannot be construed as inner specifications of the one substance, and therefore we must dismiss them as products of our subjective minds, products that we project upon the structure of the substance. In this criticism, again, Hegel gives a fundamental interpretation to a well-known Spinozistic problem. Spinoza defines an attribute as "*what the intellect perceives* of a substance, as constituting its essence" (*Ethics*, pt. 1, def. 4); and Hegel reads this as if the attribute is only subjective, explaining this by the lack of inner negativity in the absolute, which deprives it of objective self-differentiation. Hegel here again takes sides in a well-known interpretive controversy over the nature of the attributes; indeed, he starts it.

All the former points indicate a nondialectical construal of totality. Ever since the Milesian school, in fact, the problem of totality—the relation of the One and the Many within a single system—has not been satisfactorily resolved. Either the One was put forth as predominant—

in which case, as in Parmenides, *even* Plato, and (Hegel thinks) certainly Spinoza, the Many could not be done justice; or else the Many were predominant, in which case the One was sacrificed and a form of nominalism or empiricism ensued. Dualism, too, was not the answer—at least not for an avowed monist like Spinoza. The only coherent construal of the totality, Hegel argues, is by way of dialectical logic; any other construal breaks down into a new dualism, or sacrifices one of the sides for the sake of the other. The very concept of totality implies a contradiction: a system that is at once One and Many, Universal and Particular, Being and Becoming. Indeed, in the dialectical construal of the concept of totality, all the old Platonic opposites are considered as mediating each other in a single process. The universal becomes such only by way of its self-particularization, from which it is reconstituted as a "concrete" universal. The One becomes what it is only by way of the Many which evolve from it and, in their regained unity, constitute the One. The identity of the system is constituted by a process of self-differentiation and as a movement of "return to self" from this differentiation. Identity is not immediately and simply given, but is the result of a process of *reidentification*. A dialectical construal of the totality would require, first, understanding the absolute as involving negation in its inner constitution, and consequently as being the result of a process of self-particularization, by which it regains (or constitutes) its dialectical unity and its very status as absolute. For this reason, the major flaw that Hegel finds in Spinoza's theory of substance is that the modes depend upon the substance unilaterally; the substance is first *causa sui*, independently of the modes, and then it is also supposed to be the cause of the modes as a distinct and secondary act.

The First Dialectical Correction

Most of Hegel's attempt in the chapter on the absolute in the *Logic* is to refute this view and present his first dialectical correction to Spinoza's outlook—a correction, we have seen, that takes place still on the level of substance and "Objective Logic." In Hegel's corrected version, the absolute is the result of its own process of self-constitution, a process that takes place by the mediation of the finite modes. Certainly, the substance is the cause of itself—but what is this "itself" of which it is the cause? Is it a tautological identity, or is it its own "self" in the form of an "other"? Only the latter would satisfy the dialectical concept of totality, as well as the coherence conditions for maintaining such a concept. The substance is cause of itself in that it is the cause of the infinity of modes which is nothing but itself in the form of its opposite;

or, the infinite, eternal, unitarian aspect of the universe is cause of itself in that it is the cause of the finite, temporal, pluralistic aspect of the universe—both being opposite moments of the same system, of the same dialectical unity. The world as *natura naturans* and the world as *natura naturata* are one, Spinoza says; let him then construe them in such a way that *natura naturans* will be *causa sui* not directly and in itself, but in that it is the cause of the *natura naturata*—which is nothing but itself in the form of "otherness." In a word, the concept of *causa sui* is realized in that the one substance particularizes itself into the modes and becomes cause of itself *through being the cause of the modes*. Only as the result of this mediation, can the absolute totality emerge and be constituted as such.

The Second Dialectical Correction: The Absolute as Subject

By introducing negativity into the absolute and viewing it as a result, we have reinterpreted the substance as an organic totality. A dialectical totality is organic in that its unity is the result of the interrelation of the many particulars—which also are not primordial, but emerge from their unifying principle while at the same time reconstituting it. An organic totality, however, is a subjectlike system. The concept of subject denotes in Hegel not only a conscious being, but—in a more primitive sense—any organized totality whose governing logic is the same as the one governing the activity of the "ego." The unity of a subject in the sense of "ego" or self-consciousness is such—as Kant has already shown—that identity is not given beforehand, but is a result of a process of self-identification. Only by ascribing to himself, as his own particularizations, the many thoughts he has, can the subject also constitute and recognize his own identity as self. The main difference between Kant and Hegel on this count is that for Kant the manifold of cogitations is given externally, while Hegel speaks of this manifold as self-particularizations of the subject. But they agree on the other point, namely, that the identity is constituted and not given immediately. In this way, *the structure of the subject as "Ego" is a model of the structure of any dialectical totality*. The Ego, Hegel says, is the concept of the Concept. And since on the level of substance we have already found a dialectical (or organic) totality, this means that we have discovered there a subjectlike structure. In other words, we have recognized our own logical image, as human subjects, implicit in what had seemed to be a merely "objective" and "thinglike" substance. The first dialectical correction thus leads to the second: performing an *Aufhebung* of the whole sphere of the substance with its Objective Logic, and making, with Kant, the revolutionary discovery that the structure of the object is basically the same as the structure of the subject. Hegel associates the idealistic discovery of the subject as constitutive of the actuality of the object—with his own dialectical logic. The latter is a coherence condition for maintaining the former. The way in which a subject particularizes itself and gains self-identity through the manifold—its "other"—which he becomes, is the paradigm for all philosophical logic.

By introducing a dialectical logic into the Spinozistic totality we have not only brought the Objective Logic to its climax but negated the purely objectivist approach to the world. With Spinoza's totality made organic, we discover our own subjective image in what we have all along considered as something purely external that merely confronted us. But contemplating the external world in terms of a totality, and in trying to make the Spinozistic view more coherent, our thinking was driven back to itself, finding its own shape and mark in what seemed to be an inert substance. It is not to itself as mere subject, confronting an object which is merely eternal, that our thinking was pushed back—but to itself as a principle of the objective world, too; this is the principle of idealism—the basic unity of the structure of the object and the structure of the subject—that has now come to the foreground.

Again, at this crucial point, the Spinoza-Kant synthesis makes its appearance. Dialectical logic, as we have seen, is to Hegel the logic of subjectlike systems. As such, it provides the true significance of Kant's principle of the "I think" as constitutive of its object (the Copernican revolution). Only under a dialectical construal can this great Kantian discovery, unknown (and surely objectionable) to Spinoza, be properly explicated and maintained as coherent. But at the same time, Spinoza's own major idea of absolute totality (to which Kant objects) can also be maintained as coherent only if it is construed dialectically, that is, in subjectlike manner. Dialectical logic thus provides the mediation, the bridge, and the ladder by which Kant and Spinoza are each led outside their actual—which are one-sided and vulnerable—positions into a more coherent stand, while being reconciled to one another. And this, in turn, yields Hegel's own momentous *Aufhebung* which, although built as a synthesis of former systems that seem to contradict each other, is so novel and daring that it can count as revolutionary in its own right.

SUBJECT AND SPIRIT: THE ROLE OF HISTORY

The subjectivation of the absolute by Hegel has made it a result and invests it with a kind of becoming. But as long as this change is confined to the sphere of the Logic (or of pure metaphysics), it does not exhaust the meaning of spirit. Subject and spirit are not synonyms. There is still some distance to go from the first, logical subjectivation of the absolute to the realization of the spirit in its full sense. To view the absolute as spirit is to endow it, first, with self-consciousness and personality, and second, with a becoming mediated by human history. Only in this way, Hegel maintains, can we "feel at home" in this absolute and actualize our dialectical identity with it. For Hegel, this is also a correct way to interpret the myths of revealed religion, including their anthropomorphic elements, which conceal a profound philosophical truth beneath metaphors and sensual images (*Vorstellung*, resembling Spinoza's *imaginatio*).

The historization of the absolute by Hegel does not mean its relativization. (This would, indeed, be a contradiction in terms.) There is an end to the process in Hegel, in which all former stages culminate and become sublimated (*aufgehoben*) and the absolute standpoint of the spirit emerges. Prior to this stage, indeed, everything was partial and thereby relative; but it was relative to something absolute underlying the process and emerging from it. Moreover, the very status of each stage as partial is determined by the ensuing absolute which they make possible and by which they are superseded.

The historical becoming of the absolute does not relegate it to social and political history alone. The latter is the substrate and the precondition for the becoming of the absolute, but not its essence. Hegel, like Aristotle (and Spinoza)—and unlike Kant or Marx—sees philosophical knowledge and contemplation as the highest achievement, indeed, the supreme state of being. But to make this possible (here lies Hegel's originality) the whole intellectual history of mankind is necessary, based upon the evolution of social and political practices and institutions. Philosophy conceptualizes the actual human experience embodied in life, current practices, norms, religious beliefs, and artistic sensibilities of a given period or *Zeitgeist*. No single individual, however gifted, can attain philosophical truth if his culture and *Zeitgeist* have not ripened to it. This ripening presupposes the entire history of philosophy—and of society, state, and culture generally. Thus, only when freedom has been realized, in principle, in the social reality and the religious consciousness of the time, can its philosophical counterpart, absolute knowledge, be possible as well.

The subject of philosophical knowledge and education, which since Plato has been the individual thinker (a Glaucon, a Theaetetus, etc.), becomes in Hegel the human race in its historical evolution. The self-development of this collective subject has taken over the role of the education (*Bildung*) and intellectual biography of the individual philosopher in Plato. Moreover—and this already follows from Hegel's Spinozism—since all being is a single totality, what occurs in history to the human race in terms of its self-consciousness can be attributed to the totality as a single, organic whole—that is, to God. Through the historical evolution and vicissitudes of mankind, the totality gains self-knowledge and God, as absolute spirit, is being actualized.

In Hegel's evolutionary idealism, self-comprehension is a mode of being, a higher degree of actuality, both for the individual person and for the totality. The historicization of the absolute has therefore in Hegel not only a cultural and sociopolitical significance, but an ontological significance as well. It is not exclusively a human goal but the *telos* of reality itself. Through human history and collective consciousness (always mediated by actual individuals), reality, the object, attains self-knowledge and actualizes itself as subject-object. The evolution within the totality, or God, leads to a stage in which the conceptual comprehension of this totality occurs within it as part of itself. By this self-consciousness, the absolute is not simply known to itself but becomes actual, that is, attains a higher (the supreme) state of being. Only at this stage can there be an absolute entity at all, a subject-object superseding its partial moments, inner dualities, and contradictions. We may say that God attains self-knowledge and actualizes himself through human history (both cultural and social), though in the final stage he transcends his historicalness and moves into dialectical timelessness.

This is totally unheard of in Spinoza or in any other of Hegel's major predecessors. In Spinoza, the absolute lacks personal self-consciousness altogether,[10] and it enjoys a supreme ontological rank eternally, regardless of time and change and certainly regardless of the trivial vicissitudes of human history (or, for that matter, of any particular events in the universe). In Aristotle, God does have self-conception—indeed, he *is* this pure conception of himself, which moves the rest of the universe as prime mover; but this again is an eternal, timeless state of pure actuality. Only Hegel turns this stage into the result of a temporal process, mediated by the whole history of mankind.[11]

This radical shift follows from Hegel's dialectic but can also be said to translate for him the myth of Christ, the son of God. Hegel's philosophy of history has a strong semireligious undercurrent.[12] Unlike Spinoza, who dismisses historical religion as outright *superstitio* (see chapter 1), Hegel's dialectical approach offers a philosophical reinterpretation of some of the major myths and symbols of historical religion, taken as metaphorical expressions of a covert philosophical truth. Thereby, it also grants rational validation to certain anthropomorphic drives in religion—above all, to their archetypal embodiment in the myth of the God-man.

Since the absolute spirit can actualize its eternal and supratemporal status only in time and within human history, it acquires, dialectically, a human dimension which Hegel believes the myth of the "son of God" has captured. It is the whole human evolution, with its suffering, passions, ambitions, and struggles—its real human flesh and blood— that serves as the dialectical embodiment, or "incarnation," of the absolute spirit and mediates between it and the human individual. In this sense, God is "incarnated" in all men and evolves through them toward his own self-knowledge and actuality. Human history is thereby the true mediator not only between individual humans and God but also between God and himself. It is only by becoming man that God becomes God, Hegel's philosophy of history (and, fundamentally, his metaphysics) tells us. God does not exist as absolute spirit from the outset, eternal and perfect. God himself has a becoming which is essential to his self-constitution; and he himself, in order to become actual, requires mediation with individual human persons in whom alone he lives and becomes known to himself.

Using a religious idiom (which Hegel himself avoids) we could say that Christ redeems God no less than he redeems man; or, put differently, through Christ, the symbol of dialectical mediation, man redeems God no less than God redeems man.[13] The mediation between the finite and the infinite consciousness is equally necessary for both in order to become actual. In this respect, Hegel's *Phenomenology of Spirit*, his greatest systematic work prior to the *Logic*, has a tacit Protestant-heterodox structure no less than his more popular philosophy of history. The mediator between the finite and the infinite is not simply church history, a suprahistorical institution, or any ecclesiastical bureaucracy, but universal history; it is not confined to some clerical institution or bureaucracy (Hegel says to the Catholics), but resides in the heart and life of real human experience—in the minds, actions, conflicts, and suffering of men and women, in whom God must become man and whose history, though seemingly arbitrary and contingent, has in fact this latent totalizing significance that through it God is alienated, then is redeemed and becomes known to himself. Hegel departs from orthodoxy (even Protestant orthodoxy) in that his philosophical conceptualization of the religious symbol cancels (*aufhebt*) its direct religious import (this is Hegel's own dialectical way to perform a critique of historical religion); and also (perhaps primarily) because Hegel states that God must be temporalized and incarnated in history in order to become truly God. This is not something God does in addition to being absolute, but is a condition for his becoming such; and no act of grace, love, or compassion is involved in God's becoming man—only dialectical necessity.

Herein lies a true and profound difference between Hegel and Spinoza, which even a deep-structure analysis can no longer remove. Dialectical logic and the doctrine of the becoming God are essential to Hegel's system; both interpret his demand to view the absolute as spirit—and both must necessarily be rejected by Spinoza.

Spinoza cannot admit a dialectical logic because it infringes on the law of contradiction, for him the cornerstone of rationality, and because of its latent theological nature.[14] Spinoza prefers instead his own logic of the complementary aspects of the same, which he believes can do the necessary job without breaching the framework of (causal-type) rationality. As for the notion of the (historically) "becoming" God, Spinoza must reject it because it implies teleology, anthropomorphism, and a tacit providence or "sacred history" guiding the world. All three are metaphysical fictions whose removal is a fundamental systematic principle on which Spinoza's philosophy rests.

Spinoza thus has sufficient systematic reasons to reject Hegel's demand to view God as spirit. But are these reasons exhaustive? Are we not entitled, in a Spinozistic manner, to look for a complementary context of explanation, external to the system yet transformed into its logical texture by the same kind of intellectual alchemy that, in a different (esthetic) context, we have already encountered in Fernando de Rojas?*

The Existential Context: Former Marrano versus Lutheran

On several occasions, Hegel stresses the Jewish (or "oriental") origins of Spinoza to explain certain basic features of his thought. Hegel also mentions Spinoza's Portuguese ancestry and recounts his dispute with the rabbis.[15] It was the Jew in Spinoza, Hegel maintains, who rejected Descartes' dualism and insisted on the absolute unity of God—the strictest possible form of monism and of monotheism. It is again the Jew, or the "oriental" in Spinoza who refused the (rather Christian) idea of setting a "third" term to mediate between the finite and the infinite in God.[16] This idea is the proper message of Christianity for Hegel, just as its absence is the main feature he usually finds in Judaism. In his *Philosophy of Religion* and elsewhere Hegel describes the

* See volume 1, *The Marrano of Reason*, chapter 4.

unbridged gap between the finite and the infinite as the origin of the terrifying fear and trembling which the Jewish God inspires in his subjects, alienating and reducing man to nullity.[17]

These familiar anti-Jewish tones may echo in Hegel's comments on Spinoza;[18] but Hegel, perhaps unwittingly, may have made a pertinent remark. It may well be the Jew, or former Marrano, in Spinoza who views the Christian idea of a mediating "son of God" as an even greater *superstitio* than the myths of the Old Testament.[19] It may also be the former Marrano in Spinoza who, stepping outside all revealed religions and engaged in a momentous combat to secularize history altogether, must be opposed to the subtle way in which Hegel reinstates a new version of providence and sacred history under a philosophical and allegedly rational guise. Moreover, in questioning the rational legitimacy of this move (its underlying dialectical logic) it may again be the former Jew Spinoza who refuses to acknowledge such trinitarian logic with its avowed denial of the law of contradiction—just as Spinoza's forefathers, the medieval rabbis in dispute with Christian theology, refused to admit trinity and incarnation and clung to the law of contradiction in their attempt to show that these ideas, and therefore the whole basis of the Christian teaching, were illogical and incoherent.

It is again the strict rationalist Spinoza, the Jew and disciple of Maimonides, who rejects all forms of anthropomorphism, including teleology and, above all, the Christian archetype of anthropomorphic thinking, the myth of the God-man. Hegel demands to view God in human terms, as spirit—that is, as person, and as historically embodied—for otherwise we could not "be at home" in him. This familiarity Spinoza finds false. We do not approach God by reducing him to human dimensions, but rather by elevating ourselves to the "third degree of knowledge," where all humanlike features disappear from God and we identify with the absolute on its own infinite and eternal terms. If Hegel complains that in such a lofty and thinglike absolute we "are not at home," Spinoza will retort that this, precisely, was intended; for only thus can we attain God and not an imaginary projection of our own self. Spinoza's way is certainly more difficult psychologically, intended for those of rare capacities—just as Nietzsche's later version of it will be. When Spinoza concludes his *Ethics* with the remark that "every excellent thing is as difficult as it is rare," he might have addressed it to Hegel as well.

The divergence between Hegel and Spinoza may thus be construed also, though not exclusively, as a cleavage between a Protestant heterodox philosopher and a ex-Marrano Jewish heretic. Hegel remains fundamentally faithful to a Christian, even Lutheran outlook. He puts forth a dialectical form of trinity as the highest philosophical logic; he stresses the need for God, or spirit, to become "incarnated" in the lives and passions of humanity; and he insists, more generally—and speaking explicitly against the "Jew" Spinoza—on the need for a mediator between God and man, the infinite and the finite, not simply in the form of a church as Christ's mystical body but in the actual life experiences of humanity. History is thus the new *corpus christi* in a symbolic way—but it is also *corpus dei*, the necessary embodiment and alienation of God himself by which he becomes absolute. This dialectical necessity for God to be a result of his self-engendering process makes Hegel a revisionist and heterodox even in his own camp—as does also, perhaps in a lesser degree, the preference he ultimately gives to philosophy over religion, to the "concept" over its metaphorical expressions.

Nature, History, and Divine Presence

Hegel's historical pantheism continues Spinoza's philosophy of immanence, but also departs irremediably from Spinoza. Despite its heterodoxy, this Hegelian stand can also be seen as a roundabout return to Christianity, spurning what Spinoza did to both nature and history. Nature cannot be deified, and history should not, in substance, be secularized.

Hegel transfers the divine presence, the pantheistic element in Spinoza, from nature to human history as a higher and more comprehensive domain of reality. Thereby he tacitly sacralizes history while desacralizing nature which Spinoza declared to be identical with God. There can be no *natura sive deus* in Hegel, but rather *natura sine deus*. Nature as such is an inert substance, a low form of being, unfit to host the divine presence. Using the metaphor of Christian dogma, nature represents to Hegel only the moment of "creation"—the spiritless externalization of God as natural substance—but not yet of "incarnation," which alone can reinstate the divine presence within a natural universe which in itself is devoid of it.[20] Incarnation, however, requires spirit—first the finite spirit of individual persons, real particular men and women, and second, the universal Spirit which evolves and is constituted through their interrelations. The latter is Spirit in the divine sense, God becoming man and moving through human history to self-knowledge and actualization. Nature is incorporated in this process as the inert substrate of human life and action, which serves history and is superseded by it. Human history acquires a special ontological status

(46)

and a hidden sacred sense; it is the embodiment and vehicle of God's self-creation.

This stands in diametrical opposition to Spinoza's theory of history (as we sketched it at the end of chapter 1). Spinoza sets out to explode the notions of providence and sacred history altogether, reducing all events and entities in the universe to a single system of purely natural causes. He thereby totally secularizes history and allows it no special domain of its own; Whatever divine presence there is in human affairs is no different from the divine presence there is in any other segment of nature—and is expressed by the purely causal laws that govern nature throughout.[21]

"The laws of God are inscribed not in the Bible, but in nature"—thus ran a saying among Marrano heretics, which Spinoza shared and systematized. The divinity of nature is manifested in its omnipresent causal laws and in their intersections that produce the singular essences of all things. Spinoza's universe as substance is full of divine presence in that it is intelligible and rationally transparent throughout—without, however, allowing any such categories as purposes, inherent trends and goals (not to mention divine guidance and miracles), or other such man-made images and fictions which, Spinoza claims, we project upon the neutrally causal universe from the depths of our desires and the self-delusory visions they engender. It is rather with the universe stripped of such man-made fictional attire that the human mind is to be united through the third degree of knowledge, turned into a powerful love and procuring supreme emancipation.

Such emancipation is the contrary of self-deception, which is the state of servitude; it requires giving up the metaphysical comforts of manlike God, a teleological universe, and a providential history (under any guise), and learning to extract the infinite meaningfulness of the universe from its eternal causal links (as the sufficient and only valid expression of the divine).

This attitude made Spinoza—in contrast to Hegel—one of the major "dark enlighteners" of modern thought. It also highlights a line that goes from Spinoza to other dark enlighteners, all philosophers of immanence, in the post-Hegelian period, including Freud and, especially, Nietzsche. While Hegel says in reaction to Spinoza that in a universe without teleology and without a humanized God we cannot be at home, Nietzsche, on the contrary, will argue that even the *causal* rationality of Spinoza is still a "shadow of the dead God," another fiction we project upon the universe because of our desire for imaginary comfort and for control over a totally chaotic and irrational universe; and that it is the latter, as such, that we must come to grips in a supreme act of celebrating acceptance—*amor fati* replacing Spinoza's *amor dei intellectualis*.

Assessing Hegel's Critique

How are we to assess Hegel's critique of Spinoza? Hegel seems to confuse interpretation and criticism when he says that the finite things are unreal in Spinoza's system and the attributes of God are merely subjective projection.[22] Whatever the difficulties Spinoza may have in sustaining his views, there is no doubt that for him the attributes are real aspects of the universe, and that (this is even more obvious) finite things have their own mode of real existence (*duratio*), and their own form of actual individuality (*conatus*); they even have eternal essences, derived timelessly from God. Moreover, looking upon the relation of the finite and the infinite from the perspective of *scientia intuitiva*, it can be concluded, as a plausible interpretation of Spinoza's position, that they are mutually dependent. God in the aspect of infinity, as *natura naturans*, is the cause of himself only by being the cause of his own finite aspect, as *natura naturata*.

This will render superfluous the first dialectical correction demanded by Hegel. Moreover, if we consider that Spinoza preceded Hegel in rejecting an a priori method in philosophy, that his true method, under the "deductive" mantle, is the inner explication of a basic *idea vera*, and that his analysis of the infinity of God as qualitative and not quantitative and open-ended preceded (and clearly inspired) Hegel's own, we can see that, in the deep structure of his system, Spinoza had already come a great deal closer to Hegel than the latter recognized or admitted.

And yet a rigid gulf still separates them.[23] Spinoza is barred from taking the second and decisive step—viewing the absolute as subject and spirit—and deifying history instead of nature. This is no default on his part but a matter of philosophical principle. Spinoza may criticize the Hegelian system in turn, especially its trinitarian logic, its pervading teleology, its deep-seated anthropomorphism, its deification of history, its restoration of the notions of providence and sacred history in a new guise, and its seeking metaphysical comfort in a merely natural universe by projecting a false human image upon it and then performing an imaginary "unification" with this fiction. On these major points (all of which are implied by Hegel's spiritualization of the absolute) no reconciliation is possible between these two philosophers—and certainly no *Aufhebung* of Spinoza in Hegelian style. If our analysis has lessened the differences between Spinoza and Hegel, it has also hardened their core.

This does not mean, of course, that Spinoza is right. On the contrary, Hegel is fully justified in his major complaint against Spinoza—that is, if we take it as criticism and not as interpretation. There is indeed a break between the finite and the infinite aspects of the universe—a rather adverse result from the standpoint of Spinoza's intended monism.[24] Given Spinoza's view of negation,[25] he cannot, in fact, sustain the mutual implication he seeks to establish between the particulars and the totality, and the two facets of the universe must, against his wish, remain unbridged. Moreover, Hegel may well be right in claiming that only a dialectical construal of totality can render this concept coherent and that dialectics, in general, could remedy the flaws and impasses of dualism as we know it since the Pre-Socratics.

Yet Hegel's way is impossible for Spinoza because of the reasons we have just mentioned. Hegelian dialectics goes hand in hand with teleology, and with various illusory implications of the absolute as spirit. If Hegel was right in diagnosing Spinoza's logical troubles, he offered an alternative that only worsened the situation, for it depended upon man-made fictions which the whole thrust of Spinoza's philosophy set out to abolish. In the final analysis, Hegel was not a dark enlightener but rather an indirect metaphysical soother.[26]

Crossroads after Hegel: Passage to Nietzsche and Marx

Is there available, then, another alternative, that will avoid the teleological fallacy and illusion (including its appearance as disguised Providence) and yet remain a strict philosophy of immanence? This challenge will provide our guiding question as we look past Hegel at other major attempts to construe a philosophy of immanence, linked to Spinoza by affinity and rivalry. What they had to give up was, first of all, the divine nature of the universe, and even (as did Nietzsche) the very idea of rational totality.

Why should a world of pure immanence be conceived as a rational and organized totality? This is how we can rephrase Nietzsche's objection. Is this not still another, more deep-seated form of anthropomorphism, which Spinoza justly shunned? A more consequential Spinozism, so the argument will go, must strip the universe even of the causal-mechanical relations in which Spinoza saw its divinity, but which Nietzsche identifies as vestiges of the same metaphysical illusion which Spinoza recognized in teleology. The universe is thereby deprived of any rational and, needless to say, divine attributes and is seen as pure formless immanence, an eternal "will to power" in which no rational meaning inheres. Yet precisely this stripped and dehumanized universe is to be the object of a joyful and celebrating stance, even of a kind of paradoxical love, an *amor fati* as rare and as difficult as Spinoza's *amor dei* and requiring the same, or similar, mental strength.

Another alternative to Hegel's inherent teleology was offered by Marx. While raw nature, as such, has no inherent goals, the purposive form is imparted to nature by human work, above all by goal-oriented material production, which takes in Marx the role that the "pure subject" had in German idealism in determining the world and the fate of the human race itself. Marx thereby retains the general pattern of the Copernican revolution started by Kant and expanded by Hegel, but changes its substrate and brings it down to earth and back to nature—that is, back in Spinoza's direction.

Moreover, Marx shared with Hegel the view of history as the vehicle of progress, even of that which religious metaphor labeled "salvation"; but, like Spinoza, he objected to Hegel's view of history as a divine Spirit superseding inert nature. He saw history, in Spinozistic fashion, as completely secularized, an integral part of nature itself, evolving by the immanent laws of nature—whose concept was thereby dialectically enriched.

Marx and Nietzsche thus represent two great nineteenth-century alternatives to a Spinozism that refuse Hegel's idealistic correction, and fight, like Spinoza, against cultural ideologies and self-deceptions. Yet Marx, like the left-Hegelians preceding him, still views the immanent reality as intelligible and even as leading, by its own dynamics, to a form of human salvation other than the one which historical religion had promised. Nietzsche, on the other hand, belongs to (and climaxes) the trend of irrationalist Spinozism (of which Schopenhauer before him and Bergson after him are other representatives). It is in Freud that the Nietzschean kind of Spinozism makes its peace again with scientific reason, sacrificing the "divine" features which reason had in Spinoza but not its emancipating powers. This may offer a systematic angle for considering the history of later Spinozistic influences and the adventures of the idea of immanence.

Spinoza in Heine, Hess, Feuerbach: The Naturalization of Man

Marx's Spinozistic affinities were already present in the left-Hegelian milieu in which he grew and from which he took his departure. The radical young Hegelians brought man back to Spinoza's *natura* from what they saw as the abstract heights of Hegel's *Geist*, and proclaimed a unity of spirit and matter which was considered an essential Spinozistic principle and which led some of them to socialist conclusions. I shall discuss three left-Hegelian figures, especially Heine, both for their intrinsic interest and as a telling bridge to Marx.*

Spinoza was a left-Hegelian hero. "The Moses of modern free-thinkers and materialists"—so Ludwig Feuerbach, a major influence on the young Marx, anointed Spinoza. Unquestionably, Feuerbach thought of himself in the same terms. Spinoza appealed to left-Hegelians both in his negative and his positive philosophy. First, his critique of religion had branded the world of transcendence as illusory. This was, to the left-Hegelians, a major avenue to human emancipation, provided that religious images were not simply rejected outright, but explained in the light of their origins in the needs, mental conflicts, aspirations, and false self-consciousness of man. They were to be brought back to the immanent domain as its own aberration, its own world stood on its head and projected outward. A critique of religion, going beyond Spinoza's Enlightenment mood and enriched with Hegelian categories and techniques, stood at the center of left-Hegelian efforts. The left-Hegelians deepened the analysis while demoting its

---

* The aim of this chapter and the next is not, however, to lay out the complete panorama but to trace the contours of a post-Hegelian philosophy of immanence free of teleology and of Hegel's implicit theology—or at least seeking to renounce them—while retaining the emphasis Hegel put on the human subject and on history. This is the main perspective from which Heine, Hess, Feuerbach, and especially Marx will be considered.

results to an almost one-dimensional claim; and many excelled in a high-powered, sloganish style that sacrificed depth to what they considered as "practice" (i.e., the need to persuade).

Beyond his critique of religion, Spinoza appealed to left-Hegelians because his so-called pantheism was understood as restoring worth and solidity to earthly, this-worldly life and to man as a natural (and corporeal) being. The unity of matter and spirit was a left-Hegelian byword and ideal which Spinoza, not Hegel, was perceived as satisfying. Hegel saw man basically as spirit superseding and overpowering his sensual nature. In that, Hegel remained a Christian thinker. Spinoza alone, among modern philosophers, put matter and spirit, extension and thought, body and mind on the same level, as two equal manifestations of the same immanent humanity and in equal need of each other. This was the substantive message, proclaiming a free, self-emancipated human existence, which left-Hegelians drew from their own critique of Christianity and which they found clearly defined in Spinoza. The dissident Jewish thinker, who two centuries earlier had abandoned all transcendent religion, was the new hero of modern times, the "philosopher of the future" as Heine called him, a new Moses, on a par with Jesus of Nazareth, and like both these prophets, the harbinger of a new era.

This young Hegelian enthusiasm deserves some attention. In mood no less than in content, some of it found its way into Marx's system and personal action. Of course it lost its puerile appearance and a good deal of its naiveté in Marx, but not its secular-messianic fire, which the heavy load of scientific analysis and jargon in the *Capital* could at best screen off but not extinguish. Salvation did loom on the horizon; yet it was not to come about by imposing a moral utopia upon an indifferent nature, but rather, in Spinozistic manner, by uncovering and sharing in the inner laws and forces of nature itself (humanized nature, of course—that of economic production). Spinoza, at best, was only the secular St. John of this process, baptizing an era he did not belong to. The true new Moses (or Christ), the scientific prophet of salvation, was still another former Jew, born two centuries later, not in Amsterdam but in Trier.*

HEINE

"All our contemporary philosophers, perhaps without knowing it, are looking through the eyeglasses that Baruch Spinoza polished." The

---

* Marx's native town.

writer of these words, Heinrich Heine, does not deny that a similar pair of spectacles is sitting on his own nose.[1] Heine is best known for his poetry, which won him a place in German letters at Goethe's side. He was, however, also an outspoken social critic, essayist, visionary, journalist, cultural historian, the greatest wit of the nineteenth century—and one of the first left-Hegelians. As a student, Heine attended Hegel's lectures in Berlin (1821–1823) and established personal contact with the master whom he understood—with a typical left-Hegelian twist—as saying that man has taken over from God and has been deified. This idea was to impress Heine's prose and part of his poetry for a long time.

At twenty-eight Heine converted from a Judaism he no longer believed in to a Christianity he never truly adopted. It was a conversion of convenience that failed to produce the practical rewards Heine had hoped for. His millionaire uncle, Solomon Heine, had to go on supporting his renegade and left-wing revolutionary nephew, earning for himself and for Jewish capitalists a number of well-aimed barbs from Heine's pen.

When "the sun of the July revolution rose in France" Heine, then thirty-three, went to Paris, "the fatherland of Champagne and the Marseillaise,"[2] where he lived for the rest of his life. In Paris he became an expert on the German intellectual scene, rivalling Victor Cousin and Mme. de Staël. Pantheism, Heine told the French, was the liberating essence of contemporary German culture, and Spinoza was its prophet. For a while he was also caught up with Saint-Simonian socialist ideas—the secular "New Christianity"—which tainted but did not dominate his left-Hegelian thinking. Later he was drawn toward Marx, with whom—despite differences in character and age (Marx was two decades younger)—he struck up a personal friendship. "I wish I could pack you up and take you with me," the unsentimental Marx ("my hard-nut friend," Heine called him) told the poet when forced by the French government to leave Paris.[3]

Heine philosophized as he evolved; he was a philosopher-poet, given to subjective moods and variations and to the temptations of style and *bon mot*. His carefree, witty prose flew over an unmistakable personal depth studded with suffering, an earth-bound yearning for salvation, and an occasional heartening naiveté.

Heine's predilection for epigram and *bon mot* is not the only trait that unites him with Nietzsche. A deeper link lies in Heine's worship of life, pure, self-invigorating life in a Godless world. Heine preceded (and possibly inspired)[4] Nietzsche in declaring that God was dead, "massacred" by the hand of Kant who left the overlord of the world "swimming unproved in his own blood."[5] Elsewhere Heine describes the ancient God *Jehowa* preparing to die as the church bells toll his last sacrament.[6] The Jewish God, as it turns out, has been baptized, like Heine himself, and dies a Christian.

The death of God leaves man not an orphan, but his own potential master—a mini-God, creator of all values and of his own universe. However, man is still subdued and exploited by himself, that is, by other men; hence the need for a social and political revolution to complete the religious one. Here Heine's socialism and commitment to politics take over and incorporate his proto-Nietzschean stance. That both these seemingly opposed trends should reside in the same person—and branch off, as I think they do, from the same stem: his Spinozistic experience of life as pure immanence—will surprise only those accustomed to think in rigid, ex post facto categories. Marx, in any case, through his friend Heine, could have become acquainted with something like the Nietzschean universe, and perhaps identify in it more affinities to himself and to his own background than later official Marxism could ever dare admit.

As in Nietzsche, life reigns supreme in Heine—pure, sensual, this-worldly life, of which "every instant is to me an eternity."[7] Earthly life as such, says Heine, should regain the spirituality which the Jews and, even more so, the Christians had denied it for centuries, but which Spinoza (who was, like Heine himself, neither Jew nor Christian) finally restored. Life, Earthly life, is the be-all and end-all, and is passionately affirmed by Heine, as by Nietzsche, both in its exuberant vigor and in the face of tragedy and suffering (and Heine knew them both). "I need no priest to promise me a second life, for I can live enough in this life," Heine declares in his youthful *Reisebilder* (ibid.). "Red life pulses in my veins, earth yields beneath my feet, in the glow of love I embrace trees and statues, and they live in my embrace."

These are the words of an Olympic man, experiencing cosmic liberation. He enjoys life, first, as the very act of living—pure, immanent life as such—and thus enjoys particular pleasures and fulfillments, exhausting every instant to its depth, extracting the spirituality embedded in the realm of the sensual, and shaping pleasure into a liberating human experience. His enjoyment is both sensual and metaphysical, material and spiritual in the same act. And this, too, is Spinozism to Heine, the "pantheist" message he professes in his *History of Religion and Philosophy in Germany* and sings poetically in *Germany: A Winter's Tale*.

Winter's Tale begins with Heine's trip to Germany after a thirteen-year absence. He meets his old world in the form of a little girl singing in a charming voice a little out of tune, a well-known, mystifying song:

> *She sang of love and lover's woes,*
> *Of sacrifice, till the morrow*
> *We meet up in that better world*
> *That knows no pain or sorrow.*
>
> *She sang of this earthly vale of tears,*
> *Of joy one never recaptures,*
> *Of the great Beyond where souls are glad,*
> *Transfigured in deathless raptures.*[8]

Heine recognizes the song. It is the old device by which the people, that "giant fool," has always been hypnotized and brought to submission. Heine brings the girl another song:

> *A newer song, a better song,*
> *My friends, let's bring to birth now!*
> *We shall proceed right here to build*
> *The Kingdom of Heaven on earth now.*
>
> *The soil produces bread enough*
> *For all mankind's nutrition,*
> *Plus rose and myrtle, beauty and joy,*
> *And green peas in addition.*[9]

Heine goes on in a famous couplet:

> *The heavens we can safely leave*
> *To the angels and the sparrows*

This again is Heine's "Spinozism": abolishing an imaginary world of Beyond while raising earthly, material life to spiritual status. The divine is retained in mankind and nature itself; and the joy of life for its own sake replaces the false "spirituality" of Christian mortification. True life is concrete, earthly, sensual, made of bread and green peas but also of roses, beauty, and joy; and as such it is divine, the stuff of which the kingdom of heaven is made.

We may, at this point, remember Fernando de Rojas, another neo-"pagan" artist of Jewish descent, who four centuries earlier had also proclaimed a world without transcendence.* Yet Rojas was left thereby with a metaphysical desert with no inherent meaning, a mere "vale of tears."[10] Heine rejects the "vale of tears" motif as a Christian

---

* See volume 1, *The Marrano of Reason*, chapter 4.

invention and depicts the world of immanence as spiritual and meaningful in itself, even as divine and potentially satisfying—if it is reformed by man into what it can and should become. Heine is in this
respect closer to Spinoza than to Rojas, though he colors his Spinozism with man-centered Hegelian elements that Spinoza rejects. Next
in the poem-cycle[11] Heine passes through customs and watches the
Prussian officials do their duty on his luggage. The poor blockheads,
he muses, are unaware it is not in his bags, but in his head that Heine
carries the contraband. For indeed he is smuggling precious stones,
"the crown Jewels of the future," promulgating an un-Christian "God
of the Renewal." Heine even announces a new, earthly Holy Family.
The maiden Europe is already making love to the Spirit of Freedom,
and although no priest has blessed them with holy waters, they have
become inseparable. Soon there will be children born of their holy
wedlock.

A human messenger performing a new annunciation, a secular apos-
tle of a new creed, Heine does not lose his self-irony. When he crosses
the Rhine, the old river inquires about the French, whom it remembers
pouring victorious waters into its current under Napoleon, and seems
to miss their dash and *esprit*. Heine reassures the river:

> *Oh fear you not, dear father Rhine,*
> *These jibes in the French tradition;*
> *They're not the Frenchmen of old any more,*
> *And they wear different pants, in addition.*

> *They philosophize now all over the place,*
> Kant, *Fischte [Fichte] and Hegel extolling;*
> *They smoke tobacco, they guzzle beer,*
> *And many even go bowling.*[12]

But who got the French interested in "Fischte" and Kant, if not the
same "*Henri*" Heine who now makes fun of his own success?[13] Heine's
De l'Allemagne, the French version of his *History of Religion and Philosophy in Germany*[14] and published about a decade before *Winter's Tale*,
expresses in vivid essay form the same basic philosophy of immanence
as the poem-cycle.

The *History* is written in semi-Hegelian fashion, its material organized from the vantagepoint of the result to which it purports to lead.
This result is Hegel's philosophy, bringing to its climax the idealist
revolution in Germany, which Heine calls "the last consequence of
Protestantism."[15] The same Hegelian result, however, is also called
"pantheism" and identified with the "point of view" (though not the

literal system) of Spinoza—who thus enjoys a privileged position like Hegel himself. If Hegel brings the process to its apex, Spinoza underlies it throughout.

Heine speaks very little of Hegel directly. The Hegel that emerges from Heine's account is the philosopher who did everything that Schelling should have done and failed to do. He is also a reformer who undermined the social and religious order and heralded a new era of freedom. Like Spinoza, he is a pantheist and a naturalist, imbued with Enlightenment ideas and wearing a mask of prudence (to shield him from the rigors of the Restoration). Heine not only revises the conservative image of Hegel, he also views himself as unveiling the German idealists since Kant, whose true, subversive message was couched in foggy jargon and "draped in scholastic formulas" that clouded and even reversed its meaning. Kant had performed in the German mind a revolution as profound as, and far more lasting than, the political revolution in France. "As in France no privilege, so in Germany no thought is tolerated without providing its right to exist. . . . And as in France fell the monarchy, the keystone of the old social system, so in Germany fell theism, the keystone of the intellectual *ancien régime.*"[16] Kant is perceived as completing the work of Spinoza. He is an "archdestroyer in the realm of thought" who "far surpassed Robespierre in terrorism"[17] (though he shared his "shopkeeper's" self-righteousness). The French only killed a king, but Kant and his followers killed a God.

Associating Kant with Spinoza's "pantheism" is more than dubious. But Heine, I think, has here in mind their role as critics of transcendent religion, or as he calls it, "theism."* With Kant, human reason—that is, mankind as immanent existence—is left to itself as its own lawgiver and subject at once, the master and the slave of itself; it is thus autonomous or inherently free, with no divine authority to guide (or subdue) it from above (see chapter 1).

On this negative and quasi-formal basis Heine observes a more full-bodied pantheism taking shape. With Fichte, the Kantian "I" has become a "universal world-I endowed with self-consciousness,"[18] and thus a subjectivized form of the Spinozistic world-substance. Likewise Schelling, "while he was still a philosopher, put forth a philosophy of nature which is basically nothing else than Spinoza's idea of pantheism,"[19] the most outspoken proclamation of "the sanctification of nature and the restitution of man into his divine rights." In art, pantheism

---

* Here and elsewhere Heine uses the word *deism* but means what we usually call "theism," namely, belief in the existence of a transcendent God, separate from the world he had created.

was "expressed most unmistakeably" by none other than Goethe; his *Werther, Faust*, and above all, the *Ballads*, moved Heine to say that "the early philosophy of Spinoza has shed its mathematical shell and now flutters about in Goethe's poetry."[20] "Goethe," says Heine, "was the Spinoza of poetry,"[21] an avowed pantheist who occupied himself with Spinoza's philosophy his entire life.

With Hegel, "our revolution is terminated" and the circle is complete.[22] Heine, curiously but characteristically, sees Hegel's system as a kind of *Naturphilosophie* (philosophy of nature), an odd label for one which had put spirit over and above nature and saw the latter as inert substance, a mere self-"externalization" of God. Heine reads (or rather, misreads) Hegel with the same glasses "that Spinoza had polished"; he tries to perform a synthesis between them that tends back in Spinoza's direction, and so his Hegel, too, seems to give equal status to nature and spirit as two aspects of the same immanent totality, and to view the human mind as a self-reflection of nature that remains an integral part of it. This is a definite departure from the real Hegel toward Spinoza.

Besides being interwoven into the rest of the story, Spinoza also occupies a chapter for himself in Heine's account of *German* philosophy.[23] Heine, like Hegel, takes time to recount Spinoza's life and background—an exception in both these writers. Spinoza is extolled in rare language. Reading him, "one inhales the air of the future"; there is an "inexplicable breath" in him, "a *grandezza* of thought" which must come from his direct ancestors, the Hispano-Jewish martyrs; moreover, "the spirit of the ancient Hebrew prophets seems to hover over this distant offspring of theirs" who, in personal purity and in the crown of thorns he wore on his head, also resembled another divine parent of his, Jesus Christ.[24] It is no wonder that Heine's customary scoffing and mockery, which spared neither himself nor most of those he admired or agreed with, totally evaporates at Spinoza's doorstep.

Like Hegel, Heine also makes much of Spinoza's Jewish origins, but in an absolutely different mood and in close existential intimacy. Heine clearly feels Spinoza to be his brother in non-Jesus, in non-Moses, in something new transcending both. Heine pricks at Spinoza's excommunicators with their bombastic blowing of the shofar, the ancient symbol of religious awe which Heine, in cool, profane vengeance, strips down to the prosaic piece of ram horn it actually is. The rabbis, Heine says, declared Spinoza "undeserving to carry the name of Jew," yet "his enemies were magnanimous enough to leave this name to him."[25] Heine knows this experience all too well. Spinoza heralds for him the lot of the modern Jew who, projected beyond Judaism and

Christianity alike, still carries over with him a new creed, a new earthly route to something resembling redemption. The hope, the message, and the messianic drive are injected into secular society—and Heine, when drifting for a while toward the Saint-Simonians, could not have been surprised by the number of Jews in their leading ranks,[26] as he was surely not astonished by the ex-Judaism of his "hard-nut" friend Marx, the scientific prophet, nor by the latter's convoluted and almost auto-antisemitic struggle against this transcended part of his own self.

Spinoza, however, is not only a person; his life is interwoven with the pantheism he announces. What does this concept mean to Heine? In brief, it has two major and connected aspects.

Pantheism is first the metaphysical doctrine of God's identity with the world. "The God of the pantheists distinguishes Himself from that of the theists in that He is within the world itself, while the latter is outside it or, what amounts to the same thing, is above the world. The God of the theists governs the world as a separate institution from above."[27] Heine here puts the ethical and political corollaries of theism into its very definition. Being outside the world means that God rules over it as an absolute monarch. It is only with regard to the mode of this government that the theists are divided.

> The Hebrews think of God as a thundering tyrant; the Christians as a loving father; Rousseau and his disciples, the whole Geneva school, think of Him as a clever artist who fabricated the world more or less as their *Papa* [Daddy] used to fabricate his clocks, and, being *connoisseurs*, they adore the work and praise the Master there-above.[28]

Heine must be aware that this "clockwork" theology (which alone among his examples merits the term *deism*) is not a Genevan monopoly; it was professed by Leibniz and certain "occasionalist" Cartesians, and marks, in a more general sense, the whole trend of the "God of the philosophers"—excepting, of course, Spinoza. What Heine tells us under his jokes is that Spinoza was unique and solitary not only among Jews and Christians, but also among the rationalist philosophers themselves. But not any more, at least not in Germany:

> Pantheism is the open secret of Germany. In fact we have out-grown theism. We are free and want no thundering tyrants. We are of age and need no paternal care. Nor are we the artifacts of a great craftsman. Theism is a religion for slaves, for children, for Genevans, for watchmakers![29]

Geneva notwithstanding, Heine's rhetoric shows that he has little use for metaphysical arguments per se. Theism is wrong and pantheism is right because of its implications for man's self-image, life, ethics, and politics. Nor is theism so much refuted as it is outgrown. It is a phase in human development signifying immaturity, and is shed when mankind, through self-education, grows up to assert its own autonomy and divinity. Heine follows here Kant, Herder, Schiller, and other thinkers of the *Aufklärung*, whom he clothes in a Hegelian mantle and leads back to Spinoza.

However, when speaking of the divinity of man and not simply of his autonomy, Heine also Hegelianizes Spinoza, far beyond what the latter's doctrine will support. Rather than bringing Hegel back to Spinoza, Heine takes here the opposite direction. God, says Heine, is identical with nature. He manifests himself in plants and animals, yet humans have a distinct advantage—in man the divinity attains self-consciousness, Heine states in familiar Hegelian terms. Moreover, "humanity as a whole is the incarnation of God" who is "the true hero of human history."[30] This, precisely, is the aspect of Hegel's "absolute as spirit" which Spinoza must unequivocally reject. Yet this is not the Hegelian *Geist* superseding nature; it is nature itself, in its very individuality, which produces self-consciousness in man. Even where Heine oversteps Spinoza toward a specific Hegelian idea, he Spinozises, as it were, this idea too.

The second major sense of pantheism for Heine is the unity of matter and spirit. Here, again, Heine leads Hegel back toward Spinoza. He abolishes the superiority of the Hegelian *Geist* over nature and restores their parallel and complementary status. Pantheism, Heine explains, entails "the rehabilitation of matter, its restoration to dignity, its religious recognition, its moral sanctification, its reconciliation with spirit."[31] "Holy Matter!"[32] Heine exclaims, paraphrasing the Christian Holy Spirit in reverse. He does not wish to abolish spirit but to unite it with matter on an equal basis. Thereby he returns to Spinoza and stands, like him, against centuries of Christian and Jewish culture. The Jews, says Heine, despised the body and espoused austere spirituality, which they bequeathed to the pagan world in the form of Christianity. (Elsewhere Heine sees this as a subtle revenge of Judea over the Rome that had crushed it—another proto-Nietzschean idea.[33]) Christianity went even further, insisting on unnatural demands that were impossible to fulfill and thus introducing evil and hypocrisy into the world. Christianity mortified the flesh and condemned the body as vile and evil in itself. Thereby it forced every person into sin, then subdued him or her by the fear of divine retribution in the next world. The two aspects of theism are here united from a political standpoint. Christianity, moreover, had to relinquish the real world to the dominion of Caesar "and his Jewish pages"[34]—to sheer power, greed, ambition, and the oppression of the people in which it ultimately joined; dialectically, by demanding lofty and abstract spirituality, Christianity had actually drained the real world of all spirituality.

Heine, far from being a materialist, seeks to restore the link between the real and the spiritual. He insists that spirit resides within the material world, within the needs and sensual aspirations of humanity, the only subject of divinity and worth, and that the highest degree of spirituality, the kingdom of God itself, is "baked with leaven" and made with "green peas aplenty" along with more refined pleasures.

This conception has various consequences, both political and esthetic-moral. Restoring the value of matter adds a new socialist (and economic) dimension to politics. Henceforth, the political revolution must put forth the material welfare of the people as its objective, as something carrying moral and spiritual worth in itself,[35] and not be satisfied with formal democracy and political freedom alone, as if this were a "purer" domain in which, as in Hegel, spirituality might manifest itself. This anti-Hegelian and proto-Marxian demand is also made by Heine as a corollary to the pantheism he finds in Spinoza.

Moreover, socialism could not cherish a cult of poverty or austere personal morality. Heine chides the self-denial of many revolutionaries, which is but a new form of Christianity. It is not the sharing of want he is after, but the plenitude of life—rich, abundant, sensual, celebrating.

> We are founding a democracy of Gods equally holy, blessed, and glorious. You desire simple dress, ascetic morals, and unseasoned enjoyment; we, on the contrary, desire nectar and ambrosia, purple mantles, costly perfumes, pleasure and splendor, dance and laughing, music and plays.[36]

One is reminded, even by the phrasing, of Spinoza's well-known words:

> The greater the joy with which we are affected, the greater the perfection to which we pass. . . . It is the part of a wise man to refresh and restore himself in moderation with pleasant food and drink, with scents, with the beauty of green plants, with decoration, music, sports, the theater and other things of this kind. (*Ethics*, pt. 4, prop. 45S)

Pleasure, for Heine, is sensual and metaphysical experience, enjoying the self as autonomous by way of enjoying sensual existence. Such pleasure should not be construed as merely hedonistic or utilitarian.

But, equally, it must not lose its concrete sensuality and be interpreted as a metaphor (the usual strategy of theologians). Matter and sensual existence are spiritual in their own being, in their very naturalness, and both aspects reside in each other: Matter, the stuff of life, is ambrosia throughout. Even bread and green peas are ambrosia, if we care to look at them this way, as Heine suggests we do.

In May 1848 Heine walked the streets of Paris for the last time. He died after eight more bedridden years—in his "mattress-grave," as he dubbed it, suffering from advanced muscle degeneration, living on morphine and opium, his new ambrosia, fighting his enemies, his nocturnal ghosts, his past, his self-pity, and writing new poems and polemics. Heine's financial support collapsed along with his health, and he was always mindful of money. These long last years were Heine's most truly Nietzschean period—affirming life with passion in face of acute pain and impending death, and mobilizing the resources of art, beauty, wit, and humor to transform suffering into a life force. But Heine was no longer a theoretical Nietzschean. His atheism was shattered along with his health and income (and both are needed in abundance, Heine half muses in his *Confessions*, in order to be a solid atheist). This was Heine's "conversion," as it is sometimes called, perhaps exaggeratedly.[37] Heine says he has committed a manuscript on Hegel's philosophy to the flames,[38] and he retracts the main ideas of his *History* in a new preface composed in 1852. God is alive and well, Heine now reports. The good Kant never really meant any great harm to him. In fact, as Heine now recognizes, Kant did not disprove the existence of God but left the matter unresolved in principle, with mankind having only its autonomous reason to rely upon; and all the "spidery Berlin dialectic" (Hegel, of course) cannot even kill a cat, let alone a God.

"Now the shipwrecked metaphysician clings fast to the Bible."[39] Through the Bible Heine tries to come to terms with his assumed Protestantism and with his never quite betrayed Judaism. He returns to his Jewish origins, not in religious affiliation but in historical sentiment and pride,[40] composing his *Hebrew Melodies*. But, no less, Heine finds in the Bible—the Protestant book, rediscovered and disseminated by Luther—a new vindication of his apostasy, which seems to have weighed more on his mind than the simple "change of clothes" he had at first said it was. Much as, in his *History*, Heine claimed paradoxically that Protestantism was the origin of the liberating atheism that later emerged in Germany, so now he sees Protestantism as the genuine religion of the Bible, its newfound spring of life. Luther is never accepted by Heine as such, yet is always put at the source of whatever spiritual merit the Heine of the day recognizes.[41]

Heine's social vision, too, darkened toward the end. He was a friend of Lassale, but recoiled with horror from the "most communistic communism" which, like industrial capitalism, threatened to level all humanity to shallowness and kill beauty and poetry. He started seeing the people as plebians, and was frightened by a future more ominous than his youthful enthusiasm seemed to promise. His former integral Hellenistic dream was now broken into scraps of relief sculpture from his own sarcophagus, where Heine, in one of his later poems, imagines himself lying, as bits fallen from his coffin, some engraved with Greek and some with Hebrew motifs, mix and fight all around him, and the mysterious *Mouche*, the martyr's flower made of Christ's blood, flourishes over the poet before turning into a sensual, loving woman. * This was the tombstone Heine created for himself while lying in his other, mattress sarcophagus.

It was not an inaccurate self-portrait, though perhaps not complex enough. Despite his alleged "conversion" Heine died the dualist he had always been (even under his deeply assumed Hellenism), wavering between Athens and Jerusalem, between socialism and art, and, above all, between an atheism he no longer believed in and a new religious feeling he did not quite trust.

It is, however (perhaps unfortunately), not the later Heine who interests us here, but the Heine up to 1848 and especially between the two revolutions. Let me conclude by summing up his relation to Spinoza and his role in the broader picture.

The context in which Heine wrote was drawn by the *Pantheismusstreit* (the strife over pantheism) that had raged in Germany about a generation earlier. Friedrich Heinrich Jacobi, the proponent of supersensible faith, claimed that no rational philosophy can establish the truth of religion. On the contrary, when rational metaphysics is most coherent it is doomed to end in Spinoza's pantheism, which is fundamentally atheistic. Jacobi also alleged that Lessing, before his death, had confessed to him that he agreed fundamentally with Spinoza. Jacobi challenged Moses Mendelssohn, Lessing's friend and a rationalist metaphysician (i.e. maintaining that God's existence, immortality of the soul, and other religious ideas have rational proofs), to respond. The controversy that ensued sparked like fire; Kant, Goethe, and Herder among others found themselves involved, Kant trying to "cleanse myself of the suspicion of Spinozism"[42] (as he wrote to Jacobi), Goethe and Herder trying to exculpate Spinoza of the charge of atheism. This

---

* *La Mouche* ("Fly") was the nickname Heine used for a young woman, Camille Selden, who became attached to him and was his last love.

strife was, sociologically, a far more important event in German culture than the mere merit of the case may suggest; and as Heine recognizes, it put Spinoza at the heart of German idealism, with Fichte, Schelling, and Hegel trying to unite Kant and Spinoza, each in his own manner.

A generation later, Heine looks back on the battle and finds himself within it. He pours derision on Jacobi in every possible way, calling him an "old woman," a nonphilosopher in disguise, and the like; but when all is said and done and the sarcasm subsides, we see that Heine had subscribed to Jacobi's thesis: Spinoza's pantheism is indeed the logical consequence of rational philosophy, and it is indeed atheism. But there is nothing to hide or to be exculpated from: this is the new maturity of the German spirit, heralding, in Spinoza's name, a new era of liberation. Jacobi won the exegetical battle, but lost the substantive war.[43]

How does Heine relate to Spinoza and Hegel? Heine started with Hegel, but in several ways brought him back to Spinoza. First, he reinvested Hegel with elements of the Enlightenment that Spinoza had foretold but Hegel already transcended; his Hegel is refreshingly less dialectical, more a critic (especially of religion) than a system builder, a Hegel returned to his youth and made a young Hegelian. Thereby, inevitably, he is also flattened, and suffers from the same one-sidedness which the real Hegel saw as the flaw of the *Aufklärung*.

Second, Heine abolishes the superiority of spirit over matter that dominated Hegel's thought and replaces it with a strict Spinozistic parallelism. Hegel's pantheism was historical; Heine, following Spinoza, restores nature as a primordial and comprehensive category, of which matter and spirit, the ideal and the real, are equal and complementary aspects. This enables Heine to "sanctify matter," as he says, and to restore it to moral and religious worth. Heine, however, is no materialist; like Spinoza, he rejects metaphysical materialism—the view that spirit is reducible to matter or derived from it as an epiphenomenon— as well as materialism as ethics, the hedonist (and utilitarian) emphasis on crude matter as such and for its own one-sided sake. Heine's disgust with the purely carnal lasciviousness of the Roman Empire equals only his aversion to its antidote: Christian supraspirituality.

Heine joins Spinoza in his anti-Christian (and, he believes, with much less reason, anti-Jewish)[44] rediscovery of the spirituality inherent in matter and the sensual being of man. This leads Heine, on the one hand, to his anti-ascetic morality, celebrating this-worldly life, and on the other hand to his socialism. The kingdom of God can be established only on earth and must entail material welfare and the sharing of wealth. Formal democracy is not sufficient, but calls for economic democracy as well. Not only is there nothing vile in the material needs and interests of mankind, they are genuine expressions of humanity and the necessary substrate for all human liberation.

This leads well beyond Hegel and, through a return to Spinoza, onward, via Feuerbach to Marx: Hegel abandoned the world of economic production and exchange to the reign of egoistic particular interests, a war of all against all, devoid of inherent rational meaning and basically spiritless. Only the domain of politics and right was "spiritual" for Hegel, and thus the appropriate field in which human liberation is to be achieved and the old religious ideals secularized and projected into history. Heine and the other left-Hegelians—up to and including Marx—by their Spinozistic rehabilitation of matter as the only place where spirit can inhere, made it possible for socialism to emerge as a worthy human prospect, replacing the transcendent religious ideals and introducing ethical worth and rational meaning into the world of economic forces and interest.

Heine thus performs a kind of synthesis (as Lefebvre suggests)[45] between Spinoza and Hegel typical of left-Hegelianism more generally, a synthesis sprinkled with elements of the Enlightenment and leaning largely in Spinoza's direction. Yet this "return" to Spinoza is future-oriented: it serves to transcend Hegel and move toward a new version of Spinoza's naturalism, enriched with contemporary concerns and marked by a socialist tendency. This new naturalism is historicized, as in Hegel, without giving history the supreme "spiritual" status that Hegel did, but rather leaving history, in pure Spinozistic manner, within nature itself as its own integral manifestation. Heine, like D. F. Strauss, Hess, and Feuerbach, sees the divine as best embodied in human history; but even this Hegelian step, which Spinoza himself could not allow, is clothed in Spinozistic garb. No concession is made to the overriding "spirituality" of history as compared to nature. History itself is naturalized, just as self-consciousness becomes an inner reflectivity within nature, and the Spinozistic parallelism of equal aspects of the totality—the crucial point allowing left-Hegelians to remain naturalists—is strictly preserved.

Heine's was only one of the very first expressions of this new thinking, where Hegel was brought back to Spinoza and the latter was historicized without ceasing to be a naturalist. The most outstanding system of thought that developed from this is that of Marx. And the most influential young Hegelian expounding on Marx was not his friend Heine, but the more systematic Feuerbach.

SPINOZA AND HESS

Several years after Heine's *History of Religion and Philosophy in Germany*, the first socialist book was published in Germany, a curious, half-baked work, but also revealing in many ways. It came from the pen of the young Moses Hess, the future socialist leader and Marx's uneasy colleague and sometime companion. Hess entitled his book *The Holy History of Mankind* and signed it, anonymously, "by a junior (disciple) of Spinoza" (*von einem Jünger Spinozas*)—a rather paradoxical title page, considering that Spinoza was the first to abolish the notion of "sacred history" and could not allow it even in the metaphoric Hegelian sense that Hess is surely using.[46]

The paradox is heightened as we see the role which the young Hess assigns to Spinoza as the third Jewish prophet after Moses and Jesus. The sacred history of mankind (its latent meaning) unfolds in a trinity of realms. First, there is the realm of God the Father, marked by ancient Judaism and the Old Testament; then, with Jesus' birth, the realm of God the Son takes precedence, marked by Christianity and the New Testament. Christianity is then superseded in turn with the birth of "our Master," Spinoza, who opens the third and final realm, that of the Holy Spirit, the realm in which we still live. This last era will lead, through a series of revolutions (spiritual in Germany [cf. Heine], political in France and the United States, and more to come) to the ultimate redemption of the human race, when the New Jerusalem will be established in the heart of Europe. This will be a perfect socialist society, abolishing private property and the right of inheritance, dethroning Mammon and his dehumanizing regime, and allowing the inner solidarity of the human heart to assert itself freely, unhindered by the devious social institutions which, so far, have perverted it into an egoistic strife of all against all. This, says Hess in prophetic exultation—a new Isaiah transcribing the old one—will herald the end of days in which the ancient Jewish message, liberated from its narrow religious shell, will be properly translated and realized on a world-historical scale. And all this will take place under Spinoza's banner and to the awesome sound of the Jewish shofar—the same instrument that accompanied Spinoza's ban (and of which Heine spoke in derision).

The young Hess indulges in a fascinating mixture of Jewish and Christian symbols formerly known mainly among the Marranos and their descendants. But Hess is no Marrano; he is a left-Hegelian Jewish heretic who, while transcending the historical religions, tries nevertheless to recapture his own lost Judaism within the socialist utopia, the final outcome of history. This is an unmistakable drive in the young

Hess. He proclaims a spiritual recall of the Jews, just as, two decades later and after several variations, he will recommend the material recall of the Jews as well.

This drive also explains a distortion Hess makes. What Spinoza saw as the flaw of ancient Judaism—its union of politics and religion—Hess, in Spinoza's name, declares to be an advantage. The Jews, says Hess, knew no distinction between the inner and the outer man and between reality and its spiritual meaning; Christians broke this unity, severing God from Caesar and abandoning (as Heine has charged) the real world to the dominion of brute force, greed, and exploitation. With Spinoza, however, the unity of matter and spirit, the real and the ideal, is restored; now we can proceed to reunite politics and its religious meaning on a higher level, that of the communist society, which will embody a moral vision within the actual workings of economic and political forces.

Hess in later years renounced his early book, which was more enthusiastic than coherent and immature in its socialist thinking. But to Hess's biographers the work remains indicative of the lasting concerns of its author; and to us, it represents the characteristic link between Spinoza and the secularization of religious messianism in left-Hegelian socialist thinking. This Hegelianizes Spinoza, but also undercuts Hegel's philosophy of the spirit in favor of a Spinozistic "unity of matter and spirit"—and the latter could be construed as implementing an ethical vision within the brute machinery of politics and economics, a main gate for the socialist assimilation of Spinoza which the "utopian" socialists share with Marx himself. Marx's difference from the utopian socialists makes him even more Spinozistic, for he allows no role for the pure moral will as such—an illusion to Spinoza—but assigns the task of producing communist society to the inner (dialectical) determination of the socioeconomic system itself—Marx's new *causa sui* and world of immanence.

Hess never became a Marxist in this sense. He had inspired Marx; he had won Engels over to the idea of communism; he was attacked by Marx and Engels (in the *Communist Manifesto*) under the mock title of "the true socialism"; and he later came partly under Marx's influence and for a while also under his political tutelage. The mature Hess became persuaded (or believed that he was) that pure ideas and the moral will were insufficient in and of themselves to change the world, and that the forces of production, economics, the proletariat, labor organization, and self-interested action were fundamental in bringing about the society of the future. Nevertheless, Hess's approach to socialism remained predominantly ethical, and in later years he associated himself with Lassale. Hess could not live in peace with the "hard-nut" side of Marx, as Heine had dubbed it, the ruthless amoralism put in the service of human redemption and which Lenin later infused into Bolshevik theory; and Hess remained too much of a moralist for the more "scientific" (and, in this sense, more Spinozistic) Marxists to accept.[47]

Hess was, in the words of a noted historian of socialism, "a deeply honest thinker, and a man incapable of animosity, universally loved and respected, a sort of Jewish saint fallen among revolutionaries."[48] Yet it was no accident that brought Hess into such company. It was precisely as a Jew—in the modern, heretical sense created by Spinoza and which Hess shared with Heine, Marx, Lassale, and the Jewish Saint-Simonians—that Hess became a revolutionary. He had not so much "fallen" among them as he had grown toward them.

The socialist vision as Hess saw it was the new messianic call, which went beyond Judaism and Christianity but restored an ancient Jewish message on a secular and universalized level. Unlike Marx (who repressed his Jewish origins) or Heine (who saw Judaism as an object of ethnic identification and cultural historical research) Hess, who never converted, attempted to recover the old Judaism, whose religious form he had left, within the new messianic socialism that transcended it.[49] For Hess, modern Jews, like himself and his Master, Spinoza, had to serve as channels and mediators for this process and to embody it in their persons. At first Hess believed that only Jewish individuals could be redeemed by serving in such roles; decades later, however, Hess returned to Judaism also as a national entity and became the father of socialist zionism. In *Rome and Jerusalem* (1862) he advocated the return of the Jews to their ancient land, where they should set up a model socialist society, thus having the vision of universal redemption fulfilled by the same nation that had cherished it most intimately throughout the ages while lacking it the most.

From across a considerable distance, one is tempted to think of another messianic dreamer, announcing the "recall of the Jews," Isaac la Peyrère. Hess was more realistically oriented, a man of action who, in retrospect, also had the advantage of having part of his dream come close to what may seem true. But in messianic drive he did not lag behind La Peyrère, and, like him, in his early days, he used a threefold periodization of *historia sacra* to express, albeit metaphorically, the march of humanity toward an immanent form of salvation.

Even in maturity, Hess retained the link between communism as the culmination of historical religion and the humanized pantheism he attributed to Spinoza. This can be illustrated by a popular text he wrote a decade later to educate the working Christian masses. Hess defines communism as a "creed" (*Bekenntnis*) and as a "universal religion" which, far from being un-Christian, serves to bring Christianity to its completion. This it does by preserving the original Christian ideas—love and humanity—but bringing them back from a world beyond into this world, where they are to be realized by the communist society. And here, like Heine, Hess becomes pantheistic (or Spinozistic) in a left-Hegelian manner:

71. Is our God . . . anything else than the *human race*—or *mankind united in love* [socialist solidarity and affinity]?
—No, nothing else.

72. Why did we believe until now that the devil was within the world, and that our God was not within us, but in heaven?—Because we ourselves did not live in love but in separation and hostility [earlier he said "under the dominion of *Mammon*, who indeed is the devil"] . . . therefore did we believe that our God was outside us and beyond this bad world, whereas the devil was in us, in this world, the very essence of the world.[50]

This sounds close to Feuerbach and Heine, but there is a difference. Hess shares Marx's disbelief in pure philosophical criticism as the way to change our false self-consciousness. The pantheist revolution that Heine and other Germans had praised was ineffectual, for one has to change reality first. This is because the false self-consciousness implied in dualistic theism is partly true, not fundamentally but *historically*, that is, as long as exploitation and private property prevail. Hence, Spinoza cannot win beforehand in mere theory. Verifying his theory—we may complete Hess's idea in a Marxian vein—means changing the world to suit it.

Hess was, indeed, the first to proclaim the need to unify theory and practice—another facet of Spinozistic parallelism that he bequeathed to Marx. Reality, says Hess, is determined by acts, not merely by concepts. The inherent end of understanding is action, and action creates a new ground for understanding. Here again Hess relies on Spinoza. In an unpublished commentary on the *Ethics*,[51] Hess stresses that Spinoza's is indeed an ethical theory. The metaphysical part of the *Ethics* is preparatory for the practical doctrine in part 3. Freedom resides primarily in the acts of an individual who clearly understands his or her actions and emotion as they follow causally from the nature of desire; and this entails social implications as well. Socialism is then actually anchored in the ethical part of Spinoza's system, even though he had not yet been aware of this. According to Hess in the *Philosophy of Action* (1843), the future philosophy of action is but a further development of Spinoza's *Ethics*.

Spinoza, Hess adds in the *European Triarchy*, was also unaware that his absolute was already, in itself, a subject–object and not merely an object; these implications of his doctrine could only be uncovered by Hegel and Schelling. Hess means that, implicitly, Spinoza has already attributed to the immanent God a historical dimension as well as a natural one. God exists and is realized through the human race as it evolves toward redemption. This is an exaggerated, indeed a false view of Spinoza; but Hess's reliance on Spinoza is not merely intellectual but also personal and existential. Spinoza was to Hess what Socrates, Moses, Jesus, or Buddha are for thinkers or believers passing from one view to another while always clinging to the same teacher-figure. Also, Spinoza was not a remote and half-legendary figure but a concrete person with whom Hess could identify, a Jew who, like himself, had left the traditional community to confront, singly, the modern world.

When Hess claims Spinoza as a source while misrepresenting his literal meaning, he does use some actual Spinozistic motif adapted to his own philosophic and rhetorical interests. But this adaptation is too farfetched. For example, Spinoza was adamant about freeing government from the influence of religion, whereas Hess repeatedly demanded a link between them and praised the ancient Hebrew state—in Spinoza's name!—for having so tightly united religion with the state. This is paradoxical. Spinoza specifically criticized the ancient Hebrew state as a paradigm case of theocracy, and the source of two other, even worse, theocratic distortions: (1) Jewish life in the diaspora, in which religion functioned as an imaginary state; and (2) the varieties of Christian theocracy—from the pope, claiming metaphysical authority over terrestrial matters; to the Inquisition, enforcing a monolithic religion by the sword (and the stake) of the secular government; to the wars of religion and the compromise they produced (*cuius regio eius religio*—"state religion goes by the ruler"—implying that there *is* a state religion); and, in a privileged place, to the Dutch Calvinist establishment which pressed the lay government to implement its directives and claimed to constitute, in Spinoza's words, "a realm within the realm" (*imperium in imperio*). Spinoza's objection to all theocratic forms had theoretical grounds, powerfully systematized, but not unrelated to his triple existential situation (as a son of former Marranos who suffered from the Inquisition; as a heretical Jew expelled for his views; and as a political modernizer close to the republican party, who wished to emancipate state government from the clergy's impact and to have each individual relate to the state directly as citizen).

How, then, do we explain the fact that Hess praises the ancient Hebrew theocracy and in Spinoza's own name?

Perhaps the clue is to be found in the most paradoxical text of all. In *Holy History*, Hess praises the ancient Hebrews for recognizing no split between a person's inner and outer life (as in Protestantism) or between reality and its spiritual meaning (as in Catholicism). It was Christianity that shattered this ancient unity and posited a dualism instead, separating God and Caesar and thereby abandoning the real world to the domain of greed and brute force. Only Spinoza, in his pantheism, restores the unity of the real and the ideal, the material and the spiritual. Henceforth it becomes possible to unite the world of money and politics with its religious (i.e., spiritual) meaning—and this is realized in socialist society where a sublime moral principle informs the material world.

Socialism is for Hess the highest form of religion; hence what he actually wants is to unite *socialism* with the state. Hess rejects the liberal state that serves as a neutral framework lacking an ideological (= spiritual) content of its own. It is an instrument of capitalist exploitation that drains the actual world of any spiritual dimension and abandons it to a war of all against all. In objecting to the separation of state and religion Hess really objects to separating the state from moral and spiritual values; and since the highest political morality resides in socialist ethics (= true religion), the ideal state Hess has in mind is the socialist state, which actualizes a moral vision in its politico-economic institutions.

At the same time—and here Hess takes a major leap, almost a *salto mortale*—realistic conditions of progress also require a coarser, more concrete religion, whose established influence on the state will express the latter's spiritual dimension (hence the link that Hess insists must exist not only between the future state and the socialist religion of reason, but also between the existing state and the historical religion of its inhabitants). Hess does not mean, of course, government by the clergy or a mandatory religion; rather, he wants the government to embody the nation's moral-religious spirit in its ways and institutions. But Hess fails to explain why this national morality should be entrusted to the religious establishment. Perhaps he did not have much trust in the profundity of secularization and expected the public's mind to be imbued with religion for a long time to come. In any case, in the *European*

Triarchy he writes with approval of the English example, where an official state religion exercises a pragmatic influence on state affairs without excluding other religions. Hess also demands religious toleration, emancipation for the Jews, and civil marriage, and criticizes the Prussian state for having failed to institute this.

Hess's pronouncements sometimes border on the deification of the state.[52] In a characteristic mistake he attributes to Spinoza the sacralization of the state and of terrestrial institutions in general. Perhaps he was misled by a sense of symmetry. Since religion is secularized and redemption takes on a terrestrial dimension, then political institutions may well acquire a sacred dimension. But the latter is not true in Spinoza. The state inherits the authority that religious institutions used to have but not their inherently sacred status; it has absolute sovereignty but not a religious aura.

Spinoza in Hess's Zionism

In his middle period Hess did not refer much to Spinoza or Judaism. Addressing a predominantly Christian audience, he had to rely on Christian attitudes and symbolism as a basis for promoting his socialist religion of reason. But in the sixties two significant turns occurred in Hess's evolution, and both brought him back to Spinoza. One turn was the foundation of the German Social Democratic party, in which Hess collaborated with Lassale; the other turn (which Hess's friends considered a personal whim bordering on lunacy) was his return to Jewish nationalism and the publication of *Rome and Jerusalem*, by which Hess became the precursor of secular Zionism.

Hess had always believed that modern Jews like himself and Spinoza, who had stepped outside the religious community, were particularly suited (Hess nearly said "destined") to serve as mediators in mankind's passage from historical religion to socialist liberation and the religion of reason. For a long time Hess also believed that this required the Jews to relinquish their special claim to peoplehood and mingle as individuals in the society of the future. But in the sixties, disillusioned by European liberalism and by the attitude of part of his fellow socialists, Hess turned to Judaism as a national entity and, drawing inspiration from Giuseppe Mazzini and the Italian national movement, he wrote *Rome and Jerusalem*. The Jews, he now maintained, will fulfill their universal mission in history not as assimilated individuals but as a national entity which assumes its place in the family of nations and, regaining political independence, will establish an exemplary socialist society in its ancient homeland.

Over twenty-five years later Herzl, the founder of political Zionism, published *The Jewish State* without knowing of Hess's book. When he finally read *Rome and Jerusalem*, Herzl remarked that despite the Hegelian jargon, Hess was "the finest fruit of Judaism since Spinoza."[53]

No one would have welcomed the comparison more than Hess, who in his maturity returned to Spinoza both as the prophet of modernity and the precursor of Jewish national emancipation. Hess relied on a famous passage in chapter 3 of the *Theologico-Political Treatise* where Spinoza invokes the possibility that the Jews will reestablish their state and "God will again elect them." Hess seems to have been the first to read this text in modern Zionist vein, as did other Zionist writers and activists who admired Spinoza, like Nahum Sokolov, Joseph Klausner, and David Ben-Gurion, Israel's first premier who actually proclaimed the Jewish state. Yet Hess and these other Zionists stretched their case too far. Spinoza raised the possibility of a renewed Jewish state, but did not call for its establishment. The cited passage constitutes his answer to the messianic frenzy which raged in 1666 around the false messiah Sabbetai Zevi. The Sabbateans expected the imminent redemption to occur by a grand historical miracle; Spinoza, the rationalist disciple of Maimonides and the philosopher of secular history, retorts that, as history is full of vicissitudes, there may indeed one day arise a situation favoring the recall of the Jews; yet nothing will occur by providence and miracles. Sacred history—*pace* the young Hess—does not exist, and everything in the life of nations and individuals should be explained by perfectly natural and necessary causes. This is the main significance of Spinoza's "Zionist" dictum. He says little about the *desirability* of a new Jewish state, only about its *probability* and the only way in which it may come into existence.

Spinoza does, however, view the Jews as a nation or ethnic group over and above their religious affiliation. Even to the Christian Marranos he refers as Jews, and cites their history in Iberia as paradigmatic of Jewish history at large.★ Spinoza may also have endorsed (and indirectly inspired) a major claim of classical Zionism, namely, that whatever redemption the Jews may attain does not depend on the Messiah, but on what the Jews themselves will do in the context of actual, secular history. In this limited sense, Hess was indeed entitled to say of the modern messianic trend among the Jews that "its false prophet was Sabbetai Zevi, and its true prophet was Spinoza" (ibid., p. 52).

★ See volume 1, *The Marrano of Reason*, epilogue.

SPINOZA AND FEUERBACH

Ludwig Feuerbach was not a socialist,* but no other left-Hegelian had more influence on Marx or better knowledge of Hegel.[54] Soon, however, he developed his own critique of Hegelian philosophy,[55] which led to his self-styled "materialism" and to claiming Spinoza as master. Feuerbach's kind of materialism preserves the element of spirit within matter (and thus his Spinozistic heritage); he reverses Hegel by giving priority to the sensual over the conceptual form of reality, but without abolishing their substantive unity. This is a Hegelian view which Feuerbach attributes to Spinoza as well.[56]

Feuerbach is a strict philosopher of immanence. All transcendent entities are explained back to their origin in the human world, as its own projection and self-alienation. There is only man, sensual man within nature (whose thinking is a self-reflection of nature itself). But man projects his essence outward, into a separate, divine world, from where it confronts him as external and oppressive. What we are, what we wish and desire, including our craving for infinity, we objectify as an alien being which usurps our own divinity as humans. Religion is thereby a false and roundabout self-consciousness of man, though the religious believer is not aware of this and is therefore mystified.

> [In religion] the object of any subject is nothing else than the subject's own nature taken objectively. Such as are a man's thoughts and dispositions, such is his God . . . Consciousness of God is self-consciousness. . . . God is the manifested inward nature, the expressed self of a man.[57]

> Religion is the relation of man to his own nature . . . but to his nature not recognized as his own, but regarded as another nature, separate, nay, contradistinguished from his own.[58]

This is not only Spinoza, nor is it the traditional critique of religion rejecting the notion of "God in the image of man."

Feuerbach adds a new tier to this critique, based upon the concept of self-alienation, especially religious self-alienation, which Hegel had analyzed in relation to the "unhappy consciousness" and illustrated using Judaism as his prime example.[59] Elsewhere I have argued that this idea takes its departure from Kant's analysis of sublimity in *Critique of Judgment*: by an imaginary reversal (*Subreption*), the infinity belonging to humanity (Kant says: by virtue of its cosmic-moral destiny) is trans-

---

* Except in his last two years, when he joined the German Social Democratic party after reading Marx's *Capital*.

posed to an external natural object, in front of which we feel over-whelmed.[60] What Kant had diagnosed as the structure of an esthetic experience, Hegel and Feuerbach extend to religion and Marx carries over into economic and social phenomena.

Feuerbach, however, turns the Hegelian model against Hegel him-self. Whereas other left-Hegelians such as Heine and Strauss attributed to Hegel the deification of mankind, Feuerbach complained that Hegel had failed to accomplish this because he reduced the actual essence of man—which is natural and sensual—to a rarified abstraction, a pure self-conscious *Geist*, in which alone Hegel placed the element of divin-ity. This left the real existence of man outside the divine and confined the latter, in the manner of Christian tradition, to spirit alone, as a distinct (and hypostatized) "divine part" in man. Hegel thereby re-mained a Christian theologian in disguise, suffering from a character-istic self-alienation. Instead of uniting the human and the divine within the totality of human existence (as did Spinoza), Hegel only gave their separation a new and more developed form—a fact that, according to Feuerbach, "the learned mob" was too prejudiced to recognize.[61]

For Feuerbach, abolishing the world of transcendence requires that man be retrieved as divine in his very natural being. A true philosophy of immanence will make humanity, or man-within-nature, into the new totality in which everything else inheres and through which the rest of reality is apprehended. This implies that anthropology, the study of natural man, should replace theology and metaphysics as the fundamental and comprehensive science, a new kind of *prima philosophia*[62] (suited to the "philosophy of the future" which Feuer-bach, in a book of the same name, attempts to prepare).

Here again, when determining the essential features of humanity, Feuerbach performs a Hegelian-inspired reversal of Hegel. The essence of man lies in his sensibility; yet sensibility itself is humanized in Feuer-bach. "We need not go beyond the domain of sensibility in order to recognize man as a being higher than the animals."[63] "Man does not distinguish himself by his thinking," nor by any other special faculty such as free will, religious sentiment, and the like. These are all deriv-atives, necessary corollaries of the state of humanity but not its consti-tutive causes. What distinguishes humans primordially is the "*universal sensible being*" (a category paving the way to Marx's anthropology). Our universality inheres in our very sensibility or natural existence, the features of humankind which Christianity and its philosophical counterparts—but not Spinoza—hypostatized into special "faculties" and relegated to a separate, God-given "spirit."

Spiritual Materialism

This does not mean that Feuerbach's materialism excludes spirituality from man; it only reinterprets it. "Universal sensibility is spirituality" Feuerbach declares. We are spiritual beings by the natural fact of belonging to our species and by sharing its peculiar sensibility. Moreover, since this sensibility pervades the totality of our existence, it also humanizes us throughout. We are human not only while performing certain "exalted" functions, but in whatever we do (or suffer); not only do we see and feel differently from animals, we also breathe, digest, and copulate differently. Our body, both the subject and the object of our sensibility, is the first expression of our distinct humanity; and it is, says Feuerbach, to this material existence of man, invested as it is with spirituality throughout, that the divine attributes should be restored as their proper and sole legitimate bearer.

Feuerbach's brand of materialism (like Marx's) is distinguished from that of the eighteenth-century French materialists, or the Epicureans; it does not reduce reality to a play of material particles in motion but to a humanized substratum, sensibility, taken as both subject and object, body and spirit. Feuerbach, like Marx, rejects Hegelian "spirituality" without espousing crude materialism either as physicalism or as hedonism. Matter has its own spiritual dimension, because it is the object side of the same fundamental principle, human sensibility, which is spiritual in itself.[64]

This is certainly a turn—typical of all left-Hegelians and of Marx—away from Hegel in the direction of what was perceived as Spinozism. But at the same time—and this is equally characteristic, even essential, to the position we are investigating here—it retains from Hegel (and from Kant) the privileged position of humanity, the "subject," as a special focus in relation to which the natural universe is approached and apprehended. This anticipates Marx and, in a different way, Heidegger; more generally, it also indicates that Feuerbach remains within the bound of the Copernican revolution initiated by Kant (and usually known as "idealist"—which shows how misleading labels can be) which assigns to human subjectivity a central role in determining the shape of reality. Marx will convert this role from an epistemological to a practical-historical one, but will retain it throughout.

To sum up: Feuerbach offered a man-centered pantheism, not *deus sive natura* but *deus sive homo naturalis*. With the abolition of transcendence, man is restored to the center of being and reflection, a place he occupies as a pure child of nature, a being of absolute immanence. He no longer has a God-given soul or other gifts and faculties emanating from an imaginary metaphysical "Beyond." As such he becomes the focus through which the totality of being is approached. This is a new humanism, to be sure, but also tainted, perhaps unwittingly, with a sensualist version of Kantian (or rather Hegelian) idealism.[65] In Feuerbach, as in Marx, nature is seen through man no less than man is seen through nature. Humans are not one of many entities within a uniform natural substance, as in Spinoza; they maintain, as in Kant, a privileged position, as the prism through which nature itself and the whole realm of immanence is qualified and perceived.[66]

This difficult synthesis, if one may call it that, between Spinoza's standpoint and a Kantian-like idealism (or Copernican revolution), is the central theme of this chapter and the next. The left-Hegelians, including Marx, revert from Hegel's spirit to nature as the fundamental category of a philosophy of immanence, while retaining the special position of the subject which Hegel was right to stress against Spinoza. How can the (Spinozistic) principle of immanence be "subjectivized" without losing its strict natural character and without falling back upon teleology and disguised theology?

This is the perspective from which I shall now approach Marx. My aim is to examine the kind of philosophical option he construes in response to the Spinozistic heritage and its Hegelian turn. Consequently, I shall deal predominantly with Marx as *philosopher*, and not as social thinker, economist, or revolutionary, even though all these aspects are tied together from Marx's *own* viewpoint.

CHAPTER 4

Spinoza and Marx:
Man-in-Nature and the Science
of Redemption

At the age of twenty-three—almost the age Spinoza was when he was banned—another son of Jewish parents, two centuries later, plunged into the study of Spinoza's *Theologico-Political Treatise* and *Correspondence*. He copied extensively from Spinoza's original Latin and from an extant German translation, arranged the excerpts in a slightly peculiar order, and penned the following title to the manuscript:

Spinoza's
Theological-Political Treatise
by
Karl Heinrich Marx, Berlin 1841

By Karl Marx? If so, this was a perfect case of plagiarism. There is not a single sentence in this notebook which Marx had not copied from Spinoza. But this may be an act of philosophical appropriation.[1] For indeed, Spinoza's thought, adapted to the philosophical needs of the time, remained at the foundation of Marx's later thinking, almost as deeply rooted and as present as it had been to Hegel and as Hegel had been to Marx.

Marx used Spinoza's thought far more than he admitted. Spinoza was above all a counterbalance and corrective to Hegel, restoring the concept of nature and man as a concrete, natural being from what seemed to Marx his immersion in the lofty and semireligious heights of the Hegelian *Geist*. Marx did not take this move independently; he was rather the child—a prodigal child, to be sure—of his own *Zeitgeist*, especially of the left-Hegelian milieu in which he grew up, and from which he took his departure toward the socioeconomic analysis that became associated with his name.

When Marx denounced the left-Hegelian critique of religion as fundamentally insufficient, he also saw it as a necessary stage that had been completed;[2] its flaw, in Hegelian terms, was that its one-sided role has been fulfilled. Marx was looking past the purely philosophical analysis of consciousness, and was searching for the *fundamental* causes of the self-alienated mind, in which Feuerbach had rooted the religious illusion. These causes Marx found in the economic forces of production and the network of social relations they involved. Here was the true reality underlying all human affairs, including man's dialectical relations with nature, himself, and other humans.

This economic substrate Marx made into the *arche*, the first principle, the foundation of the whole realm of immanence. Viewed in ontological terms, it was for him what water was for Thales, fire for Heraclitus, *Geist* for Hegel, and *deus sive natura* for Spinoza. It was neither physical matter nor pure spirit, but a practical★ synthesis of the two produced by human labor and producing man himself in turn. Religion, law, politics, art, and all the metaphysical *Weltanschauungun* were different configurations in which this practico-material substance—a kind of Spinozistic *causa sui*—was reflected in cultural images and institutions.

In making this move, Marx returns from Hegel's absolute spirit to a Spinozism of his own, entailing a new version of nature. It is no longer Spinoza's uniform nature, in which man is a simple member among others, on a par with snakes and rainbows. Nature has been humanized in Marx but, unlike Hegel, without spiritualizing it and without involving an inherent teleology. Through human labor and material (and mental) production, man and nature constitute a dialectical unity, in which everything else inheres. It is their separation that becomes an abstraction—a false reflection of reality that is, however, inevitable under the economic alienation in which we live and thus must affect and prejudice our minds, beliefs, and culture.[3]

Marx's new philosophy of immanence, though strongly influenced by Hegel and his milieu, goes back to Spinoza in more ways than one. Indeed, Spinoza is almost always present in Marx's thought. But, we may add, the actual presence of Spinoza in Marx far surpasses his direct mention by name.[4] In what follows I shall try to reconstruct this presence in three major areas of Marx's thought: (1) in the preparatory critique of religion, which Marx—like Spinoza, but under more restrictive conditions—takes to be a real power of change; (2) in the way Marx construes the practical relation between man and nature as a new

---

★ I use "practical" as a derivative of praxis in its philosophical sense (following Aristotle, Kant, and Marx himself), meaning roughly, deliberate or reasoned human action affecting some matter.

immanent totality, and makes room for a man-made teleology as an objective feature of reality; and (3) in the alleged scientific form that the *Capital*, as a "science of salvation," gives to Marx's early ethical vision. The *Capital* spells out the dynamic by which the goal of human emancipation can be attained "Spinozistically," by the inner laws of reality itself—the same practico-material (or economic) reality which Marx from early on had come to see as the new immanent substance.

THE CRITIQUE OF RELIGION AND THE ROLE OF THE MULTITUDE

Just as the young Marx was ploughing his way through Spinoza's *Theologico-Political Treatise* and affixing his own name to the excerpts he diligently copied from it, Feuerbach's *Essence of Christianity* (1841) was bringing Spinoza's critique of religion up-to-date. The link between the two books was too timely and apparent for Marx to overlook. Feuerbach's attack on religion translated Spinoza in terms of Hegel's concept of alienation and, more importantly, updated him historically in terms of the modern German situation. Thereby, as Marx saw it, Feuerbach completed the work of the left-Hegelians, which was not merely theoretical but also a form of action, a kind of social praxis: it cleared the way for a still deeper and more radical fusion of criticism and practice which Marx came to see as his task to unleash.

In Spinoza's *Theologico-Political Treatise* Marx could have found, if not the first suggestion, then at least strong support for his idea that theory itself can serve as practical force and lever of change, once it is made to suit the minds and real interests of the multitude.[5] As chapter 1 has shown, Spinoza wrote the *Theologico-Political Treatise* with precisely this aim in mind—to get involved as philosopher in the subtle mechanism of social and cultural evolution. But the *Theologico-Political Treatise* is more than a one-time act of engagement; it also contains a generalized *meta*theory, demonstrating how theory can become a practical force and offering specific tools and strategies for achieving this end. Among other things, as we have seen, Spinoza devises a certain use of language, of myth, and of hermeneutics as a permanent institution suited to the level of consciousness of the multitude and serving to shape their minds in a socially beneficial way.

But here Marx takes issue with Spinoza on two major counts. First, Marx rejects Spinoza's conception of the multitude as a lower group, incapable of true salvation and requiring some sort of religious illusion and an inferior state of knowledge. In Marx it is the multitude itself, transformed into the proletariat, that is to bring about redemption for the rest of humanity; it is the subject of rational emancipation as well as its object, and to perform its role it must have as clear, as sober, and demystified a consciousness of itself and the world as any philosopher can possess—perhaps expressed in simpler terms than the philosopher's, but enjoying the added advantage of being immersed in real life. Whereas Spinoza had separated the multitude and the philosopher as two distinct entities, Marx unifies them: the proletariat is philosophy incarnate, the material weapon and embodiment of philosophy.[6] Perhaps paradoxically, but also typically, Marx transports the qualities of traditional esoteric groups to his own kind of multitude, undermining this category altogether and forming instead the concept of the proletariat as the avant-garde of revolution and redemption.

Second, Marx insists that for theory to be translated into practice, it cannot merely express a timeless truth (as in Spinoza), but must rouse the consciousness of the masses to some real predicament they experience, so that their actual want will prepare them to become aware of it. "Theory," he says, "is actualized in a people only in so far as it actualizes its needs"[7]—and Marx means this in the historical sense, as a Hegelian correction of Spinoza. A theory that simply states the woes and deficiencies of humanity in general, in some ahistorical way, will not do, for it will not have reality on its side and will therefore lack a significant chance to further affect reality.

While this is certainly an implied criticism of Spinoza, it is clearly made very much in Spinoza's own spirit. Both Marx and Spinoza view natural causality as the sole vehicle of social change, though they give it different interpretations. Spinoza, an avowed determinist, would accept without qualms (indeed, he foretells) Marx's principle that changes recommended for the future should not be projected as mere dreams of the utopian will, but must have a scientific grasp of what the actual situation already foretells. Yet Spinoza, child of the seventeenth-century and its scientific revolution, understands all natural causality under the semimechanistic model of the physical sciences, whereas Marx, following Hegel, views social change as dialectical and bound and determined by history.

At this crucial point, Marx's naturalism takes on a distinctly historicized* complexion: it is Hegel's legacy brought back to Spinoza without the Hegelian *Geist*. Nature itself is now taken as the substrate of history—an approach that presupposed, of course, a reinterpretation of what is understood by "nature." No longer seen as a finished

* By "historicized" or "historicist," I do not mean "relativized" but only the property of being understood through history, and being subject to its dynamics.

and alien entity that merely confronts us, nature is conceived by Marx as the synthesis between practical human subjectivity and the raw stuff of the universe.

As Marx sees it, Spinoza's critique of religion came before its time and was therefore anticipatory and historically abstract. Feuerbach and the left-Hegelians had a clear advantage over Spinoza, since they were operating when conditions in Germany were historically ripe. Now an enthusiastic young Marx can declare that "for Germany the critique of religion has been completed," adding that "the critique of religion is the presupposition of all critique."[8] This is a twofold statement, using, like Hegel, partial approval as a means of criticism. On the one hand, it hails the work of Feuerbach and other left-Hegelians, since on the level of ideas—of *mere* ideas, as Marx will add—they have abolished the fiction of transcendence and exposed religion as a mental form of self-alienation, an inverted consciousness of this world and an illusory consolation for its woes ("the opium of the people," as Marx dubs it for popular consumption).[9] Yet Feuerbach's critique was self-defeating because it was not radical enough. The twofold statement above also means that the critique of religion is fundamentally insufficient; it is only a presupposition of true social criticism, and if left at that, it will only add to the mystification and thereby reinforce the oppression that lies at the bottom of religion.

As Marx puts it in a well-known aphorism:

> The abolition of religion as the people's *illusory* happiness is the demand for their real happiness. The *demand to abandon illusion about their condition is a demand to abandon a condition which requires illusion.* The critique of religion is thus in embryo a critique of the vale of tears whose halo is religion. ("Towards the Critique," p. 250; emphasis added)

> The critique of religion ends with the doctrine that *man* is the highest being for man, hence with the categorical imperative to overthrow all conditions in which man is a degraded, enslaved, neglected, contemptible being. . . . (Ibid., pp. 257–58; emphasis added)

While these tones may remind us of Heine, Marx carries them even further and against the left-Hegelians. Marx condemns immature and superficial calls for action, driven (as Heine's) by an abstract social conscience that impedes a sober (i.e., Spinozistic) analysis of reality. The critique of the "holy" form of alienation—religion—must become an overall critique of its "unholy" forms, first as a critique of law and politics and then, more thoroughly, as the critique of wealth, property, and economic production, the fundamental conditions of which political and religious alienation are consequences.

Since the left-Hegelians failed to fathom the meaning of their own work, they stopped at the symptoms and neglected the root of the malady. It is on both sides of the theory/practice equation that Marx takes issue with them. Either they shunned social action, believing that by mere intellectual analysis they could move the world and emancipate man, or they plunged into crude and hasty calls for action—and to mere *political* action at that, unguided by fundamental theory and blind to the underlying economic substance. In both respects they missed the true function of theory, either by aggrandizing its power or by making do without it; and in both respects they were doomed, not only to failure but, dialectically, to serving the cause of the same ruling powers they wished to rout.

Does this criticism apply to Spinoza as well? In its broader outlines, certainly; but we must also remember that Spinoza's critique was part of a theologico-*political* treatise, which provided an elaborate and fairly radical theory of political action. This theory, moreover, not only stated what was desirable, but also delineated a good part of the sociopsychological mechanism by which to advance it. Marx may be at odds with parts of Spinoza's social theory, including his concept of the multitude and his view that some sort of illusion is required to maintain a stable polity; and Marx certainly views Spinoza himself as prisoner of the traditional illusion of metaphysics, lacking true fundamental theory—the analysis of economic forces and their presuppositions.[10] But Marx, diligent student of the *Theologico-Political Treatise*, could not fail to see the link it established between theory and practice on the one hand, and between political and religious emancipation on the other. This will mitigate, though not revoke, Marx's criticism of Spinoza's critique of religion.

IMMANENCE AND MAN-MADE TELEOLOGY

The New Causa Sui

In abolishing the other world and God, the critique of religion leaves man with himself as the be-all and the end-all, a new beginning and the true context of being and reflection. Man is not only the highest being *for man* (replacing God in this respect), but he is also the active creature who confers meaningful form on the rest of being, and through which his own environment—and thereby he himself—is molded and produced.

Yet man inherits these formerly divine roles as a finite being. It is not man as self-sufficient, but as a creature of wants, placed in dialectical relation to his natural environment, that becomes the overall principle. Because of his finitude, man does not have his being all in himself; he is not self-sufficient nor can he sustain his existence by his own resources. He is in constant need of something that comes from the outside, from a nature that in itself is alien to man and contains an element of the "other." Yet this otherness is not absolute, since nature is constantly changed and reshaped by the human race and acquires forms and meanings—primarily usage-meanings (later transformed and alienated into other socially determined configurations)—which are conferred upon nature by human work and praxis.

The finitude of man needs objective nature as a complement, and together, in their dialectical relation, they constitute the new immanent totality, replacing Spinoza's God or substance while establishing its divine connotations. Marx thereby follows Hegel in giving man, as subject, a special constitutive role in being, whereby being is not only an object, a mere substance, but is subject. Yet this is done by human work and production, not by knowledge; the role of man in being is to shape and humanize it through praxis, not to raise it, as in Hegel, to speculative self-consciousness. Moreover, the human species fulfills this role as a natural entity, and not as superior *Geist* that surpasses or *aufhebt* nature.

In this way, the privileged position Marx gives man as subject does not place him in Hegel's camp, because man performs his world-shaping role from within nature and in the practical mode of work. This, as we shall see in the following section, is a practical and material Copernican revolution, a new form of mediation between Spinoza and Hegel which performs a naturalist "subjectivation" of being (as required by Marx's first Thesis on Feuerbach).[11]

A methodological remark is in order at this point. Marx's ontology—for this is what interests us here—is not easily determined. Marx rarely discusses it as a subject in itself, but his views are embedded in his anthropology and in the socioeconomic doctrine he later offered *instead* of pure philosophy. Moreover, although no major gulf divides, in my opinion, the early from the later Marx on this issue, dualities do exist in each period. Marx's views on ontology did not so much change with time as they had their ambiguities at any given time.

This leaves us with the uneasy task of reconstructing Marx's underlying ontology from contexts that seldom refer to it explicitly.[12] A key concept I shall use for this purpose is "man-in-nature," with the new type of relation it entails between being and action, object and subject, the in-itself and teleology.*

The In-Itself in Nature

The status of nature prior to any human agency and outside its actual (or potential) scope is ambiguous in Marx's thought. While he frequently recognizes a raw or "inorganic" nature (as he calls it) confronting man,[13] he sometimes seems to dismiss this idea as a transcendent abstraction.[14] Without trying to resolve the ambiguity or to attribute to Marx a more coherent position than he holds, two points can be made with some confidence.[15]

First, Marx at least recognizes an in-itself *ingredient* in nature, whose rigid givenness must be admitted and reworked as such. Although a correlate of human sensibility (an idea the young Marx borrowed from Feuerbach), this natural in-itself cannot be reduced to anything human; it is a thinglike being that confronts man and in which we cannot find a trace of our own image. Or, to use the term of the Spinoza-Hegel dispute, it is mere "substance" with no inherent subjective features.

Second, however—and in the final analysis—this "raw" natural ingredient cannot meaningfully be approached outside the interaction of man and nature, whereby both shape each other while retaining the element of duality and confrontation within this primordial link.[16] If so, we may say that nature in the concrete sense is a shaped, even a humanized being, and that Marx starts with a unity of subject and object (a practical, not a cognitive unity) which serves as substrate to all that follows. The subject-object as practical unity is a latent structure in Marx that generates and underlies the historical process all along. This also explains the alienation that occurs in the meantime, for only against the background of a latent unity of subject and object, or man-in-nature, can their unnatural separation be seen as "alienation" and not simply as dualism.

---

* The entity which Marx considers ontologically self-sufficient is not "nature" in the homogeneous sense of Spinoza, but a dialectical interaction of nature and man, whereby each affects the other in a practical mode (work, shaping, reproduction). The hyphenated term *man-in-nature* seems more adequate to express this idea than Marx's *man and nature*, since Marx clearly does not have a simple conjunction in mind but a dialectical reciprocity. However, the whole system can also be called "nature" in a secondary and expanded sense, since, as we shall see, man who shapes the natural world is a natural agent himself and is shaping and reproducing himself in the act.

"Man and Nature Exist on Their Own Account"

The primordiality of man-in-nature precludes any query about their origin or "creation." In a strong Spinozistic train of thought, the young Marx argues in the *Economic and Philosophical Manuscripts* that once the world of transcendence has been eliminated, there is no sense in wondering about the origins of the world as a whole. "Man and nature exist on their own account,"[17] and immanence as the first principle asserts itself of itself.

> If you ask a question about the creation of nature and man, you abstract from nature and from man. You suppose them *non-existent* and you want me to demonstrate that they *exist*. I reply: give up your abstraction and at the same time you abandon your question. (*Manuscripts*, "Private Property and Communism," *Early Writings*, p. 166)

Marx continues:

> Or else, if you want to maintain your abstraction, be consistent; if you think of man and nature as non-existent, think of yourself too as non-existent, for you are also man and nature [*sic*]. Do not think [= do not engage in the act of thinking], do not ask me questions, for as soon as you think and ask questions, your abstraction from the existence of man and nature becomes meaningless. Or are you such an egoist that you conceive everything as non-existent and yet want to exist yourself? (Ibid.)

These are two different arguments. The first is fundamentally Spinozistic. It establishes the necessity and self-suffiency of the immanent world by dismissing the idea of its possible nonexistence as a logical absurdity. Immanent being ("man and nature") is overall being to Marx; as such it is there necessarily—self-contained, self-grounded, allowing of no external explanations and calling for none. While Kant banned transcendent statements from philosophy, Marx, in a Spinozistic vein, expels transcendent questions as well. Any talk about "creation" (i.e., searching for external sources of reality) presupposes that the universe is contingent and conceivable as nonexistent; but this, as Spinoza, too, had argued, is the foremost philosophical fallacy.

In the second part of the quotation, Marx starts with the human *ego cogito*, the subjective act of thinking, and no longer with the universe at large. At first his move may seem Cartesian, but Marx, in effect, departs from Descartes in Kant's direction and finally ends up with Spinoza again.

In the act of thinking, Marx says in essence, I assert my own existence as a first unshakeable datum. But I do not do so in a Cartesian
manner—as a bodyless, worldless ego—but rather as being *in* the
world and *with* the world. Here Marx, perhaps unwittingly, espouses
Kant's paradigm argument in the transcendental deduction, according
to which the ego's self-conscious thinking is possible only if the ego
confronts an objective world distinct from itself. In other words, I can
be conscious of my own thinking self only if there is also a world other
than myself to which I relate (Kant says: constitutively) and of which
I am equally conscious.

To the inherent link established by Kant between the "I think" and
the world, Hegel added a *practical* link between the "I think" and other
persons as an additional structure that makes self-consciousness possible. All these links—between the self, the world, and other persons—
are considered primordial, that is, they are preconditions to the very
first datum of self-conscious thinking.

Marx, even without spelling it out, accepts this primordiality and
reinstates it within a Spinozistic context. Man-in-nature is the primordial datum, inexorably implied in self-conscious thinking; and this
complex datum with *all* its ingredients (the individual, nature, and
other humans—or the species) now enjoys in Marx the status of *causa
sui*, or self-sustaining being; it can no longer be open to doubt or sub-
jected to a search for its transcendent origins, because—here the former Spinozistic train of thought takes over again—in doing so we imply that the new immanent totality, man-in-nature, can be conceived
as nonexistent.

Thus, in a somewhat roundabout way, the semi-Cartesian beginning is reversed through Kant and Hegel and is planted in Spinozistic
terrain again.

A word of caution is in order here. The new *causa sui* which I attribute to Marx is, of course, meant to be taken with a grain of salt. Marx's
overall principle of immanence is neither a divine nor a necessary being
in the semitheological sense of Spinoza. Marx avoids the high-flown
religious connotations that Spinoza deliberately emphasized as pertaining to his nature-God and exploited in his theory of salvation. The
significance of Marx's new *causa sui* is more prosaic: it is the underlying
principle of all natural entities which, as such, are necessarily finite and
dependent. "A being which does not have its nature outside of itself is
not a natural being,"[18] Marx says in a statement that, if taken strictly,
would abolish the idea of a singular and infinite nature-God—an entity
which, indeed, is absent in Marx.

Marx, in other words (and using Spinoza's own terms), abolishes

Spinoza's *natura naturans*. What is left is the *natura naturata*, that is, the immanent totality seen from the standpoint of finitude; and this now becomes the overall being in Marx, a new (and different) kind of *causa sui*. It is a universe where pure immanence is inevitably linked with finitude, allowing of no divinity either without or within; and as such it exists primordially, out of itself, barring any transcendent queries and serving as the absolute starting point for action and for all meaningful discourse and reflection.[19]

Man, Nature, and Production

There is a different sense in which a variant of *causa sui* applies in Marx: man as self-creator. Human practical activity transforms the natural in–itself and thereby creates the historical universe by which man himself is produced and transformed.

Marx follows an idea advanced by Vico, giving it a far-reaching new interpretation. History, of which man is both child and parent, is not only a distinct realm of being alongside nature, but becomes an extended domain that comprises nature itself as a moment of man's self-productive activity. The relation "man-in-nature" acquires its concrete meaning only within a historical context. Man-in-nature implies, first, the social dimension of human existence—the distinctive "species-activity" of man as determined by his communal ties; and second, the self-productive activity in which "raw" nature is transformed and the human race creates and reshapes itself in the process. However, in historicizing the man-in-nature relation, Marx does not elevate history to a semitheological status like Hegel's *Geist*. History is rather brought back to nature, as the latter's fully developed and dialectically enriched sense.

The self-productive role of man-in-nature has not only social and anthropological implications in the early Marx, but also ontic ones. Natural entities are objects of human sensibility (both practical and cognitive), a fact that belongs to their very constitution. Being natural *means* being related to human sensibility as its actual or potential object—not only to our perceptions but equally, and primarily, to human needs and desires (whether actual or projected) and, of course, to our practical reshaping. This is not a Berkeley-type idealism but rather an extension of Feuerbach's peculiar brand of materialism, where material objects are seen both as real and as necessarily related to human sensibility as its "objectivized" side.

Moreover, human sensibility itself is not a fixed and timeless factor, but evolves in history along with its objects and as a result of its relation with them. As new material products and cultural experiences become available, as taste, knowledge, and life-styles and patterns evolve, so do the forms of our sensibility. "The creation and cultivation of the five senses is the work of all previous history" Marx notes in a salient epigram (in "Private Property and Communism," *Early Writings*, p. 161). Not only are our needs and desires socially determined; perception itself is affected by culture (both material and spiritual), which in turn is the historical product of man changing nature and thereby also changing his own "nature" to reflect the most primitive modes of feeling and perceiving.

The manner in which the human race creates and humanizes itself is by embodying itself in its material objects. Man breaks away from his state of animality by imprinting a humanized (his own) form upon objects in his environment, that is, through a teleologically oriented transformation of the material objects around him. The distinctive human element, which the Greeks saw in *logos*, Christianity in a God-given soul, Kant in the transcendental ego, and Feuerbach in a universal kind of sensibility, Marx sees in the production of the means of our subsistence. This is "the first historical act" and the most fundamental human feature.* Consciousness, religion, logic, and other mental products of culture (which also distinguish humans) are only derivative of the fact of material production, which is, to Marx, the primordial expression of the man-in-nature relation and of the dialectical totality it establishes.

The concept of production has thereby a metaeconomic function, grounding Marx's economic theory within his anthropology and its implied ontology.[20] Earlier I have attributed to Marx a kind of economic monism, even fashioned on the pre-Socratic model; yet the "economic" substrate of reality draws its meaning from the metaeconomic premises (man-in-nature, production as the teleological subjectivation of matter, etc.) and should be understood as their *concretization*.[21]

Material self-production is also more fundamental than the universal

* Man can be distinguished from the animal by consciousness, religion, or anything else you please. He begins to distinguish himself from the animal the moment he begins to *produce* his means of subsistence, a step required by his physical organization. By producing food, man indirectly produces his material life itself (*German Ideology*, in *Writings of the Young Marx*, p. 409).

The first *historical* act, the act by which they [human individuals] distinguish themselves from animals is not the fact that they think, but the fact that they begin to *produce their means of subsistence*. The first fact to be established, then, is the physical organization of these individuals and their consequent relationship to the rest of nature. (Ibid.)

sensibility by which Feuerbach's self-styled materialism sought to define man's uniqueness. Marx accepts the general (and rather Spinozistic) trend of Feuerbach: to maintain universality as the distinctive human feature while reintegrating it within man's natural being; and Marx, of course, subscribes to Feuerbach's view of humans as "species-beings," related by nature to other humans and making this their primary object. But Feuerbach, here again, was not sufficiently fundamental. The distinctive human sensibility is not a first natural datum but rather the historical product of our self-humanization, which is rooted in material production—above all in producing the *means* of production. This now assumes in Marx the universal character distinctive of the human race:

> Of course, animals also produce. They construct nests, dwellings, as in the case of bees, beavers, ants, etc. But they only produce what is strictly necessary for themselves or their young. They produce only in a single direction, while man produces universally. They produce only under the compulsion of direct physical needs, while man produces when he is free from physical need. Animals produce only themselves while man produces the whole of nature. The products of animal production belong directly to their physical bodies, while man is free in face of his product. Animals construct only in accordance with the standards and needs to which they belong, while man knows how to construct in accordance with the standards of every species. . . . Thus man constructs also in accordance with the laws of beauty. (*Early Writings*, p. 128)

As the essential life activity of man by which objective reality itself is shaped, material production inherits in Marx the role of the Kant's transcendental ego in expressing (1) man's universality (and thus also freedom); (2) his inherent link to his community (here to the "species" taken as a natural entity); and, above all, (3) his shaping and constituting powers vis-à-vis the world of objects, whereby nature appears as his work and his reality.

Work and Self-Alienation

Marx's anthropology of production also provides the source of his ethics of work as self-expression and self-actualization.[22] Through his productive work, man engraves his image on inorganic nature, reproducing himself in the object and thereby coming back into his own as actually human:

The object of labor is therefore the *objectification of man's species-life*; for [in material production] he no longer reproduces himself merely intellectually, as in consciousness, but actively and in a real sense, and he sees his own reflection in a world which he has constructed. ("Alienated Labour," p. 128)

This is an analogue of the typical relation of consciousness and its object as put forth by German idealism since Kant, which Marx now translates into a practico-material context. Man asserts his actual (and natural) species-being by imprinting himself in the world of objects—an activity that has no other purpose than self-expression.[23] Material production is not merely utilitarian but an essential activity for humans, whereby they express and actualize their being; as such it carries the value attributes that were formerly attached to loftier human activities such as knowledge, rational speculation, religious or moral devotion, and so forth. Material production has in this sense a spiritual significance inhering in its very materiality. It represents a unity of matter and spirit which left-Hegelians, as we have seen, were prone to view as the foremost Spinozistic trait.[24]

True humanity entails demands that work be done in a self-oriented (and thus free or autonomous) mode. In the state of alienation, however (which therefore is, strictly speaking, less than human), the workers view their "life activity," labor, only as a means for maintaining their sheer physical existence; and in selling it to another they turn the most genuine expression of their being into a commodity. As Marx notes:

But labor is the worker's own life-activity, the manifestation of his own life. And this *life-activity* he sells to another person in order to secure the necessary *means of subsistence*. Thus, his life-activity is for him only a *means* to enable him to exist. (From "Wage Labor and Capital," in Marx-Engels, *Collected Works* [New York: International Publishers, 1977], 9: 202)

This alienation creates a self-sustaining circle. Viewing my genuine life activity as merely a means of subsistence is a form of false self-consciousness, forced upon me by the alienated material conditions in which I live and at once reinforcing these conditions. The product of work—the purported objectification of my own self through which I am to realize and enrich my life as a person—is not only taken away from me by the market forces but actually turns against me, because from the outset it is integrated within, and serves to sustain, a system that blocks, deprives, and supresses the very subjective humanity it is supposed to enhance.[25]

Here Marx comes close—perhaps dangerously so—to the classic teleological pattern whereby humans are to rise to a higher level by realizing something considered as their essence. The human race can humanize itself either genuinely or deviously, the latter being the current historical condition under capitalism. Anything short of communistic life and the liberation of work and its products is still a dehumanized and unnatural way for humans to exist, even if it is a necessary preparation for their emancipation. Thus, neither avoidable nor an eternal human lot, alienation with its several faces marks the long intermediary state between animality and salvation—the two poles traditionally reified into separate worlds, the natural and the divine, with man partaking of both—but which Marx incorporates within history as a single, dynamic, and natural totality.

While this is a definite Spinozistic move—immanent, naturalistic, and monistic—it also resembles Hegel's attempt to undergird history with a latent structure borrowed from religious consciousness. Alienation in Marx is a secular version of "fallenness," a state of defective being from which, indeed, not a transcendent God or his Son but the natural course of history is to redeem the human race through toil, suffering, and the deepening of alienation that will serve as a lever in its conquest.

The semireligious undertones are unmistakable. The eschatology of the Jewish prophets is translated into immanent economic terms (a Spinozistic unity of spirit and matter), and the hope for the second coming is transformed into a theory of revolution, with the proletariat playing an avant-garde role in this natural-dialectical drama of redemption.

Is this a tacit theology (as in Hegel) and a radical departure from Spinoza? To answer this question we must draw a line between theology in general and historical providence in particular. Spinoza was the first to suggest a semitheological hermeneutics as the vehicle of secularization. But not all religious motifs were acceptable even as metaphors, and providence was the first to be banned. Moreover, as the Marrano of reason, Spinoza was no less motivated by the pathos of secular redemption than Marx, but for him redemption was a personal matter, affecting a minority and leaving the multitude outside its scope (see vol. 1, chap. 6). It had no global historical aim and no utopian dimensions. With Marx, on the contrary, utopia served both in envisaging the highest human liberation for the masses, and in assuming that the forces of reality can yield this formidable result by their own dynamic. It was, paradoxically, by trying to avoid utopia and opt for Spinozistic realism that Marx ended up with a tacit, new historical providence, because he assumed an unlikely correspondence between what the forces of reality will bring about and what humanity deeply needs and aspires to.

I shall return to Marx's utopia in my discussion of the *Capital*. Meanwhile, we should address the broader question of teleology, which prompted our discussion of Marx in the first place. Based upon the foregoing analysis of man-in-nature, how does Marx's philosophy of immanence—lacking an inherent teleology while maintaining a historical perspective—trace its own way between Hegel and Spinoza?

TELEOLOGY, ALIENNESS, and ALIENATION

The road, I think, leads through Kant. Indeed, on this issue Marx offers his own synthesis of Kant and Spinoza, which we shall now examine.

Kant and Teleology

Kant inherited the problem of teleology from Leibniz and the seventeenth-century scientific revolution. The natural universe must be conceived as a purely mechanical system, with no inherent ends and purposes. As such, it confronts man as an alien power, indifferent to human needs, aspirations, and moral tasks. In his attempt to reconcile this mechanistic "kingdom of nature" to a teleological "kingdom of grace," Leibniz conceived of them as two complementary systems between which God had preestablished a permanent harmony. With Kant, however, the transcendent principle of God is no longer available. Instead of God, it is man who has to create the harmony (or synthesis) between nature and teleology, by imprinting his practical and moral goals upon nature as given; and instead of the harmony being preestablished from the outset, it becomes in Kant the task and the result of human efforts in history.

This is not simply a logical-systematic change, but a whole new *Weltanschauung* and mental revolution. It introduces the modern historical outlook to which Marx was a (prodigal) heir. It is also significant for our analysis that Kant tried, but failed, to discover a cognitive way in which man gives reality an objective teleological form.[26] This failure in particular points the way from Kant to Marx. Already in Kant it is man as practical agent and *homo faber*, not as *homo sapiens*, who brings nature and teleology objectively together. This is ex-

pressed in Kant's wider move from the traditional cognitive metaphysics into his new metaphysics of moral practice. Actual reality can
take teleological shape only by the action of man, who uses the mechanistic laws of nature to transform nature in accordance with human
interests and moral demands. This is done through all forms of civilization—technical, political, and, above all, moral. While nature itself
is devoid of inherent purposiveness, man as practical agent must im-
print his image upon the world and reshape the existing nature (including his own "inner" nature) into a "new nature," modelled on the
moral idea. This generates history as the overall teleological context,
and even gives the world itself its objective "final end."[27]

Marx's Synthesis of Spinoza and Kant

With certain important modifications (all Spinozistic in spirit), Marx
adopts this basic Kantian scheme, including its primacy of practice.
The world as such has no inherent teleology; it is man as practical
being (*homo faber*) who introduces purposive form into a nature that
lacks it in itself. But once this is performed, the teleological form is
interwoven with the texture of reality and becomes an actual determi-
native factor.

In assuming this position, Marx splits Hegel's synthesis of Kant and
Spinoza into its basic components, and then builds a new one in its
place. Hegel claimed that a subjectlike feature can be discovered in the
deep structure of what seems to be a thinglike, objective reality, because it is underlaid by dialectical logic—the logic of subjectlike systems. In this view, the universe as a natural system already has a latent
humanlike form, so that in "subjectivizing" it we only explicate and
realize its inherent structure. This view, which I shall call "ontological
anthropomorphism," led Hegel to the further *Aufhebung* of nature
within the God-like Spirit and to his semitheological reading of history.

Is there a similar ontological anthropomorphism in Marx? Certainly
not, if by this we understand the ascription of a human feature to the
natural world itself, as inherently latent in it. Marx, on the contrary,
aligns himself with Spinoza in viewing nature with no inherent principle of subjectivity. The subjectivation of nature occurs through the
human race as a distinct natural principle, a power that confronts and
subdues the natural in-itself without initially recognizing its own image within it. The human image, as in Kant, is only imparted to raw
nature; it is neither discovered in it nor explicated from its latent structure.

The most we can ascribe to Marx, by logical implication, is that the natural in-itself can lend itself, at least in part, to human shape-giving action. But this does not involve in Marx an extraneous postulate (like Kant's divine guarantee) since for Marx both man and nature belong to the same immanent domain.

This is where Marx remains fundamentally Spinozistic. While following the Kantian scheme, he rejects Kant's dualism of reason and nature and its consequences (such as utopianism, the identification of humanization with moralization, and the view of practical reason as a transcendental principle that imposes itself upon nature from without). In Marx man becomes a natural being himself, albeit in a special (dialectical) sense. Man is no longer a dual creature who partakes equally in nature and in a supranatural domain of "pure" reason. Hence, his practical activity is material and sensuous, not purely moral and a priori, and in fulfilling his ontological role he acts as a real empirical entity and no longer as a transcendental ego.

In this sense it may be said that it is nature itself that works upon itself through the human being—a reflexive feature that preserves the immanent Spinozistic framework of Marx's system. But we must also recognize a major difference that tends in Hegel's direction. Man does not belong to nature in the simple uniform sense of Spinoza's *res*, but in a dialectical manner, that is, both as object and as subject. Man in his work is a natural principle of subjectivity, a natural for-itself which depends on the in-itself of nature for both subsistence and for exercising man's distinctive ontological activity (production); yet he cannot be reduced to this in-itself, nor be fully explained and constituted by its merely objective and mechanical causality. Marx's materialism, as has been frequently observed, is practical and economic, but not ontological.

A Materialist Copernican Revolution?

This, I think, is Marx's major novelty with respect to both Hegel and Spinoza. He does not take a "middle way" but engenders his own distinctive synthesis from their opposition. It can be seen as a naturalist way of maintaining man's privileged role as a world-shaping subject, or as a materialist Copernican revolution. Nature in the broad sense, as the overall realm of immanence (N_1), is marked from the start by an inner bifurcation; on the one hand there is an inert natural in-itself (N_2, or nature in the narrow inorganic sense), facing a natural principle of subjectivity that transforms this in-itself into a "humanized" world. Neither of these natural principles can be reduced to the other, and their interrelation constitutes man-in-nature as the overall totality (N_1). And it is as a natural (and practical) being (in the sense of N_1), and not as self-conscious *Geist*, that man retains his distinct power and ontological role in the immanent natural system to which he belongs as both subject and object.

In this sense, Marx remains within the tradition of German idealism (or better, within the Copernican revolution) though he gives it a practical and metaeconomic interpretation.[28] Marx's self-ascribed materialism implies, above all, the primacy of praxis over speculative knowledge (against Hegel) and of sensuous, or natural-material praxis (production) as against the moral-transcendental one (Kant). This is a naturalization of the role of the subject as conceived in German idealism (or the Copernican principle), but not its abolition. Marx's materialism means that the Copernican principle is materialized and man, through material production, performs his role as a natural and practical entity. The result can be seen as "practical materialism," which is to be distinguished from ontological materialism and, indeed, is incompatible with it.[29]

To sum up: In Spinoza nature was pure and uniform substance, and no subjectivation of nature was possible, either from within (as in Hegel) or from without (as in Kant and Marx). The teleological projections of the subject were pure fictions that had no share in the shape of reality. In Hegel, on the contrary, a teleological and subjectlike feature was latent in what seems to be a thinglike substance. In Marx, following Kant, man as a practical being introduces purposivity into a natural in-itself that lacks it initially; he does so by work and production and their loftier cultural derivatives, and first of all by producing the means of production—a second-order teleological pattern. This is a material relation that subjectivizes nature in a real sense. The purposivity it engenders is no longer fictitious and illusory as in Spinoza, but becomes a determining factor in the natural texture of the world. It constitutes the "economic" substrate of reality whose investigation provides the new *prima philosophia*.[30]

Alienation Reconsidered

This also explains the major role of alienation as a philosophical problem in Marx.[31] The crucial point about alienation is not that nature is alien to man, but that it is distortingly humanized. If man had not initially existed by imprinting and objectifying himself in his natural products, the ontological problem of alienation would not have arisen.

In the state of alienation, man's self-objectification turns against him. Instead of promoting liberation and self-realization, it takes the form of (and helps to sustain) a social and economic system that degrades and impedes his humanity. For the purpose of the present analysis we need not elaborate the social and ethical details of alienation but only indicate their underlying philosophical principle. The problem is not that man is impeded by an alien power that simply confronts him; this would be *alienness*, but not (self)-*alienation*. Rather, the problem is that the impeding power is my own material embodiment by which I was to impart a purposive form to alien nature in order to realize and liberate myself. While nature is initially supposed to be subjectivized through praxis in a way that enhances human development, the human image, as embodied in the socioeconomic system of production, is projected back to us as a power that distorts our humanity. Marx's major problem—alienation—is thus rooted in the same theory by which he addresses the issues of teleology and anthropomorphism, moving away from Hegel in Spinoza's direction.

Marx's way to overcome alienation is again Spinozistic, though in a different sense. It posits the goal of secular redemption and demands a scientific way to it.

Spinoza and the Capital: The Science of Redemption

Later in his career Marx broke completely with pure philosophy and felt uneasy about the ethical vein of his early reflections. But this does not mean that his ontology and anthropology significantly changed or that he dismissed philosophy in the manner of the positivists. On the contrary, Marx's economic theory is laden with elements whose metaphysical parentage is unmistakable. Yet metaphysics no longer had an independent posture or claim. Having fulfilled its role as pure theory, it was not to be submerged and *aufgehoben* (which also means preserved) within the more concrete theories of economic and social change, and also within the revolutionary action into which they should be translated.

"You cannot cancel [*aufheben*] philosophy without realizing it," Marx already said in an early essay ("Towards the Critique," p. 256). This is a special unity of spirit and matter which left-Hegelians, as we have seen, understood as the prime meaning of Spinozism. The young Marx implied this unity as well when he declared the proletariat to be "philosophy incarnate"; later, as he set out in the *Capital* to provide the proleteriat with its theoretical self-consciousness, he also supplied the new substitute for pure philosophy, its practically embodied transformation.

Hence, despite the undeniable differences in style, scope, and scientific mood, I see no real rift between the early and the mature Marx. The *Capital* expands and concretizes Marx's original vision, to which it gives scientific expression and thereby, we may add, a Spinozistic form. Already the early Marx had discovered what he saw as the economic substrate of reality, including the self-shaping activity of man-in-nature that underlies economic production. The mature Marx, in a Spinozistic mode, proceeded in the *Capital* to explicate and spell out the basic categories and dynamics of this reality, offering not only an economic theory in the narrow sense but a kind of "first philosophy"—Marx's own immanent substitute for traditional theology and metaphysics. Marx's economics, indeed, is not to be conceived as one distinct discipline among others but as a comprehensive and fundamental science—the concrete explication of that humanized substance and new *causa sui* that constitutes immanent reality.

The *Capital* has, moreover, the difficult task of reconciling reality with ethical utopia. If Heine said that the kingdom of heaven was baked in leaven and made of green peas, Marx in the *Capital* spells this idea out as scientific theory. The dry and sometimes scholastic bulk of this magnum opus is Marx's own way, following Spinoza, of discussing ethical vision and powerful human aspirations as if they were points, lines, and bodies. Economic analysis replaces Spinoza's *mos geometricus* and offers instead a *mos economicus* as a road to salvation.[32]

To be more specific: the mature Marx preserves the wish, indeed the fire, that animated the early *Manuscripts*: to establish a Kant-like "kingdom of ends" within the domain of economic production and exchange—the very domain which Kant and Hegel considered as fit only for strife and competition and therefore abandoned to an egoistic war of all against all. The same universality, based upon mutual recognition of the other's humanity, which Kant made the basis of inner morality and Hegel projected into the political institutions of the state, Marx seeks to embody within the world of socioeconomic relations (Hegel's "civil society"), as the most fundamental domain that determines all the others.

But to do this, Marx insists, one must go by the laws of socioeconomic reality itself, as it determines its own dialectical course in a manner open to scientific analysis and prediction. At this crucial point, Marx's Kantian drives make way for his fundamental Spinozism. Whatever emancipation is in store for humanity will be attained by the inner working and immanent laws of reality itself, not, as in Kant and the utopian socialists, by imposing an external moral will upon reality. The *Capital* was to serve as the theory of this development—at once a fundamental philosophy, an empirically usable science, a moral vision brought down to earth, and the formed self-consciousness of the proletariat, the new "universal class." As such it also offers the kind of theory that suits the era of the "end of philosophy," since it is submerged in practice and is potentially a practical tool itself.[33]

Marx's demand to approach society scientifically distinguishes him from very early on. Even when still marked by a blend of Enlightenment and left-Hegelian thought and centering on politics as the major area for reform, the twenty-four-year-old Marx wrote:

> Philosophy had done nothing in politics that physics, mathematics, medicine, every science has not done in its own sphere. Bacon of Verulam declared theological physics to be a maiden consecrated to God and barren; he emancipated physics from theology and she became fertile. . . . Similarly Machiavelli and Campanella earlier, and Hobbes, Spinoza, and Hugo Grotius later, down to Rousseau, Fichte, and Hegel, began considering the state from the human viewpoint and developed its natural laws from reason and experience. ("Religion, Free Press, and Philosophy," in *Writings of the Young Marx*, pp. 128–29)

This scientific, realistic attitude is even more constant than Marx's economic materialism. Philosophy, says the young Marx, must discover the inner laws of society, taken as natural laws, no less than the laws of physics. The mature Marx extends this approach from politics to economic theory and conceives of the "laws" in question as dialectical and no longer in association with physics or mathematics;[34] but he maintains this basic Spinozistic approach and amplifies it in the *Capital* into a full-fledged new science.

Marx's approach is Spinozistic on two counts: not only because he views society as scientifically determined by its natural processes (this, as Marx recognizes, was suggested by Machiavelli and Hobbes before Spinoza), but because he combines this view with a perspective of secular salvation which the science in question is to serve and help approach. This combination is what distinguishes Spinoza and Marx—and also what constitutes for each of them a major problem. Rejecting utopia and voluntarism, denying a role in the affairs of history (or of one's personal evolution) not only to God but also to the alleged moral will, Marx and Spinoza, each in terms of his own system, must explicate reality in such a way that its own evolution will serve as a vehicle of redemption.

In Spinoza this problem takes on the form of a paradox: liberation seems to be the product of coercion. Metaphysical freedom, where it exists, is not attained but, rather, *occurs* to us. Every person starts out unfree, and his or her passage from external to internal determination (Spinoza's definition of freedom) must itself be determined by the chain of external causes that preceded it. The person living in freedom is, indeed, supposed to enjoy internal determination, but to get there he or she must depend on the same coercive causality which his or her freedom reverses. No hiatus, no spontaneous jump or revolutionary "instant," is allowed by the logic of Spinoza's universe, even though his theory of liberation seems to call for something of the kind.[35]

Marx's version of the problem is more serious—at least from the standpoint of teleology and providence. Spinoza, who views salvation as a personal affair, is able to account for its occurrence by a deterministic probability affecting the happy few. He cannot—and does not—make a tacit appeal to some overall teleology or secular providence; his problem arises, so to speak, from a surplus of determinism. But Marx, because he historicizes redemption and sees the entire human race as its subject, must indulge in some sort of secular eschatology. Redemption can no longer be predicted by a calculus of deterministic probability, and the shadow of illicit teleology again looms on the horizon.

All that Marx can logically do is affirm that, as a matter of historical fact, we are nearing the goal, grounding his claim in a dialectical analysis of the rise of capitalism and its inherent conflicts, in which a new era seems to be incipient. But, precisely at the latter point, prediction and teleology seem to be intermingled (which may be the reason for some of Marx's rash prognostics which so far have failed). Moreover, even assuming the prediction to be austerely grounded in its own theory and facts, what, on the metaphilosophical level, can account for this wondrous correspondence, in which reality by its own dynamics eventually agrees with the deepest desires and aspirations of humanity? As Sartre has recognized, in a world truly devoid of providence, no such guarantee can exist.[36] But Sartre, indeed, is far more Spinozistic in this respect than Marx, who still clings, in the final analysis, to a residue of providential theology. As in Leibniz, as in any view that accepts some version of the "moral world-order," there seems to exist in Marx at least a factual harmony between the realm of nature and the realm of freedom, even though no God, no providence, and no preestablished harmony are officially allowed to guarantee this wonder.

Marx's historical utopia (in which he certainly conflicts with Spinoza) is related again to their differences on the question of the multitude. For Spinoza, the universalization of redemption was neither a conceivable goal in itself nor a precondition (as in Hegel and Marx) for redeeming the individual. This is why Spinoza needed a separate theory (and strategy) for the multitude, as it will always remain outside the scope of true salvation. Marx, on the contrary, because he envisages redemption on a grand historical scale—but expects, like Spinoza, everything to happen by the immanent forces of reality—turns to the multitude, in the form of the proletariat and the masses, as the lever of universal redemption.

Here a whole complex of differences between Marx and Spinoza can be discerned. Spinoza, too (common opinion notwithstanding), had a historical perspective and a plan for the future, based upon the multitude as the substrate of change (see chapter 1). Yet in the absence of providence and of any hidden teleology, this meant to Spinoza that all changes must be suited to the lower natural faculties of their medium, the multitude. All that can be expected (though this is a revolution in itself), is raising the multitude to the level of purified imagination, where semirational conduct is produced through obedience to authority, while all private beliefs and sentiments (even the lower ones) could flourish. This—the tacit program of the *Theologico-Political Treatise*—will create an enlightened social environment, based upon freedom, security, tolerance, and institutionalized solidarity—but not upon the third degree of knowledge. True redemption, though perhaps more accessible, remains a matter for the minority.

With Marx, the democratization of redemption becomes the inevitable and most utopian feature of his theory. Paradoxically, this is a result of Marx's Spinozistic attempts to avoid utopia and to base his expectations on the forces of reality.[37] This led him to endow the masses with far higher powers of enlightenment and self-awareness than seems realistic, and, more generally, to presuppose the providential correspondence of reality and the ideal indicated above. Here Marx is as utopian as Kant while claiming to replace Kantian utopia with Spinozistic natural determinism.[38]

This is not only a theoretical flaw; historically, it became the source of much suffering and repression. The unrealistic view of the masses led to an inevitable split between these masses and their alleged representation in leaders and institutions, usually bureaucratic, who, within the dictatorship of the proletariat, were supposed to embody the avantgarde principle of history while actually dominating the masses with superior knowledge and frequently with despotism and terror.

While Spinoza's political theory is not immune to possible infringements on freedom,[39] its greater realism makes it more humane, especially with respect to the multitude. People are not compelled to rise to levels above their reach;[40] they are neither seen from the outset as mobilized in the cause of an ideology supposed to express their "true" being, nor considered traitors if they fail to devote permanent service to the cause. Recognizing the different levels of human consciousness and the right of humans to indulge in lower-than-ideal states of mind is a basic principle of humanism, because it shows respect for humanity as it actually is and wherever it is found; whereas the attempt to lift all people to the height of some rational ideal (or a moral, religious, nationalistic one, etc.) may open the way to tyranny and terror.[41] Imposing utopia upon an unwilling world or upon a naturally unsuitable one will easily turn utopia into its opposite—a fact that history attests in recurrent waves of suffering. Spinoza could have learned it from his fellow Marranos and the Inquisition, and some of Marx's disciples have given it new expression in our own century. And while Marx is not responsible for every abuse committed in his name, there is still a self-defeating element in his utopia that almost inevitably invites abuse. On the whole, if a tautology can be allowed to sum up this chapter, Spinoza is far more Spinozistic than Marx.

On the other hand, Marx had a more penetrating view of social reality, which led him to add the indispensable economic dimension to both the concept of freedom and the project of self-knowledge. Here we may find in Marx an advantage over Spinoza and in terms of Spinoza's own philosophy.

Spinoza defines the aim of the state as freedom, but understands freedom mainly, if not exclusively, as mental and political. Marx, however, added the crucial modification that freedom has also, and primarily, an economic side. As a result, freedom must not be seen as the aim of the state alone, but of social organization in general, and must be embodied within the socioeconomic system that underlies the state itself and makes it possible. Second, self-knowledge and demystification in Spinoza are based upon discovering the true, if hidden, natural causes that affect our existence. This is a major Spinozistic idea. But Spinoza understands these causes mainly as physical and psychological. Ignorance of how the universe works breeds religious superstition and mental instability; ignorance of the natural way the mind operates breeds passivity and oppression of the self. Spinoza traces here a way which both Marx and Freud will follow and enrich, each in his own manner. In this respect, Marx's discovery of the economic forces that covertly determine our lives and the images we form of them is very much a Spinozistic move—but it carries Spinoza's program into further regions and adds a richer dimension to it.

However, Marx failed or refused to follow Spinoza's rigorous rejection of all forms of teleology and anthropomorphism. In projecting a worldwide ideal of redemption and putting forth his own, secular kind of messianism, Marx outreached the limits of immanence which (as I shall argue in the Epilogue) are inseparably bound with finitude. Messianic communism is a failure. But so is any other messianism. The value of Marx's discoveries, and his enrichment of the philosophy of immanence, will be retained only if a much more modest view of emancipation, a partial, finite view, is to replace the hopes and pitfalls of utopia.

Spinoza's antianthropomorphic rigor, which Marx failed to observe, will be taken up by Nietzsche who, had he known Marx's doctrine, would certainly have said that although in Marx, too, God seems to be dead, his "shadows" are still alive and thriving. As we shall see, if Marx was less Spinozistic than Spinoza, Nietzsche, in a sense, was more so.

CHAPTER 5

Spinoza and Nietzsche:
Amor dei and *Amor fati*

Amor fati—love of fate—is the defiant formula by which Nietzsche sums up his philosophical affirmation. The term, never before used in philosophy,[1] is clearly a polemical transformation of Spinoza's *amor dei intellectualis*, rejecting the primacy of the intellect and putting *fatum* (fate) in place of Spinoza's nature-God as the object of love.

The pair *amor dei* and *amor fati* provides an apt verbal representation of the complex relationship between Nietzsche and Spinoza, the two enemy-brothers of modern philosophy. Perhaps no two philosophers are as akin as Spinoza and Nietzsche, yet no two are as opposed. If Spinoza initiated the modern philosophy of immanence and undergirds it throughout, then Nietzsche brings it to its most radical conclusion—and, as we shall see, turns this conclusion against Spinoza himself.

Nietzsche explicitly recognizes his debt and kinship to Spinoza. Speaking of his "ancestors," Nietzsche at various times gives several lists, but he always mentions Spinoza and Goethe—and always as a pair.[2] This is no accident, for Nietzsche sees Goethe as incorporating Spinoza and as anticipating his own "Dionysian" ideal.

Goethe, Nietzsche says, was a "magnificent attempt to overcome the eighteenth century by a return to nature," an endeavor in which he "sought help from history, natural science, antiquity, and also Spinoza. . . ." Goethe, Nietzsche adds, wanted "totality" (of sense, reason, feeling, will); he "disciplined himself in wholeness," and he "created himself."

> Goethe conceived a human being who would be strong, highly educated, skillful in all bodily matters, self-controlled . . . who might dare to afford the whole range and wealth of being natural, being strong enough for such freedom; the man of tolerance, not

from weakness but from strength . . . the man for whom there is no longer anything that is forbidden—unless it be *weakness*, whether called vice or virtue.

This strongly Spinozistic ideal of Goethe Nietzsche then turns in his own direction:

Such a spirit who has *become free* amid the cosmos with a joyous and trusting fatalism, in the *faith* that only the particular is loathsome, and that all is redeemed and affirmed in the whole—*he does not negate any more.* Such a faith, however, is the highest of all: I have baptized it with the name of *Dionysus*.[3]

In this revealing passage Nietzsche attributes his own idea of *Übermensch* to Goethe while painting it in milder and more harmonious colors. In a certain respect, indeed, Nietzsche is a kind of intemperate Goethe, a stormy cultural radical who lacks Goethe's delicate artistic balance and is carried away by contradictory drives and by the more ferocious aspects of his naturalistic revolt. But, at bottom, as he looks at Goethe's ideal, Nietzsche recognizes himself in it, assimilates this ideal to his own Dionysus, and traces it partly back to Spinoza. Spinoza thus has a privileged role in forming Goethe's position which Nietzsche sees as the kernel of his own.

The extent of their kinship came as a flash to Nietzsche in the summer of 1881 when, probably after reading Kuno Fischer's book on Spinoza (where the concept of power is emphasized), he exclaimed in a postcard to his friend Franz Overbeck:

I am utterly amazed, utterly enchanted. I have a *precursor*, and what a precursor! I hardly knew Spinoza: that I should have turned to him just *now* was inspired by "instinct." Not only is his over-all tendency like mine—making knowledge the *most powerful* affect—but in five main points of his doctrine I recognize myself; this most unusual and loneliest thinker is closest to me precisely in these matters: he denies the freedom of the will, teleology, the moral world order, the unegoistic, and evil. Even though the divergencies are admittedly tremendous, they are due more to the differences in time, culture, and science. *In summa*: my solitude, which, as on very high mountains, often made it hard for me to breathe and made my blood rush out, is at least a dualitude.[4]

Nietzsche, in his enthusiasm, tends to minimize the divergencies between himself and Spinoza, which he attributes to the distance in time, culture, and so on. On other occasions, however, he disputes with Spinoza quite bitingly. What had incited Nietzsche's enthusiasm was, above all, Spinoza's strict naturalism with its many derivatives (which Nietzsche lists on the postcard), including the abolition of good and evil, the denial of a built-in moral world order, and an emphasis on self-interest and power as the basis of life and the lever for ethical advancement.

Nietzsche also singles out their common tendency "to make of knowledge the most powerful affect," meaning that knowledge is determined by the instinctual part of life and is no longer seen as an autonomous interest; and also that as affect, knowledge retains its role in liberating life. But here a major difference arises. Nietzsche, in a more Socratic manner, attributes a salutary affective power to knowledge in the critical, not the doctrinal sense; it is the kind of knowledge gained through disillusionment. This knowledge teaches no fixed positive truth, but purifies the individual of decadent images and false metaphysical consolations, preparing him or her for the final self-overcoming assent of *amor fati*.

In Spinoza, the immediate affective tone of knowledge is joy, the sensation of the enhanced power of life; Nietzsche, on the contrary, incessantly stresses the painful nature of knowledge and measures the power (and worth) of a person by "how much truth he can bear." Knowledge, in the sense of disillusionment or critical enlightenment, is a source of suffering and primarily a temptation to despair—which the Nietzschean man will overcome and transform into Dionysian joy. *Gaya scienza*—joyful knowledge[5]—is a task and goal in Nietzsche, not the normal outcome. Yet even when this goal is achieved, the conquered temptation to despair remains an inevitable component of Dionysian joy. Joy is not the natural outcome but the product of self-overcoming.

This already hints at some of the crucial differences between Nietzsche and Spinoza. Indeed, if Spinoza, as Nietzsche puns, redeems him of his solitude into a state of "dualitude," he also presents him with a powerful alternative. Nietzsche and Spinoza offer two rival options within the same radical conception, that of total immanence. Both declare the "death" of the transcendent God, and see life within immanence as all there is. This-worldliness is co-extensive with being in general. Moreover, the universe, *pace* Hegel, is devoid of any subjectlike features or inherent teleology, and thus offers man no consoling semblance of his own image engraved in the nature of things. Man himself is a fully immanent (or, in Spinoza's terms, "natural") being, with no supernatural gifts, obligations, or deficiencies; he neither lacks something more elevated residing in a superior world, nor is he en-

dowed with special powers emanating from such a transcendent domain. Man has no separate, eternal soul,[6] no "transcendental self" to
replace it, no a priori reason demanding to impose itself externally
upon nature and life. As a finite mode, man is, however, but a drop in
the immanent universe and as such is inescapably bound and con-
strained by it; this fact (or destiny) he must interiorize, understand, and
assent to with the full intensity of his life, if he is to endow his bare
existence with a worthwhile meaning compatible with the boundaries
of immanence (freedom in Spinoza, authentic existence in Nietzsche).
This involves some form of "love of necessity"; yet the crucial question
is how to interpret this necessity, whether as a self-justifying system
of rational laws or as opaque and indeterminate *fatum* which nothing
can justify or capture by rational categories, causes, or laws. This question is the watershed at which, upon the common ground of immanence, Nietzsche and Spinoza stand in conflict and each argues, indeed,
pleads and seduces, toward a totally different experience of immanence.

In Spinoza the immanent world inherits divine status and many of
the properties of the defunct transcendent God. Self-caused and self-
justified, it is eternal and infinite both in quantity and in perfection. Its
existence follows necessarily from its essence, governed by fixed and
eternal laws, and is also rationally intelligible throughout. As for man,
he exists "in God" and shares in the same universal rationality by
which eventually he can rise above his finitude and realize eternity
within his temporal existence. By contrast, Nietzsche's experience of
immanence leaves no room for order, permanence, fixed laws, inherent rationality, or truth; it presupposes a mode of existence from which
not only God, but (as Nietzsche says) God's "shadows" have also been
removed. Man exists here in an ever-transient flux of (cosmic) "will to
power," without redemption, without fixed truth, with nothing to explain his life or justify his death. As for the concept of necessity—the
object of love—it signifies that existence flows from the essence of God
and is rational and divine throughout, whereas in Nietzsche necessity
is opaque and unintelligible *fatum*, devoid of essence or rational ground
and pressing upon all creatures as an inescapable burden.

These are two radically opposed experiences of the world, one se-
curing order, permanence, and even, in a pantheistic vein, the sense of
cosmic meaningfulness and shelter provided by the old religions
(though it denies their historical form), the other leaving man in a
metaphysical wasteland, a world of conflicts and transience which cannot be captured by rational categories and from which all metaphysical
consolation is banned. Consequently, the assent and celebrating accep-

tance of immanent existence in Nietzsche's *amor fati* must take the defiant and self-overcoming form of a "nevertheless." *Amor fati* is based upon a fundamental dissonance between the individual and the world, as against their consonant agreement and semimystical identification in Spinoza's *amor dei intellectualis*.

Personal Affinities

The striking personal kinship of Nietzsche and Spinoza cannot pass without comment. When Nietzsche speaks about their "dualitude," he throws into relief the picture of two independent and solitary thinkers, each living in relative isolation, their lives almost consumed by their philosophical work, and both making unsettling discoveries that alienated them from most of their contemporaries (who saw them as cultural villains) and from the major bulk of tradition. (Nietzsche, however, had Spinoza to lean upon—and compete with—in building a new countertradition.) The objects of shock and horror, they were denigrated as "atheistic" or "nihilistic" (depending on the abusive idiom of the age) and shunned as socially subversive and grossly antimoral. However, both Nietzsche and Spinoza, though they rejected the concepts of good and evil, were profound moral philosophers, not in the sense of prescribing duties or grounding moral obligations, but in setting a perspective of human ascendance and perfectibility and trying to seduce their audience toward it.

The highly esoteric nature of their ideal reflects both men's existential isolation and aristocratic frame of mind. Spinoza, unlike Nietzsche, was partly equipped to deal with the problem of esotericism, since he had worked out a distinct moral perspective for the multitude, and distinguished it categorically from that of the happy few (see vol. 1, chap. 5). Not so Nietzsche, who sometimes seems to suggest that his artistocratic psychology should apply to everyone within the new culture. This is both incoherent and dangerous, a potential for inevitable abuse.

Linked to their isolation and revolutionary message—and also, in Nietzsche, to his sense of depth and aristocracy—is both men's taste for mask and equivocation. "Whatever is profound loves masks" says Nietzsche, who abundantly illustrates this belief in his work. His complex, aphoristic utterances, intentionally equivocal, loaded with allusions and ironic twists, exaggerating, pretending, over- and understating, leaving crucial points half-said while lingering upon others of lesser importance, provide the reader with a wealth of insights as well as pitfalls. This way of writing not only reflects the nature of

Nietzsche's literary gifts, or his conscious choice of unsystematic style, or his need to divert, shock, and seduce his readers, but also, I think, betrays an existential need for masks per se. Depth cannot disclose itself directly but must use the roundabout route of hide-and-seek, overwhelm and retreat, which includes irony as a necessary ingredient. Nietzsche's depth is frequently dramatic but rarely pompous; and, like Heine, he knows that good style can be used not only to pass on a message but also to erect a protective screen. Self-exposure borders on bad taste, and sincerity is the virtue of the vulgar.

Spinoza, with his geometrical method, obviously had no qualms in using a direct, unequivocal style, at least for strict philosophical purposes and when communicating with the initiated. Yet Spinoza was also a great connoisseur of masks and a master of equivocation. Few surpassed him in carrying on a discourse on several levels simultaneously, a practice he used primarily for prudence and persuasion, but which clearly also gave him intellectual and esthetic pleasure. It was not only a strategic necessity but also a *laetitia* (if not an outright *amor*) *intellectualis*.

The mask had yet another function for both philosophers. Experts in using it, they were equally sensitive to its use—and abuse—by others, especially when the mask was not put on deliberately. In this they share with thinkers like Marx and Freud, who set out to unmask accepted notions and established personal and social facades by digging into the unavowed motives and mechanisms behind them.

Spinoza, indeed, lacks a sophisticated apparatus for explaining the varieties of self-deception and ideological mystification, but he shares, and indeed triggers, the modern trend of educating the mind to be suspiciously attentive to itself and its projected images, and to seek a deeper, perhaps a darker kind of enlightenment than the one provided by the overt process of reasoning.

That such a trend of "dark enlightenment" is tied up with a philosophy of immanence will be attested by the list of its major representatives. Machiavelli and Hobbes, Spinoza, Darwin, Marx, Nietzsche, Freud, perhaps Heidegger, and Sartre were all bound by a philosophy that challenges the "divine part" in man and its alleged origin in a transcendent realm; each worked to shatter complacent self-images and comforting illusions and claimed to have discovered something dark and unsettling about the structure of man and his world. This kind of "knowledge"—always painful, as Nietzsche repeatedly says, with its critical "dark" side and disillusioning cure, and the unrelenting drive to gain it, to make it a powerful and salutary affect—is also the common ground that Nietzsche seems to have discovered between Spinoza and himself.

Nietzsche makes innumerable direct references to Spinoza. Some of his remarks are important, others are marginal, and all are biased in style and content by Nietzsche's current philosophical emphasis. Hence it will not serve our purpose to follow the line of "Nietzsche as reader of Spinoza."[7] Instead, I shall try to reconstruct their respective positions around certain key philosophical issues, especially the nature of immanence and the proper human response to it.

Conatus *versus Will to Power*

A necessary consequence of the philosophy of immanence that Nietzsche shares with Spinoza is their adherence, in their theory of man, to a strict naturalistic monism. For both philosophers there is a single natural principle active in man that constitutes his individual existence (as it does everything else in nature). This principle is not a static being but a dynamic thrust, striving, or desire; as such it is also the unique principle underlying all the affects, drives, and diverse forms of human behavior. Spinoza calls it *conatus*, Nietzsche, "will to power."

Conatus in Spinoza is basically the striving for self-preservation. "Everything . . . endeavors to persist in its being" (*Ethics*, pt. 3, prop. 6) is the first principle from which the rest is derived, encompassing all human affects from the most common to the most philosophical. For Spinoza, the mode of being of individual things is *duratio* (duration), defined not in temporal but in modal terms. It is the mode of being of a thing whose existence does not follow necesarily from its essence. As such, it needs external causes in order to come into existence, and it will endure in existence as long as external causality will permit, constantly resisting its assault and the dangers it represents. This resistance, the negative aspect of *conatus*, is not an attribute or an added quality of finite things but their very mode of being; it constitutes their individuality as distinct entities.

In defining humans by their self-centered desire, the *conatus* is (as Nietzsche recognizes with approval) the very opposite of disinterestedness. Yet its offspring includes not only common passions and desires but also the drive for rational knowledge (*conatus intelligendi*) as well as the supreme emotion and life-form of *amor dei intellectualis*. Both aggression and empathy, violence and mutual help issue from this single natural principle, depending on circumstances, the laws of psychology, and one's degree of knowledge (i.e., of emancipation).

This monism is, of course, a necessary corollary of Spinoza's strict naturalism or principle of immanence. Since there is no transcendent world, no moral world order, no a priori norms and obligations, no purposive organization of the universe, but only a world governed by a play of mechanical forces, the individual's total life must be explained and grounded in a strictly natural principle of desire that individuates him or her as a single natural entity. *Conatus*, as the striving of every natural being to persevere in existence and, for this purpose, to enhance its power to exist, is thus made by Spinoza into the single principle from which all human behavior and all civilized phenomena are derived.

This monism agrees with Nietzsche as well—and for similar reasons. Nietzsche's will to power, like the *conatus* it replaces, is conceived as "the primitive form of affect, [such] that all other affects are only developments of it." But here again Nietzsche contradicts Spinoza. "It can be shown most clearly that every living thing does everything it can not to preserve itself but to become *more*,"[8] Nietzsche writes in a note to himself, naming Spinoza as his specific opponent. Elsewhere he insists: "A living thing seeks above all to discharge its strength—life itself is will to power; self-preservation is only one of the indirect and most frequent results."[9] What especially disproves Spinoza's thesis are the frequent cases (which Spinoza is unable to explain except as "folly") in which one is ready to risk one's life for the sake of expanding and transcending oneself:

> The wish to preserve oneself is the symptom of a condition of distress, of a limitation of the really fundamental instinct of life which aims at the expansion of power and, wishing for that, frequently risks and even sacrifices self-preservation.[10]

Spinoza, too, speaks of enhancing the power of existence (and of action) as his goal.[11] Frequently he conjoins this goal with self-preservation (either as its implication or as its equivalent) but then—at least on one occasion—seems to suggest that they are independent concepts.[12] Despite this ambivalence, the only coherent way to construe Spinoza's theory is to see the one goal as subservient to the other. Enhancing the power of existence and of action is desirable because it increases the prospects of self-preservation. In Nietzsche, however, power is not an instrument of life but defines and encompasses it. We do not first exist and then seek to prolong our existence by augmenting its power; rather, we exist from the start as will to power, that is, as the dynamic projection of our being and as the built-in thrust to enhance and expand it, for which life as merely given may sometimes be jeopardized.

Will to power is thus a drive toward self-transcendence which is natural to all humans (and to all other beings as well). Nietzsche (correctly, I think) sees no contradiction in the idea that immanent entities—the only kind there is—strive by nature to go beyond their boundaries and "become more." This does not infringe upon the principle of immanence, because in transcending themselves they are not necessarily guided by a transcendent realm or by a priori norms, but express and project their own existence and constitution. Hence we need not assume a separate world in order to think that all this-worldly entities exist by nature as this self-transcending drive.

Heidegger later adapted this Nietzschean idea of self-transcendence within immanence to his own account of human existence (*Dasein*) and of the meaning of being-in-the-world (*In-der-Welt-sein*). But Heidegger restricted his analysis to human beings, to whom he accorded a privileged ontic position in being; thereby he aligned himself to the Hegelian strand within the philosophy of immanence and, like Feuerbach, performed an inner critique within it. Nietzsche, on the other hand, sides with Spinoza's anti-Hegelian view that humans have nothing special that distinguishes them ontologically from the rest of being, to which they are assimilable.

This uniformism leads Nietzsche and Spinoza to apply their principles even to physical entities. In Spinoza, the physical side of *conatus* is the resistance a body shows to external causes which threaten to dispossess it and take its place;[13] it thus displays a "defensive" posture so to speak, the effort to resist external invasion and preserve what is physically the self. But in Nietzsche, characteristically, the physical idiom or expression of will to power states the exact opposite: "every specific body strives to become master over all space and to . . . thrust back all that resists its extension."[14]

Two further points must be made. The monism of *conatus* and will to power requires a theory to explain how the diverse and opposing forms of mental and cultural life can spring from one and the same primordial principle. But only Spinoza provides such an explanation; Nietzsche leaves us wondering how the will to power takes the various forms it does, especially those forms which Nietzsche considers devious, alienated, or otherwise nongenuine. Will to power can be healthy or degenerate, Dionysian or decadent. In its negative form, it works in the morality of *ressentiment*, in the Christian culture, and in the attempt of the rationalists to dominate the world by subjecting it to an imaginary web of fixed categories and laws. What is to distinguish between these "negative" forms of will to power and its "positive" or healthy expressions? What will explain how the one can be transformed into the other (as Spinoza explains the transformation of a "passive" into an "active" affect), and why do we persist in calling "weak" a form that has dominated human life throughout two millennia of its history? Nietzsche would have been greatly served by a theory of alienation of some sort, accounting for reversals in the mode of will to power (from genuine to devious and vice versa) and explaining how it becomes a hindrance to itself and how this can be resolved.

Finally, Spinoza's insistence on self-preservation is in accordance with his metaphysics of self-identity and permanence, whereas Nietzsche's will to power, in attributing self-transcendence to all immanent entities, agrees with his general theory of flux which denies self-identity of any sort. In this way, their differences over *conatus* and will to power fall well within the broader Spinoza-Nietzsche confrontation over the nature of the immanent world, to which we shall return. Meanwhile, let us briefly consider the ethical implications of what has been said so far, and its relation to the nature of the philosophical enterprise.

Morality and Self-Overcoming

Although Nietzsche and Spinoza reject good and evil as values embodied in nature or imposing themselves upon nature from without, they are, we said, moral philosophers in the sense of stressing human perfectibility. Each inspires his readers to seek a rare ethical achievement—*amor dei* in Spinoza, *amor fati* in Nietzsche—or at least to rise to some more attainable degree of existential liberation. Ethics, however, cannot be based upon supranatural powers, norms, categories, transcendental precepts, and the like, to substitute for the transcendent God. Nor can ethics take its cue from some latent structure of the universe, as if there existed a moral world-order imprinted upon things, which has to be copied or read off them as a guideline for moral obligation. The very notion of moral obligation (or moral duty) has no sense in a strictly immanent system, and must, in both Spinoza and Nietzsche, make way for *self-overcoming* as the key ethical concept.

Ethical achievements must have nature as their sole source, substrate, and principle. As strict naturalism goes hand in hand in both Nietzsche and Spinoza with a powerful ethical project, the latter must be construed as an ethics of self-overcoming, whereby the immanent natural principle (*conatus* in Spinoza, will to power in Nietzsche) shapes itself into something higher, producing a value that neither conflicts with nature nor transcends it toward some supranatural norm, but resides in the new organization and quality of the same natural principle and the mode of life to which it gives birth.

Self-overcoming thus differs radically from what may bear a similar name in Kant, the Stoics, or Christian morality and asceticism. It does not impose external constraints upon life and the emotions, but lets life reshape and sublimate itself, with one strain of emotions working on and giving shape to another. Not reason versus life, but life molding itself and enhancing its own power, generates self-overcoming in both these philosophers of immanence.

This is also a new or alternative interpretation given to the age-old concept of "spirit" or "spirituality," though neither Spinoza nor Nietzsche use these terms in order to avoid the adverse connotations of Christian asceticism and priestliness. Restraints which depress life by subduing it to some superior principle over and above life itself are liable to produce a morbid and self-denying asceticism that Spinoza shuns as much as Nietzsche despises. Spirit, or what should serve as its adequate substitute, is not a separate principle stemming from another world or from man's pure and autonomous consciousness, nor does it serve to depress and subdue life. Rather, spirit (or, in Nietzsche, "free spirit") is life itself, with its full-blooded dash and affective power, as it shapes and gives meaning to itself by that mode of self-overcoming which enhances rather than reduces its vital and creative powers. On this understanding, the Dionysian way of life is also the most "spiritual."

The immanent ethics Nietzsche shares with Spinoza can neither recognize altruism nor accept a morality of self-denial, pity, or guilt. At the same time it rejects unrestrained licentiousness and all forms of *laissez aller*. Grounded as it is in the respective principles of *conatus* and will to power, it places virtue in the shaped and sublimated self-assertiveness of the individual, that is, in the invigorating form of self-overcoming. But here a major difference appears.

In Spinoza the sublimation of the affects is informed by reason and objective scientific knowledge; hence it obeys definite rules and universal patterns. Not so in Nietzsche, who conceives of the life of his *Übermensch* as an open existential experiment, and who recognizes no objective knowledge, only perspectival interpretations. Self-overcoming thus has a hermeneutical aspect in Nietzsche; it is linked to a personal mode of self-interpretation whereby the individual projects and gives meaning to his or her life. To better appreciate this point we must consider how Nietzsche and Spinoza see the nature of philosophy and its relation to life.

Philosophy and Life

For Nietzsche there is no objective truth, only "perspectives" and "interpretations" that serve and are bound by existential drives and interests. Hence philosophy—or rather, philosophizing—is not understood as a search for objective knowledge or as a new kind of science. It is, fundamentally, an evaluative attitude toward life, an attitude that both expresses and finds support in certain cognitive images. Accordingly, Nietzsche's so-called "genealogical" method sets out to uncover the origins of the various cognitive beliefs and claims to truth within the typical psychology and life-preferences imbued in them. (The term *genealogy* connotes a search for covert origins that are to be exposed and also evaluated as "noble" or "ignoble.")

Life is always the life of some individual; hence philosophy, as a mode of life and an attitude toward it, must have an individual focus or goal. To philosophize means that a certain individual takes a stand toward life, imparts meaning to it, affirms or negates it, and thereby gives it shape. This process is not confined to the individual's intellect alone but is carried out by the fullness of his or her life, with its affective (or instinctual) basis and the will to power which this life embodies and projects. Hence life is a kind of existential *causa sui* in Nietzsche, using the term in a weak (psychological and not ontological) sense. Life is both subject and object of the process of self-interpretation; it is the generator and the value-giver, as well as the subject matter which is being shaped and given meaning and value to. In the (rather disapproving) words of Jaspers: Man is here his own creator in the state of "self-being without God."[15]

The individual's self-creative attitude toward her or his life is not a mode of consciousness but of *being*, in which his or her instinctual life, by imparting meaning to itself and the world (through action, experimentation, inner experience, self-discipline, etc.) also transcends and shapes its raw, wild substantiality. Self-interpretation is thereby supposed to be linked to self-overcoming as well, and to the ethical perspective of life.

This view of philosophy stands of course in opposition to the time-honored ideal of philosophy as science which Spinoza had shared and renovated, but which Nietzsche traces back to Socrates and Plato. Faithful to his genealogical method, Nietzsche objects to this ideal not only as a simple philosophical fallacy, but as a decadent perspective that serves the self-image and life-preferences of an unhealthy and world-weary culture, the opposite of his Dionysian ideal.

Spinoza's geometrical method not only highlights the ideal of philosophy as science; it also seems to Nietzsche to advocate a cold, repressive attitude to life and an absolute intellectual asceticism:

> *Non ridere, non lugere, neque detestari, sed intelligere!* [Not to laugh, not to lament, nor to detest, but to understand] says Spinoza as simply and sublimely as is his wont. Yet in the last analysis, what else is this *intelligere* than the form in which we come to feel the other three at once? One result of the different and mutually opposed desires to laugh, lament, and curse? Before knowledge is possible, each of these instincts must first have presented its one-sided view of the thing or event. . . . Since only the last scenes of reconciliation and the final accounting at the end of this long process rise to our consciousness, we suppose that *intelligere* must be something . . . that stands essentially opposed to the instincts.[16]

Nietzsche adds that conscious knowledge is only the tip of the iceberg under which a struggle of instincts is raging. But he seems to forget that rational understanding in Spinoza only suspends the emotions but does not kill them; eventually, it is supposed to enhance the power of emotion while rechannelling its direction and turning its quality from "passive" (or servile) into "active" (or free). Herein lies the ethical and affective goal which philosophy has in Spinoza. (Spinoza makes this goal abundantly clear, from the programmatic opening of his essay on the intellect to the *Ethics*.) Science with all its apparatus, including the geometrical method, is but a preparation for attaining freedom, joy, active power, and the transformation of one's life into something resembling secular salvation.

Of course, to fulfill this goal, knowledge must be "pure," not in the sense that it has no bearing on existential needs and drives, but in the sense that, in order to properly serve these drives, knowledge must be free of bias and follow its own logic and the constraints of its subject matter. Otherwise, among other ills, it will fall prey to illusions and mystifications from which Nietzsche, too, wishes to liberate the philosopher.

Thus Spinoza is not the repressive or cold rationalist who alienates life from philosophy, as Nietzsche sometimes polemically pictures him. And yet their differences remain vast. Spinoza did not believe in an objective world and in true knowledge that can capture it (in the idiom of a contemporary philosopher, knowledge is a kind of "mirror of nature," though the mirror in this case is part of nature itself).[17] Spinoza deduced the concepts and postulates of modern science as if they were eternal truth. Moreover, he wished to experience the universe not only as a scientific object but as a theological one as well—as

God. Hence, Nietzsche charges, Spinoza was not a radical philosopher of immanence. He disposed of the transcendent God, but kept his "shadows" alive.

Immanence and the Shadows of the Dead God

Centuries after Buddha was dead, Nietzsche tells his readers, people were still showing Buddha's shadow lingering in a cave.[18] So it is with the dead God: his shadow still hovers in and over the world of immanence, and if not exorcised, will survive for thousands of years. But "we" (meaning the new philosophers), Nietzsche insists, must overcome not only God, but his shadows as well.

What are these "shadows of the dead God"? They include, on the one hand, the idea of a moral world-order, of good and evil inscribed in the order of things, which Spinoza, as Nietzsche recognizes, had already set out to abolish. On the other hand, these shadows also include the postulates of science and of rational thinking generally, projected upon the universe as objective and eternal truths. Here Nietzsche confronts Spinoza as a direct and, in a sense, specific opponent. Many of the rationalist postulates that Nietzsche criticizes are associated with the category of substance, Spinoza's main concept; and Spinoza's deification of nature—which many other rationalists avoid and to which the scientific outlook is not committed—adds a distinct "shadow of God" to his picture of the immanent universe. When will the world be pure of God for us? Nietzsche exclaims. Spinoza believed that in insisting that the immanent world was "substance" and not "subject," and by adhering to a strictly mechanistic explication of the world, he avoided any vestiges of anthropomorphism. Yet genealogically, Nietzsche argues, the concept of substance is tacitly presupposed in that of the subject; and mechanism is no less anthropomorphic than teleology, only more subtly so.

Mechanism presupposes the unfounded belief (characteristic of weak and life-weary people) in rational necessity and permanent laws, as well as a set of notions and postulates which make this belief possible although they have no corresponding reality,[19] but are all fictions. They are our images, serving a variety of human needs—biological, psychological, and existential.

> Over immense periods of time the intellect produced nothing but errors. A few of these proved to be useful and helped to preserve the species: those who hit upon or inherited these had better luck in their struggle for themselves and their progeny. Such erroneous

articles of faith . . . include the following: that there are enduring things; that there are equal things; that there are things, substances, bodies; that a thing is what it appears to be; that our will is free; that what is good for me is also good in itself.[20]

Later (and elsewhere) Nietzsche extends this list of fictions, which he also calls "articles of faith," to include the soul, the subject, cause and effect, form and content, geometrical entities (lines, surfaces, bodies), divisible space and time, and so on. Many of these articles of faith (especially the belief in self-identical and measurable "things" and in identical cases upon which logical and natural laws are based) are not merely intellectual abstractions; they penetrate the deepest and most immediate organic functions and build themselves into the patterns of "sense perception and every kind of sensation." They even set up for themselves a self-immuning system: "even in the realm of knowledge these propositions became the norms according to which 'true' and 'untrue' were determined—down to the most remote regions of logic."[21]

To break this vicious circle of self-immunization—or rather, to bypass it—Nietzsche turns to his genealogical method, which does not accept rational claims to truth at face value, but looks for their origins in the various needs and functions of life. "Pure logic" is neither pure nor primordial; it is the product of a life process that needs and presupposes its fictions.

The Origins of Logic

Logic is bound to the condition: assume there are identical cases. In fact, to make possible logical thinking and inferences, this condition must first be treated fictitiously as fulfilled. That is: the will to logical truth can be carried through only after a fundamental *falsification* of all events is assumed. . . . Logic does *not* spring from will to truth.[22]

Fortunately for survival, our senses help in forming this fiction, since "the coarser organ sees much apparent equality."[23] Moreover, as in the process of digestion, the organism assimilates as much of this fiction as it needs, and discards its excesses. In *Gay Science* Nietzsche elaborates this idea in a semi-Darwinian vein:

How did logic come into existence in man's head? Certainly out of illogic, whose realm originally must have been immense. Innumerable beings who made inferences in a way different from ours perished; for all that, their ways might have been truer. Those, for example, who did not know how to find often enough what is "equal" as regards both nourishment and hostile animals—those, in other words, who subsumed things too slowly and cautiously—were favored with a lesser probability of survival than those who guessed immediately upon encountering similar instances that they must be equal. The dominant tendency, however, to treat as equal what is merely similar—an illogical tendency, for nothing is really equal—is what first created any basis for logic. (§111)

And Nietzsche continues, in a passage that may directly apply to Spinoza (because it puts substance at the center of rationalist fictions):

In order that the concept of substance could originate—which is indispensable for logic although in the strictest sense nothing real corresponds to it—it was likewise necessary that for a long time one did not see nor perceive the changes in things. The beings that did not see so precisely had an *advantage* over those that saw everything "in flux." (Ibid.)

This advantage, as Nietzsche often points out, is not only biological but also mental. It is both painful and awesome to experience the world as the transient indeterminacy it is. Ordinary humans crave permanence, fixed and rigid entities in which to find order and consolation. Just as animals whose perception was more precise suffered a biological disadvantage, so the more discerning philosophers, the skeptics and critics of rational illusion, incur suffering and anxiety for themselves. Nietzsche, however, in his ideal of the *Übermensch* seeks to overcome the effects of ordinary psychology in order to create a new type of response, suitable for the powerful and the rare.

Nietzsche's critique of "logic" and rationalist postulates centers around the concept of self-identical "things," which is also the basis for the category of substance—Spinoza's major concept. A "thing," however, is also thought of as a self-identical unit that exercises (or submits to) causal agency; yet to Nietzsche, causality is as much a man-made projection as is teleology. Citing Hume with approval, Nietzsche claims that there is nothing to justify our "faith" that event *A* has something in it which effects or generates event *B*. The causality we attribute to "things" is the reified projection of our own inner experience, namely, of what we feign to be the causality of our will.

"We believe ourselves to be causal in the act of willing: we thought that here we caught causality in the act."[24] Hence we generalize from our will to the rest of the world and attribute will-like entities to external events as well, calling them "powers," "agents," or "causes." On Nietzsche's genealogical analysis, then, causes are magical embodiments of imaginary acts of will. And Schopenhauer, in his bizarre doctrine that being is willing, had therefore only "enthroned a primeval mythology."

> Man believed originally that wherever he saw something happen, a will had to be at work in the background as a cause, and a personal, willing being. . . . The faith in cause and effect became for him the basic faith that he applies wherever anything happens— and this is what he still does instinctively; it is an atavism of the most ancient origin. [25]

Causality is also based upon the fiction of the serial universe, composed of discrete, self-identical entities. Nietzsche objects not only to the causal dependence of event *A* upon event *B*, but to the very splicing of the world process into such unitary items as events *A* and *B*. "An intellect" he speculates, "that could see cause and effect as a continuum and a flux . . . would repudiate the concept of cause and effect and deny all conditionality." [26]

The myth of the will, or the subject as agent, also underlies the concept of substance itself. On several occasions Nietzsche analyzes the concept of substance as a consequence of the concept of subject, not the reverse. This is because the subject "is interpreted from within ourselves, so that the ego counts as substance, as the cause of all its deeds, as a doer." Hence,

> the logical-metaphysical postulates, the belief in substance, accident, attribute, etc., derive their convincing force from our habit of regarding all our deeds as consequences of our will—so that the ego, as substance, does not vanish in the multiplicity of change.— But there is no such thing as will. [27]

Seen in this light, the Spinoza-Hegel controversy would appear to be fictitious, since Hegel does not really transcend Spinoza, and Spinoza does not really oppose Hegel but rather includes Hegel's idea of the universe as subject in his own concept of substance.

The Nature of Immanence and the Problem of Truth

We need not go into all the "shadows of God" which Nietzsche seeks to exorcise in order to capture his kind of world-picture and experience of immanence. [28] But before looking at the positive world-image that

Nietzsche offers, a crucial question must be addressed: What is the status of Dionysian "truth"? We have seen that Nietzsche recognizes no facts, only interpretations, and no objective knowledge, only perspectives that are relative to existential interests and drives. Yet he also gives detailed accounts of the nature of the universe his *Übermensch* recognizes and experiences. Are these accounts also mere perspectives, or is there a Dionysian truth that escapes perspectivism and applies to the world prior to all interpretations?

This is perhaps the most problematic issue in Nietzsche's thought. Neither the text nor the logic of Nietzsche's work furnishes a satisfactory resolution. On many occasions Nietzsche seems to suggest that there is a sober and painful view of the world and of life that deserves the name of truth *simpliciter*. The more we can take and accept of this truth, the stronger we are and the freer we may become. Frequently, Nietzsche also speaks of those who shun tragedy, transitoriness, or the multifaceted character of existence as fearing truth or fleeing from it; and he calls the opposite beliefs, the postulates of rational science and metaphysics, by the outright name of "errors" and "fictions." It seems to me that this tendency betrays Nietzsche's more direct and spontaneous mind, as he lets his "gut-philosophy," so to speak, express itself without the critical restraints he should however have obeyed in light of his philosophical method. For on Nietzsche's official view of philosophy, nothing can evade the hermeneutical process; there can be no "bare" facts or truth prior to a value-laden interpretation; and perspectivism is the universal rule.

If so, what is the status of the latter pronouncement? Is not this theory itself yet another perspective—a *meta*perspective, perhaps, but one that also depends upon an existential commitment? Yes, a Nietzschean might answer, this is the cognitive counterpart of the Dionysian way of life, which it makes possible and to which it is relative. Existential options come together with their corresponding cognitive images; but the latter depend on the former, not the other way around.

Whether Nietzsche would have lived in peace with this relativization of what he sensed as his painful and dramatic discoveries about the universe is an open question. In the final analysis, Nietzsche can neither accept nor reject the idea that the Dionysian world-view is a truth unbound by perspective. But this important question has little bearing on our present discussion, for we are contrasting two rival experiences of immanence; and there is no doubt that, on whichever interpretation, the Dionysian world-image enjoys in Nietzsche a privileged position as the view that he pleads for and values most. Whether his reasons are partly also cognitive or only existential is a secondary consideration for the present purposes. With this in mind we may now summarize the Spinoza-Nietzsche confrontation on the image of the immanent world.

In Spinoza the immanent world is a rational *causa sui*, having its reason, meaning, and justification within itself. Eminently intelligible, it is illuminated, as it were, from within by the light of reason, which pervades and constitutes every entity. The universe inherits the role and status of God and omnipresent reason takes the place of the divine presence or grace. Man, living within the immanent universe, exists within God and may rise to a detailed knowledge of this relation—with all the mental repercussions that such a consciousness entails.

God, in other words, is not dead in Spinoza. He does not disappear from the horizon of Spinoza's philosophy but is, as Spinoza sees it, correctly identified for the first time. All the sublimity, the infinity, the supreme "wisdom" (intelligibility), the omnipresence, and the divinity of the old personal God are here attached to what is claimed to be their true and only legitimate subject, the universe or the nature-God. Spinoza not only naturalizes God, but also deifies nature.

"God's shadows" are indeed present everywhere in Spinoza. Substance and causality, self-identity and permanence are the dominant marks of his universe. And although there is also transience in Spinoza's world (every particular thing is inevitably perishable), the individual thing also has an eternal aspect whereby it is grasped (and exists) from the standpoint of eternity. Individual things are fully determined by causal laws which, far from expressing something arbitrary or "opaque" about the universe, are thought to embody its supreme rationality and divinity. Mechanical causation is seen as equivalent to logical derivation; and even particular things, which exist by external causes and not by virtue of their own essence, are considered from the standpoint of eternity as logically (not only factually) necessary.

In Nietzsche, on the other hand, the immanent world has no inherent reason, order, or justification. Even its natural necessity—the basis for *amor fati*—cannot be construed as a rational system of cause and effect. To Spinoza's banning of teleology Nietzsche adds the abolition of mechanical causality, as another, subtler form of anthropomorphism. As there is nothing fixed and capturable in the world, there are no identical and even no *self*-identical causes and events, and thus no basis for permanent universal laws. The major categories and postulates by which we understand the universe are but useful fictions; and even logic is exposed as an illusion, an imaginary fixation of what in itself is indeterminable and evades all forms of "correct" or "true" picturing.

Against Spinoza's eminently rational, law-governed nature-God Nietzsche thus opposes a world in everlasting flux—never self-identical, never at logical rest, never attaining equilibrium (by which it would be captured and defined) or a fixed final state; a world which is neither pure being nor pure becoming but always wavering between both. "Eternally self-creating, eternally self-destroying,"[29] the world must be experienced as a contingent and irrational variety of the *causa sui*. Though it has no transcendent cause or inherent rational grounds, yet it maintains itself by itself and lives of itself: "its excrements are its food." Nietzsche offers a variation of this idea in calling the world "a work of art that gives birth to itself."[30] The artistic metaphor indicates that the world has *some* organization in Nietzsche, though it is esthetic rather than scientific.[31] But the metaphor should not be pressed too hard. Even as "work of art," the world remains indeterminable and elusive, a cluster of perspectives without fixed substance; moreover, its art forms are themselves transitory and liable to constant change and transformation.[32]

Thus we are back in the domain of flux. If Spinoza's rational substance continues the tradition of Parmenides, Nietzsche sides with his opponent, Heraclitus, but goes much further than this pre-Socratic master, since he also denies the *logos*, or fixed rational order, which in Heraclitus undergirded the world-flux.[33] Thus man has nothing constant to hold on to in Nietzsche's world; his experience of immanence is that of a metaphysical desert, a yoke, the everlasting undoing of all transitory forms and the constant slipping of being from under his feet.

The following quotation from the end of *Will to Power*, where, using a mixture of poetic and semiscientific idioms, Nietzsche projects his "positive" vision of the world, sounds like the last of the pre-Socratic philosophers:

> And do you know what "the world" is to me? . . . This world: a monster of energy, without beginning, without end; a firm iron magnitude of force that does not grow bigger or smaller, that does not expand itself but only transforms itself; . . . at the same time one and many, increasing here and at the same time decreasing there; a sea of forces flowing and rushing together, eternally changing, eternally flooding back with tremendous years of recurrence, with an ebb and a flood of its forms, out of the simplest forms striving toward the most complex . . . and then again returning home to the simple out of this abundance, out of the play of contradictions . . . a becoming that knows no satiety, no dis-

gust, no weariness: this, my *Dionysian* world of the eternally self-creating, the eternally self-destroying . . . my "beyond good and evil," without goal, unless the joy of the circle is itself a goal; without will, unless a ring feels good will toward itself . . . do you want a *name* for this world? . . . *this world is the will to power—and nothing besides!* And you yourselves are also this will to power—and nothing besides! (*Will to Power* 1067)

This famous passage (over which we are told that Nietzsche toiled) seems to be written more as a metaphysical fable than as a full-fledged scientific theory. But it conveys the kind of immanent world-experience which Nietzsche suggests as the stuff of the Dionysian affirmation.

Another pertinent fable is eternal recurrence, which does not as much impose a fixed order on the universe as it dramatizes the inescapability of immanence. For it bars any perspective of life either outside the world or within it (in some better future) by which life in the present can be redeemed, guided or given meaning to. And as life has no source of meaning beyond itself, it must be endowed with meaning on the basis of its instantaneous character.

Eternal Recurrence and Amor fati

Eternal recurrence, says Nietzsche, is the chief doctrine taught by his Zarathustra. I shall not discuss the question whether eternal recurrence was also meant as a full-fledged cosmological theory, but take it as an existential fable, expressing the kind of self-overcoming which *amor fati* involves. Seen in this way, eternal recurrence serves to better explicate the content of *amor fati* and also to test its existence.[34]

Eternal recurrence derives its primary meaning in Nietzsche as the theme of a major act of affirmation. Whether in joy, routine or suffering, and although he does not see an inherent purpose or ready-made meaning in existence, the Dionysian man will say "yes" to his life as it is by wishing this life to repeat itself over and over again, exactly as it has been, without any novelty, betterment, progress, or the like. In *Gay Science* (351), Nietzsche expresses this idea in terms of an acute temptation and test:

What if one day or night a demon were to sneak after you into your loneliest loneliness and say to you, "This life as you now live it and have lived it, you will have to live once more and innumerable times more; and there will be nothing new in it, but every pain and every joy and every thought and sigh and everything immeasurably small or great in your life must return to to you—all in the same succession and sequence. . . ." Would you now throw yourself down and gnash your teeth and curse the demon who spoke thus? Or have you once experienced a tremendous moment when you would have answered him, "You are a God and never have I heard anything more Godly"? . . . How well disposed would you have to become to yourself and to life to *crave nothing more fervently* than this ultimate eternal confirmation and seal?[35]

This is the utmost affirmation of immanence. By craving that every moment, every passing "joy and sigh" be repeated forever, I recognize the closed horizon of immanence as the totality of existence, and also, in *amor fati*, transform this recognition from a burden into a celebration. It is not resignation, but the active joy of the self-created man, liberated from the external yoke of transcendent religion, morality, utopia, or metaphysics.

It should be noted that what I wish to be endlessly repeated is not only the content of every moment but its very momentariness. Immanence is here identified with the present, with what exists now as merely transitory; and in wishing it to recur time and again I equally wish it to pass away; or rather, I recognize and accept the mode of being in which transience is the rule.

Herein also lies Nietzsche's alternative to Goethe's Faust. Faust craves being able to say to the moment, "Stay forever"; he wants eternity to be placed in this-worldly moments. Nietzsche does as well, but to him this-worldly moments contain their passing away within themselves; hence Nietzsche cannot tell the moment to *stay* forever but only to *repeat itself* forever. In this way he both adheres to the moment and affirms and accepts its inevitable transience.

Significantly, Nietzsche attributes eternal recurrence to Heraclitus, his master in matters of flux and transitoriness. But Nietzsche could also have found this theme—colored in pessimistic and "decadent" tones—in the Preacher's complaint that "there is no new thing under the sun" and "the thing that hath been, it is that which shall be." The Book of Ecclesiastes concludes that all is vanity and life is a burden; whereas Zarathustra and his followers are supposed to make the ultimate confirmation of immanence a source of celebration.

Eternal recurrence dramatizes the inescapability of immanence. In being prepared to live every moment of my life innumerable times over and again, I renounce any claim or hope for a "next world." Even my hope for the future does not refer to a better state of this world (as in Kant, Hegel, Marx, and Christian and Jewish eschatology), but to the same kind of existence taken over and over again. What is to replace my present life is this same life again—that is, *nothing* is to replace my present life. Immanent life is all there is; in calling for its identical repetition I thereby assume the weight of immanence as my only horizon.[36]

But what kind of immanence? Certainly an immanence very different from that of Hegel or Spinoza. In Hegel, the historical progress toward freedom and self-knowledge offers a perspective in which the human race (and through it, being itself) is to be actualized. Although the immanent world is all there is, it has, so to speak, an inner transcendent dimension—the *telos* (goal) it has to realize and become. This also gives time a qualitative character in Hegel, as the medium of historical novelty and advancement. Spinoza admits of no such teleology, and like Nietzsche, he views time (or better, duration) as qualitatively neutral.[37] At best, the notion of progress in Spinoza has a subjective meaning relative to *conatus* and personal desire. An individual may indeed attain a rational way of life, but this occurs by mechanistic causes and does not manifest any inherent structure or goal of the world-substance as such. In other words, God (the universe) is utterly indifferent to the human lot and to human ethical and rational achievement.

This view, of course, makes Spinoza much more appealing to Nietzsche than Hegel and his followers. But Spinoza, too, must be perceived by Nietzsche as having his own eternalistic, rather than historical, form of "transcendence within immanence," because he accepts the eternal substance and laws of nature as underlying the world of change and as reflecting the inherent rationality and timelessness of God. Even what Spinoza calls *natura naturata*, the world of finite and transitory things, is not really in flux, because it is eternally shaped by *natura naturans* and because, thereby, the transient particulars have their self-identity while they last.

Moreover, in the third kind of knowledge and its accompanying experience of *amor dei intellectualis*, the transcendent element of timelessness is even said to enter the immanent particular (the knowing mind) and transform it in such a way as to abolish its finitude and make it allegedly infinite. Here, the penetration of eternity into the domain of transience has not only scientific, but semimystical connotations.

Nietzsche's eternal recurrence excludes both historicist and eternalistic transcendence.[38] The only eternity Nietzsche admits is the endless recurrence of transitory states, in which his Dionysiac philosopher will place all the worth that tradition had attributed to permanence. This will not be passive resignation but the active joy and vigor of a person delivered from the grip of transcendent religion. But this, it should be stressed, is an immensely difficult task which calls for a new type of psychology and person.

It is essential to see that *amor fati*, with its celebrating assumption of immanence, runs counter to normal human psychology. Ordinary people, Nietzsche expects, will experience pure immanence as a yoke and an oppression; their natural response to it and to recurrence is pessimism and world-weariness, the depression of their vital powers—or the various forms of escape and self-deception current in religion and traditional philosophy (Spinoza not excepted). It takes a powerful act of defiant affirmation, a supreme "nevertheless," to transform the oppression of immanence into its opposite, joy and celebrating power; and this requires a new and rare kind of psychology, the one which constitutes and expresses the *Übermensch*.

To make this transformation feasible, the individual needs support from a whole new culture, based upon the revaluation of all values (of which, therefore, *amor fati* and recurrence are the cornerstone): "No longer joy in certainty but in uncertainty; no longer 'cause and effect' but the continually creative; no longer will to preservation but to power." While these new values are diametrically opposed to Spinoza's teaching, there are others on which Spinoza himself had insisted, like "freedom from morality; . . . the abolition of the 'will'; the abolition of 'knowledge-in-itself.' "[39]

Amor fati thus differs from Spinoza's *amor dei* not only in content and mood but also in its mental structure. Spinoza's *amor dei* expresses a harmonious agreement with the universe, whereas *amor fati* involves an inner rupture and distance, bridged by an act of defiant affirmation. This has several implications.

First, the structure of defiant affirmation endows the Nietzschean *Übermensch* with a greater share of agency than can be credited to its Spinozistic counterpart. In Spinoza, any progress of the mind is determined by continuous, semimechanistic lines of logical inference and psychological determinism. Even liberation, once attained, was not caused by us, but "occurred" to us. In Nietzsche, however, a person attains *amor fati* through an act of defiant assent, by which he or she introduces a break into the ordinary course of events, negating its normal (and continuous) outcome and producing its opposite instead. Thus, even without admitting free will, the person may be credited with more agency and, indeed, freedom in bringing about the ethical state he or she values.

Second, the moment of rupture and defiance precludes all mystical connotations from *amor fati*. There can be no form of *unio mystica* here, as in Spinoza, because the defiant posture entails a distance between the affirming person and the universe he or she affirms and loves. *Amor fati* bridges this gap but does not abolish it; on the contrary, it maintains the tension of "nevertheless" as a constant feature of itself. Thus Dionysus, though he bears a mystical name, actually stands for a non-mystical attitude.

Finally, *amor fati* is an overcoming of Christianity—even in its atheistic cover. Pessimistic atheism remains at bottom a Christian frame of mind, because it denies all value to the immanent world as such. What is more Christian than feeling miserable and oppressed in a Godless universe? It is only when the temptation of pessimism is resisted and the world as divested of all "shadows of God" is accepted and experienced as a source of joy that man becomes his own creator and, for the first time, Christianity is overcome and Dionysus supplants Christ.[40]

The Temptation of Pantheism

In the rare moments of religious temptation, when his "god-forming instincts occasionally become alive," Nietzsche comes close to Spinoza in picturing an impersonal God existing beyond good and evil:

> Let us remove supreme goodness from the concept of God; it is unworthy of a god. Let us also remove supreme wisdom; . . . God the *supreme power*—that suffices! Everything follows from it, "the world" follows from it!

And in a different mood:

> Is it necessary to elaborate that a God prefers to stay beyond everything bourgeois and rational? And, between ourselves, also beyond good and evil?[41]

Yet these moments of religious (and pantheistic) temptation are declared to be "impossible" and Nietzsche resists them. Spinoza's *deus sive natura*, Nietzsche says, betrays the illicit "longing to believe that in some way the old God still lives" and "the world is after all like the old beloved, infinite . . . God."[42] But this is precisely what *amor fati* and recurrence preclude. Even Dionysus, the symbol of transient immanence, should not be deified. It is true that Zarathustra, in an imprudent moment, declared that he would believe only in a God who could dance (Dionysus). But this, Nietzsche later reassures us, was merely a manner of speaking, a counterfactual conditional: "Zarathustra says he *would*, but he *will* not"; for "Zarathustra himself is merely an atheist; he believes neither in old nor in new Gods."[43]

The pantheistic temptation and its resistance reveal something else to us. A God existing beyond good and evil could suit Nietzsche's critique of morality, but is incongruous with his sense of being in the world, with *amor fati*, and thus is rejected. In resisting the pantheistic temptation, Nietzsche makes it clear that his philosophy is not exclusively concerned with a critique of morality but centers on a revaluation of the whole experience of existence. The new values he seeks are not moral ones but existential modes and responses to life (like the love of transience, the joy in uncertainty, etc.); they constitute, indeed, a new psychology that could not co-exist with pantheism (just as, on other grounds, it is incompatible with mysticism).

Political Normativeness

Amor fati and *amor dei* are, of course, the highest achievements that Nietzsche and Spinoza offer as immanent philosophers bound by an ethics of self-overcoming. But the same principle of radical immanence also affects their views of the origins of political normativeness.

To account for the origin of binding rules of conduct in a world that has no inherent values and norms, Spinoza had recourse to the notions of contract and consent—a fact that makes him one of the first modern political philosophers and anchors his protodemocratic views directly within his doctrine of pure immanence. As there is nothing on earth or beyond it to generate binding norms and obligations, these can only be drawn from the consent of actual human beings who set up a government to use and distribute power in the service of their natural desires. Thus it is only with the state and its enforceable legislation that normativeness emerges in the world and makes sense at all.

This interplay of consent and power stands at the heart of Spinoza's view of political authority. Consent is needed to set up political institutions and state power is needed to keep them in effective existence. Moreover, consent itself is seen by Spinoza as a form of power that checks the power of the state. When a government is felt to be unjust or illegitimate, this will undermine political stability and threaten the survival of government. On the other hand, state power cannot penetrate the individual's mind and dominate his or her inner thoughts (so Spinoza, living before Stalin, believes). Hence liberal democracy (as we call it today) is the preferable system, not because it embodies a priori values or the innate rights of man, but because it is best suited to reconcile state power to the power of thought and procure a relatively stable and peaceful government. In other words, Spinoza is an early democrat, not because he believes in transcendental norms but because democracy is best suited to a world from which they are absent—a world of pure immanence.

In linking political authority to human consent Spinoza is obviously a disciple of Hobbes. But he objects to Hobbes' pessimistic portrayal of man's natural disposition to others; and, especially, he takes Hobbes seriously to task as an inconsequential naturalist. Hobbes wished to derive all human affairs, including political authority, from nature alone, but did not strictly adhere to his own principle.

Hobbes based obligation on the binding power of the contract. But why keep the original contract? This meta-obligation Hobbes could not ground within the contract itself, so he relegated it to a grey area of precontract normativeness which he called "natural law," a curious name and problematic concept for the strict naturalist philosopher Hobbes claimed to be. The notion of precontract normativeness flirts dangerously with that of a "natural moral order" to which both Spinoza and Nietzsche must object. In addition, Hobbes' construal of the contract introduces a degree of discontinuity between nature and civilized life. In overcoming the natural state of man, the original contract establishes the foundations of civilized life as a new domain, a kind of "realm within a realm." It provides for a universe where man, through this new realm, is ultimately said to spring from nature; it includes the semi-a priori moment of "natural law" with its doubtful naturalistic credentials, and causes an inner rupture within nature that gives rise to civilization as a semi-autonomous domain. Nature and reason, the natural and the civilized states, are linked but not quite continuous with each other. Hobbes seems to deviate from a strict naturalistic monism in favor of the vestiges of Christian (or Platonic) dualism, to which, at the price of logical coherence, he makes what seems to Spinoza unacceptable concessions.

Spinoza, at least in his official doctrine, makes no such concessions. He construes the passage from the natural to the political domain as continuous, and recognizes no "inner leap" in nature or a "realm within a realm" founded by civilization. Strictly speaking, the state of nature is not overcome by the political contract but continued in a different mode. This is why, in the last analysis and after allowing for necessary nuances, the idea that "might is right" has strong literal application in Spinoza. For this reason, however, *actual* consent is needed no less than the original (and abstract) contract in order to sustain a stable political life. Since nothing, including the original contract, can guarantee the keeping of contracts, state power is needed to enforce them; but as state power cannot compel the mind, it becomes indispensable to acquire the consent of the governed to the authority of their government. Again we see how Spinoza's strict naturalism—viewing the state, including a liberal democracy, as a natural play of forces—also stands at the root of his democratic tendencies. Spinoza is a harbinger of modern liberal democracy (as against Hobbes' tyrannical state) because of his stricter adherence to naturalism and the principle of immanence.

Spinoza rejects Hobbes' grim and pessimistic portrayal of man's natural disposition to other humans. To Hobbes' *homo homini lupus est*, Spinoza retorts provocatively with *homo homini deus est*. There is in man a natural potential to mutual help and mutual benefit, based upon *conatus* and natural interests. Hobbes' pessimistic picture translates the Christian myth of original sin into secular terms, but is still a prisoner of this myth. By nature, man's disposition to others depends on circumstances and the psychological laws of association and resemblance. On certain occasions they will produce rivalry and envy, on others empathy and compassion. Man is thus morally indifferent by nature—a position that no longer conceals religious motifs and which Nietzsche will welcome contra Hobbes, as he will also hail Spinoza's rejection of pity as a keystone of morality.

Nietzsche's Dionysian metaphysics of power has frequently been misrepresented as a political doctrine, leading to Bismarckian politics and also to fascism and nazism. Dispelling these gross distortions and misconceptions (which cannot be done here) does not, however, provide us with a positive political doctrine that can be attributed to Nietzsche. But there are many negatives: Nietzsche opposed nationalism, the modern nation-state, patriotism, racism, anti-Semitism, liberalism, socialism—indeed, those ideas that were most of the new trends of his time based upon the phenomenon of the mass society. In denouncing these "modern ideas," Nietzsche may seem to betray a taste for something like conservatism, yet he does so under a misleading mask; for there is very little in the past he wishes to preserve. He was a cultural radical looking forward to a future where politics would lose its importance in human affairs altogether. The only "great politics" he sometimes hints at concerns the unification of Europe and the mixing of its races; but this, too, has a cultural goal for Niezsche, not a political one.

In mood, taste, and sensibilities, Nietzsche may indeed be placed on the "right-wing" spectrum of politics.[44] Yet beyond these vague generalizations, a positive political doctrine can hardly be derived from Nietzsche's thought. His failure to provide such a theory is perhaps in the first place due to his being a profoundly antipolitical philosopher—a cultural aristocrat, aloof from the base concerns of the mass society which he snubs but cannot cope with. All political ideologies repel him because of their strong reliance on the masses. And there is little he denounces in stronger terms than the modern cult of politics and the state—that "new idol" of which Zarathustra strongly warns his followers[45] and which Nietzsche repeatedly declares to be the enemy of culture.[46]

This aristocratic disdain of politics reflects a dangerous confusion. Inevitably, modern politics is mass politics. To combine the dreams of a rare Dionysian hero with the realities of mass society (as Nietzsche in off moments is tempted to do) is as unrealistic as it is a call for abuse. Nietzsche's *Übermensch* cannot be universalized—that is, vulgarized—without incurring logical contradiction and social and political disaster. Fascism, though abhorrent to Nietzsche, is one of the tragic caricatures of such an impossible combination of the aristocratic and the vulgar. As the shopkeeper, the bus driver, and the petty intellectual worker are endowed with "Dionysian" qualities and placed beyond good and evil, the result must assume onerous dimensions. Nietzsche himself, of course, would have recognized in nazism everything he loathed—extreme nationalism and xenophobia, mass culture and the cult of the state, *ressentiment* and the identifying marks of a "slave morality" which can assert the self only by negating others. Yet Nietzsche's general paralysis when it comes to dealing with political theory, and his failure to provide an alternative way of emancipation for the ordinary man (the basis of political theory in Spinoza), place the tension and the danger of abuse well within the confines of his philosophy.[47]

Spinoza as a Genealogical Scandal

Perhaps because of their striking "dualitude," the person of Spinoza always haunted Nietzsche. "Hermit, have I recognized [i.e., unmasked] you?" Nietzsche asks in a poem, *To Spinoza*.★ Has he indeed?

Some of Nietzsche's comments on Spinoza would apply equally to himself. A "sick hermit" Nietzsche calls Spinoza, a "shy" and "vulner-

---

★ *Lovingly facing the "one is everything"*
amor dei, *happy from comprehension—*
Take off your shoes! That three times holy land—
—Yet secretly beneath this love, devouring,
A fire of revenge was shimmering,
The Jewish God devoured by Jewish hatred . . .
Hermit ! Have I recognized you?
—(Nietzsche, *Werke*
[Leipzig: Kröner, 1919], 8: 369, my translation)

able" man who has put on a "masquerade" (his geometrical method) in order to shield his most personal philosophy from a prying, vulgar world. Shifting metaphors, Nietzsche also calls Spinoza's mask a "chastity belt" and his personal philosophy "a virgin." The erotic allusion again applies to both these bachelor-philosophers (a kinship Nietzsche highlights elsewhere) and sheds more light on the term *hermit*.[48]

Yet these similitudes cease when Nietzsche comes to the core issue—the love of permanence and eternity. Here the enemy-brothers pattern takes its full force. Spinoza is denounced as the symbol of weakness and decadence, a man oppressed by his own existence, fearful of the Dionysian truth, and unable to cope with the trying implications of his own discovery: that immanent existence is all there is.

Sketching a "psychology of metaphysics" that should apply to all rationalists since Plato, Nietzsche singles out Spinoza as the prime example of those who "have feared change, transitoriness," a stand which he says betrays "a straightened soul full of mistrust and evil experiences." Even the *conatus*, Spinoza's most naturalistic principle, is exposed as "the symptom of a condition of distress," because in stressing self-preservation it puts an unhealthy limitation on will to power, the actual principle of life.[49] No wonder, Nietzsche surmises, that the survival principle has been advanced by sick philosophers "such as the tuberculosis-stricken Spinoza," since these people "indeed suffered distress."

This is not all. Nietzsche goes on to attribute rancor and subtle vengefulness to Spinoza, even as the psychological essence of his work:

> These outcasts of society, these long-pursued, wickedly persecuted ones—also the compulsory recluses, the Spinozas and Giordano Brunos—always become in the end, even under the most spiritual masquerade, and perhaps without being themselves aware of it, sophisticated vengeance-seekers and poison brewers (let someone lay bare the foundations of Spinoza's ethics and theology!).[50]

The context is Nietzsche's attack on the philosopher-martyrs who are supposed to have suffered "for truth's sake"; but with minor differences, it is also a form of *ressentiment* which Nietzsche sees at the root of Spinoza's ethics and metaphysics.* In exposing the "poison" of *res-*

---

* *Ressentiment* is the dominant attitude of the weak and decadent persons who cannot be assured of themselves unless they negate others; it is the genealogical source of the morality of good and evil, whereby the psychological "slaves" take subtle vengeance on their betters by subjecting them to their own inverted values.

sentiment in Spinoza's philosophy, Nietzsche not only burdens Spinoza with the ills of rationalism but, paradoxically, also with the ills of his forefathers, the Jewish priests through whom Christianity had taken over the world.

Here we start to note the incongruence in the portrait Nietzsche is bound to draw of Spinoza. In Nietzsche's genealogy, the philosophy of Spinoza must be seen as expressing and reinforcing the kind of person with the following characteristics. He is the lover of permanence, hence a decadent and weak person who, oppressed by the burden of immanence and by his own existence, escapes the painful perspective of Dionysian truth toward illusory metaphysical comfort. In addition, he is also petty, full of rancor and mistrust, the man of *ressentiment* who can assert himself only by negating others and who transforms (or sublimates) his vengefulness into the creation of inverted values and theories. Such a person is also bound to glorify suffering and pity, to inspire (and submit to) guilt feelings and *morsus conscientiae*. In short, he is bound to be exactly the kind of petty "slave" moralist whom Nietzsche abhorred and was exhilarated to discover that Spinoza was *not*.

Thus Spinoza upsets Nietzsche's genealogical scheme. Although a lover of permanence and eternity, he is, like Nietzsche himself, a philosopher of power and joy, rejecting the moralism of good and evil, guilt and pity, and trying to expurge the mind of the negative and self-poisonous emotions of envy, hate, rancor and *ressentiment*, which he sees as a form of suffering that depresses the vigor of life.

Something has gone wrong in Nietzsche's genealogy. Spinoza, his enemy-brother, presents him with a singular counterexample. He is both a Nietzschean and yet a lover of reason and permanence. Spinoza is thereby a genealogical scandal for Nietzsche—impossible, unthinkable, yet embarassingly real.

Spinoza had already played this unsettling role in the past. The image of the virtuous atheist he projected was an intolerable scandal to his contemporaries and to later generations. Atheism was supposed to lead inevitably to moral anarchy and destructive violence; but Spinoza's philosophy of ethical restraint and mutual help, together with the legend of his saintly life, seemed to attest to the contrary. Nietzsche, of course, is the first to claim that atheism and barbarism are not the same; but he is embarrassed by the semi-Dionysian virtues Spinoza advocates and manifests despite his decadent rationalism. This again highlights the enemy-brother relationship between the two men, for it is by being partly Nietzschean that Spinoza upsets Nietzsche's oversimplified unmasking of rationalism.

Can there be, then, a more rationalist Nietzschean? Was Goethe coming close to being one? Or Heine? I think that Freud—our next topic—will give us a better case for looking into this question. Freud continued the Nietzschean strand in the philosophy of immanence but mitigates it with the spirit of science. The fragile yet dependable achievements of science help us lead a disillusioned life in a Godless world and accept *ananke* (necessity) with fortitude and sobriety; they also (through self-knowledge) make possible a form of human emancipation which, however, falls short of the drama of *amor fati* or the rare exception of *amor dei*. Thus Freud tones down the high-flown language and expectations of both Nietzsche and Spinoza, but he still is the modern thinker that comes closest to *both*.

Spinoza and Freud:
Self-Knowledge as Emancipation

Freud is the greatest Jewish heretic of our century. Spinoza, three centuries earlier, was his foremost "brother in nonfaith" (a term coined by Heine and used by Freud). Both of them, and Nietzsche, who is in many ways like them, belong to a group of thinkers I have called the "philosophers of the dark enlightenment":[1] people who brought to light something profound and revolutionary—and often perceived as dark and frightening—about what we are and the world we belong to.

From Machiavelli and Hobbes, to Darwin and Marx, and up to Nietzsche, Freud, and Heidegger—and passing through Spinoza, as its unique and most disturbing paradigm—this process of dark enlightenment provoked a sharp awakening from religious and metaphysical illusions, incurring pain and conflict in its wake. For it challenged accepted self-images and enshrined cultural identities, and thereby endangered a whole range of vested psychological interests. But for these very reasons, it was also a movement of emancipation, serving to inspire a richer and more lucid self-knowledge in man, even at the price of unflattering consequences which often shock and dismay. This is the true "Oedipal drive"—not of Freud's Oedipus but of the original protagonist of Sophocles' tragedy, of whom Freud himself is an avid follower. The Freudian Oedipus theory (regardless of how accurate it may be) is a modern way of fulfilling the wish of the mythological king who did not rest until he discovered the hidden truth about himself and his real situation in the world, even at the price of tragedy and the loss of his two eyes. Freud, like the other "dark enlighteners," brought to light the hidden layers in human existence buried in unconscious depths and whose budding consciousness has long been repressed.

The fierce resistance with which Freud's discoveries were met can only be matched by the outraged revulsion that Spinoza's views provoked for a very long time. Freud, a servant of *ananke* ("necessity," his milder form of *amor fati*), might have consoled himself with the thought that such opposition was inevitable. Was not his own theory the first to predict and explain this reaction by the concepts of "repression" and "resistance"? But one need not be a devout Freudian to realize how difficult, indeed impossible, it is to shatter a consoling world-picture and self-image that provide a measure of metaphysical and moral comfort, without incurring pain and torment which easily turn into aggression, hostility, and outcries of shock and scandal. The image we make of ourselves is not only a cherished possession with which we are reluctant to part; it is also an integral part of our ego, a cornerstone of our identity. The crisis and suffering involved in the loss of identity are no less grave than those involved in the loss of property, and have been known to produce as much passionate aggression as human beings are capable of.

The fact that both Spinoza and Freud were Jews cannot be written off in considering their unsettling cultural roles. Freud recognized this about himself:

> Nor is it perhaps entirely a matter of chance that the first advocate of psycho-analysis was a Jew. To profess belief in this new theory called for a certain degree of readiness to accept a situation of solitary opposition—a situation with which no one is more familiar than a Jew. [2]

Replacing the word *psychoanalysis* with, say, *immanence* or *the identity of God and nature* will make this statement apply equally to Spinoza.

Spinoza, in his solitude and perhaps before his time, anticipates yet another phenomenon which later became current and which Freud strongly exemplifies. This is the phenomenon of the modern Jew who, having lost his religious faith and most of the ties that bind him to his tradition, absorbs much of the Gentile culture around him (usually in its more universal, less denominational aspects), in which he perfects himself and often excels, but which, in the process, he frequently also challenges or tries to revolutionize. (We met a similar pattern in Heine, Hess, and Marx.) Like Spinoza, Freud was the stranger within the gates, neither quite integrated in his adopted society nor fully severed from his origins, a man both within and without, or better, whose way of being within was by his being an outsider, without. This made him detached but not aloof, sober but not cynical; he maintained an interest in changing reality, which he coupled with remarkable clearsightedness, unmarred by devotion to ruling ideologies or by a slavish respect for social and religious taboos. Such a person, by his situation, may be better placed to uncover the hidden layers of life and the mind which other persons, better integrated in the ruling culture, will be prone to miss even if their intellectual gifts equal or surpass his.

FREUD AND PHILOSOPHY

Freud was ambivalent toward philosophy. In his youth he had studied some philosophy with Franz Brentano (and other members of his school) but never completed his studies, a fact which may have made him oversensitive on the subject of philosophy. Freud read philosophical books with interest, but also with suspicion. What put him off was the "speculative" nature of philosophy, which he saw as opposed to the "scientific" or "empirical" character he attributed to his own investigations. This, according to Freud, was the reason he never made a thorough study of Nietzsche—not because Nietzsche was alien to him, but precisely the contrary. Freud says he felt so drawn to Nietzsche and akin to his world that he stopped reading him for fear of being biased by a speculative thinker on matters that demand a purely empirical approach.

Not all Freud scholars would accept this statement at face value. Freud may have been better acquainted with Nietzsche than he was willing to admit. It is noteworthy that Freud had a similar problem with Schopenhauer—and he tried to solve it, or at least summed it up, with the following comment:

> You may perhaps shrug your shoulders and say: "That isn't natural science, it's Schopenhauer's philosophy!" But, Ladies and Gentlemen, *why should not a bold thinker have guessed something that is afterwards confirmed by sober and painstaking research?*[3]

This remark, which through his imaginary audience Freud seems to be addressing to himself, applies also to his attitude toward Nietzsche—and to Spinoza.[4]

Freud's References to Spinoza

Freud hardly ever mentions Spinoza by name; but when he does, it is always to acknowledge their close affinity. Here again is a philosopher whose proximity to himself Freud must treat with caution. In the Freudian corpus there appear to be only three direct references to Spinoza, written at different times yet showing remarkable consistency. They all reiterate the same idea: Freud and Spinoza share a similar "mode of thinking" and a common "atmosphere" in their backgrounds.

In his essay "Leonardo da Vinci and a Memory of His Childhood" (1910), Freud says:

> Because of his insatiable and indefatigable thirst for knowledge, Leonardo has been called the Italian Faust. But . . . the view may be hazarded that Leonardo's development approaches Spinoza's *mode of thinking. (Standard Edition* 9: 75; emphasis added)

Years later, Dr. Lothar Bickel, a Spinozist with psychoanalytic leanings, demanded of the old Freud a statement of his debt to Spinoza and an explanation why Spinoza's name is hardly mentioned. Freud replies frankly and without hesitation:

> *I readily admit my dependence on Spinoza's doctrine.* There was no reason why I should expressly mention his name, since I conceived my hypotheses from the *atmosphere* created by him, rather than from the study of his work. Moreover, I did not seek a philosophical legitimization.[5]

Freud's reply attests to his "dependence" on Spinoza's doctrine, not in its letter but in the intellectual climate and "atmosphere" it created. The affinity between them is so great that Freud feels Spinoza could have provided him with philosophical legitimation, had Freud felt the need for one; but, as in reading Nietzsche, Freud shuns the unsolicited legitimation and the speculative influence to which he might have submitted from a philosopher much too dangerously akin to himself.

Shortly after this episode, Freud was asked to contribute a paper to a volume commemorating Spinoza's three hundredth anniversary. Freud declined, saying he had nothing special to offer, but nonetheless took the opportunity to restate his feeling for Spinoza in extremely strong language:

> Throughout my long life I [timidly] sustained an extraordinarily high respect for the person as well as for the results of the thought [*Denkleistung*] of the great philosopher Spinoza.[6]

Freud uses far stronger words than mere decorum would require. His sincerity is evident. Nor is it insignificant that Freud's "extraordinarily high respect" attaches to Spinoza's person no less than to his philosophical accomplishment. In the figure of Spinoza Freud could see a reflection of himself—a solitary young revolutionary, adhering to a truth excavated from under the surface of the ruling culture, and facing hostility and scorn as a result. Spinoza is a kind of distant brother to Freud, his brother in the honesty of his thought and the difficulties of his path, in his solitude and his genius. Indeed, Freud indirectly (through Heine) refers to Spinoza as his "brother in nonfaith,"[7] a Jew who has lost his faith yet continues to bear the traits of the Jew both in his own eyes and, even more so, in the eyes of the outside world.

Freud, Leonardo, and Spinoza

An examination of what Freud says about Leonardo will help us to better understand the comparison between himself and Spinoza and show how some of Spinoza-like traits that Freud finds in Leonardo are also, to a certain extent, true of him.

The key to Leonardo's character, says Freud, lies in his view that "one has no right to love or to hate anything if one has not acquired a thorough knowledge of its nature."[8] Leonardo—like Freud himself and like Spinoza—restrains his desires, his eros, until he learns and understands; and he makes knowledge itself into his passion (cf. Spinoza's *conatus intelligendi*). Thus—again like Spinoza and like Freud—Leonardo "did not love and hate, but asked himself about the origin and significance of what he was to love or hate."

Like Spinoza, who investigated the most violent passions of the human soul as if he were dealing with geometric forms, and like Freud, who studied the most distressing and "disgusting" of human instincts with the scientist's analytic cool, so Leonardo pursued his investigations from a position outside good and evil and free of love and hate.

But Leonardo does not deny eros or repress it: he simply suspends it. Eros is converted into the passion for knowledge and thus is able in the end to manifest itself in all its power. Here we may be reminded of Spinoza's highest degree of knowledge in which eros, in the sublimated form of the "intellectual love of God," finally erupts as the most powerful affect of the human soul. "For in truth," says Leonardo, "great love springs from great knowledge of the beloved object, and if you know it but little you will be able to love it only a little or not at all. . . ." This was Spinoza's view almost exactly, at least as regards the highest (third) degree of knowledge. The love of God—that is, of the natural universe in its absolute and rational necessity—does not burst forth as fuzzy enthusiasm or an otherwise opaque and immediate emotion; it is rather mediated by the intellect and its scientific knowledge which, at its highest, produces a powerful affect that transforms and liberates the knower's life and personality. This is a form of semireligious exaltation which Freud, following Edmund Solmi, identifies in Leonardo's writings as well. "*O mirabile necessita!*" Leonardo cries out in a vein not far from Spinoza's when, at the end of a painstaking and detailed study, he discovers how all things combine and coalesce within the grand tissue of the universe. Science gives him an inkling, powerful and vivid, of "the grandeur of the universe with all its complexities" and the necessity of its laws, which makes him "readily forget his own insignificant self";[9] and Solmi, with Freud's approval, comments that here is a "transfiguration of natural science into a sort of religious emotion"—a pattern that is also essential in Spinoza.

The link Freud establishes between Leonardo and Spinoza betrays his own thinking. He partly recognizes himself in their comparison. Freud also suspended eros and sublimated its power into a relentless drive to know. This helped him penetrate his own repressions into the dimmest and most troubled recesses of the mind; it also gave him strength to persevere in the face of hostile resistance from others. Having "converted his passion into a thirst for knowledge, he then applied himself to investigation with the persistence, constancy and penetration which is derived from passion."[10] These words, by which Freud describes Leonardo (and through him, Spinoza), serve as his own self-portrait. Freud too had undergone a similar sublimation; like Leonardo and Spinoza, he suspends love and hate, value judgments, good and evil, and steps beyond them in contemplation of the world's necessity.

As Freud will agree with Nietzsche, no pure, idealistic "will to knowledge" is involved here. It is eros set against its own doings, sublimated in ways that allow it to crack the defenses it had previously erected. Thus Freud joins not only Spinoza and Leonardo but also Nietzsche in the wish to make of knowledge the most powerful affect (see Nietzsche's postcard quoted in chap. 5).

Freud, however, traces his own path within this larger intellectual family. He objects to Nietzsche's discrediting of science, but also to the semimystical expectations that Spinoza and Leonardo had of science.[11] Until Leonardo attains his goal of knowledge, eros is powerfully kept in check and reshaped by the intellectual process; then, at the end, it bursts forth as a kind of religious exaltation, taking up a universal cosmic dimension. This is not unlike the link that exists in Spinoza between the advance of knowledge and its affective climax in *amor dei intellectualis*. Freud too sees knowledge as an ethical force and liberator—but within much narrower confines and with no such broad metaphysical implications. Freud deals in therapy, not salvation; and even when considering the world at large he remains prosaic and rationalistic throughout.

THE CLIMATE OF IDEAS

To a certain extent both Spinoza and Freud exemplify the situation of the Jew who, abandoning his orthodox tradition without being integrated in the Christian world, develops a penetrating eye for both worlds and the ability to free himself from their conventions. As a result, Freud and Spinoza became uncompromising critics of historical religion, adhering to a radical philosophy of immanence while denying any transcendent horizon to existence. There are only natural phenomena, though the meaning of nature is expanded by both thinkers to include the psychic domain. Moreover, the knowledge of nature acquires spiritual dimensions. In Spinoza, it even engenders mental states which, at their height, rival those of religion, whereas in Freud, the uncompromising atheist, it gives rise to a more limited form of human emancipation.

With all their naturalistic determinism, both Freud and Spinoza are motivated, perhaps paradoxically, by the pathos of human liberation—liberation not only from illusions and inhibitions, but from what Freud called "neuroses" and Spinoza "bondage" to the passions. This liberation is hard-won and painful, forcing as it does a new understanding and self-image on man, free of illusions and metaphysical self-flattery.

Freud shares Spinoza's refutation of the image of man as endowed with a God-given soul, selfless motives, or a transcendental mind separate from nature and capable of modifying and manipulating nature from without. Human beings are fully integrated in nature and are moved by a dominant natural striving or source of energy (*conatus* in Spinoza, *libido* in Freud), which streams forth in a variety of outlets, and of which knowledge and the products of high culture are but sublimated configurations. This has an irritating ring in the ears of traditional believers, whether religious or metaphysical, who are used to thinking of man as halfway between animal and angel. Moreover, in view of the natural determinism which they hold to reign entirely over human life, Freud and Spinoza probe the fiercest passions and most complex aberrations of the human soul with the cold eye of necessity. They abstain from all moralizing; they suspend their own fears and anxieties, their passions and hopes, and the temptation to allocate guilt and to assume power through pontificating. Instead, they penetrate into the objects of their investigation with cool intellectual *askesis*—which Nietzsche criticized in Spinoza[12] but which Freud accepts as a vital ingredient in the "atmosphere" he has in common with Spinoza. He, too, treats the darkest passions of the soul as if they were lines, surfaces, and bodies, except that his scientific idiom is no longer geometrical.[13]

The climate of ideas that Freud shares with Spinoza is naturalistic and deterministic, yet the meaning of "nature" is expanded in both to include the psychic (even the logical) domain. Nature acquires an additional depth dimension; in Freud it includes the psychological depths of the unconscious, and in Spinoza it takes the form of the attribute of "thought," in which nature is internally reflected and which is considered an integral part of nature. There are indeed only natural phenomena, but nature is neither matter alone, nor is it exhausted by its apparent surface. The kind of naturalism which Freud shares with Spinoza can therefore be said to be neither materialistic nor positivist.

While Spinoza views nature as a single substance to which he transfers the divinity and the uniqueness of God, Freud avoids such pantheistic overtones. His concept (and experience) of nature remains prosaic and critical (even in the Kantian sense) throughout. There is no single totality in Freud called "nature." There are natural phenomena, but nature as such is not reified into a single substance, let alone a divine one.

The depth dimension in nature has further implications. Both Freud and Spinoza postulate hidden forces which motivate and determine the human mind without it being aware of them. This ignorance produces a wealth of mystifying fictions that mask human existence to itself. Determinism, as mental therapy, is primarily concerned with this type of hidden causation, stating its existence while making it a purely natural and explicable phenomenon. In Freud, the covert forces take an additional dimension, as a new kind of "demons" that control human fate; yet there is nothing magical about them, for they are exposed as purely natural, are located in the inner depths of the mind itself, and are capable of being "exorcised" through knowledge and interpretation. This, indeed, is the germ of liberation in both Spinoza and Freud: admitting the existence of the covert agents while demystifying them through knowledge and transforming their effects through self-knowledge.

The Critique of Religion

Spinoza sees all forms of historical religion as superstition (*superstitio*) and vain religion (*vana religio*); he wishes to see it gradually abolished and replaced with a religion of reason, of which he conceives two forms, popular and philosophical. Freud sees all forms of religion as illusion, the product of human anxiety and our sense of impotence in the world, which create the need for shelter and protection. It is the intense wish to satisfy this need that engenders the universe of religious beliefs and images as a system whose aim is imaginary wish-fulfillment.

Here Freud joins Spinoza in adopting the classic position of the Enlightenment, or even of the rationalist critics of religion who, since Epicurus, tried to reduce various religious manifestations to a few natural phenomena, especially to fear in its various forms and to ignorance of true causes, thereby depriving religion of its claim to metaphysical status and insisting on its repressive social role.

This was not a purely disinterested analysis: it had a polemical and emancipatory aim. The rationalists believed—and the old Freud, the author of *Future of an Illusion*, hesitantly endorsed their assumption (was this *his* illusion?)—that a person who grasps the natural causes of the religious mystification of which he or she has been a victim will thereby be set on the road to liberation. Once the psychosocial factors at work behind her imagining have been made clear to the subject, she will realize that her religious faith is actually a form of bondage: to her instincts, to her fears, to her ignorance, and to the social and religious establishment of the clergy which draws its power from her fears and ignorance and perpetuates their repressive effects by means of sanctified institutions and rituals.

But what should replace historical religion? Here a major difference separates Freud from Spinoza. Spinoza proposes a kind of universal religion in which the powers of passion and the imagination will be reshaped into an external imitation of reason. This religion is destined for the masses; it demands not dogmatic belief, only socially beneficial action, and its precepts are subject to the interpretation of the political authorities. To the minority of true philosophers Spinoza proposes a higher ideal, the intellectual love of God, which is supposed to attain by the power of reason the same absolute goals that mysticism and historical religion have claimed and vainly tried to achieve by irrational practices.

All the power, the plenitude (Freud would say: all the *libido*) of traditional religion has been poured here into a philosophical-ethical system entirely oriented toward this world. The soul's unity with God which mystics used to seek above and beyond the world is to be realized in this earthly world, following a natural process by which we come to know the universe by its rational laws and to know ourselves via the third kind of knowledge as part of the nature-God. This knowledge has an intuitive power of illumination; and it engenders a most powerful love (another mystical parallel). Yet the love of the philosopher toward the universe-God is not the same as the mystic's love, for it is impersonal and intellectual. God is not a person and has no singular consciousness; therefore he can be loved and be united with only by means of intellectual understanding. The latter, however (as Nietzsche realized), becomes the most powerful affect, transforming one's whole life and personality and serving as a springboard to the secular kind of salvation Spinoza sought.

Nothing of this is found in Freud. Freud offers no substitute for absolute religion and, like Nietzsche, he would certainly have rejected Spinoza's idea of secular salvation as yet another illusion. Atheism, says Freud (without concealing his subscription to it), must resign itself to man's impotence in the universe without seeking illusory compensations; all that is open to it are fortitude, sobriety, and a modest measure of self-knowledge. (Sartre, too, in many ways Freud's disciple, came to see atheism not simply as lack of faith but as an active attitude toward life where redemption is no longer a concept on the horizon; and the later Sartre criticizes himself for having sought a sense of semiredemption in his esoteric knowledge that redemption was impossible; he did not realize how difficult true atheism was.[14]) Freud lacks Spinoza's vast metaphysical horizons; he neither deifies the universe nor sets absolute goals for the individual. Nor does he experience the existential drama of the lack of salvation as intensely as Nietzsche, Camus, or the early Sartre. He is truly an atheist, with no pantheistic or other compensations, and with no sense for the mystical. All he can offer as existential virtue is fortitude, sobriety, and a modest measure of understanding and self-knowledge. The rest is *ananke* (necessity), which must also become the object of sober recognition. This is not fatalistic resignation but an active choice and attitude toward life; it is a quiet, undramatic form of *amor fati*. Unlike Nietzsche, however, it admits of objective scientific knowledge and self-knowledge as the lever for emancipation. Thus the three of them form an intellectual family in which the enemy-brother relationship we analyzed in chapter 5 obtains between *any* pair of the three. The main gap that separates Freud from Spinoza is Freud's lack of absolute goals and a pantheistic dimension. This explains many particular tensions between these two intellectual brothers, radical challengers of tradition and Jews without faith.

LIBIDO VERSES *CONATUS*: THE HUMAN BEING AS DESIRE

The naturalist view which Freud and Spinoza share is also expressed in their theories of human behavior and motivation—at least in fundamental outline. Human beings, for both of them, are dynamic natural entities constituted by some principle of desire. Spinoza calls this desire *conatus*; Freud expounds it in his theory of *libido*.

Conatus is the striving for self-preservation, which also entails the effort to enhance the power and vitality of existence. As such it is the sole and unique source of human emotions and behavior; from the basest forms of lust and aggression to the supreme intellectual love of God, all are configurations of this one natural *conatus*. In Freud, *libido*, though not the unique principle, serves as a fundamental psychic energy which all affective phenomena presuppose and which determines our conscious and unconscious processes. Both concepts (like Nietzsche's will to power) underscore the purely naturalistic character of human beings, and their dynamic mode of being as finite and striving (or desiring) entities. Whatever "higher" faculties we possess—reason, culture, concepts of justice, moral preferences, and the like—are not the product of some supranatural principle in us but special configurations of the primal natural desire that characterizes our existence from the outset.

Despite this fundamental kinship, there are important differences between *libido* and *conatus*.[15] *Libido* is conceived as the energy behind the sexual instincts, which gives it a rather restricted significance from Spinoza's standpoint (and in a way, as we shall presently see, even from Freud's). In addition, *libido* is immediately connected with pleasure, not with self-preservation; and the two, says Freud, are not the same.[16] Self-preservation in Freud is the goal of the so-called "ego-instincts," which Freud (at least the classic, or early Freud) opposes to the sexual instincts whose energy *libido* is.[17] Furthermore, *conatus* implies the endeavor to enhance power, whereas *libido* is conceived in a more static fashion, as the flow of a given quantity of energy whose outlets and distribution are determined in a semimechanistic and "economic" idiom.

The major difference, however, lies in the dualistic picture Freud opposes to Spinoza's strict monism. In his early theory of the instincts Freud had used two opposing principles, the ego-instincts and the sexual instincts, with *libido* underlying only the latter.[18] Then, for a short while, he maintained that the ego itself was the main reservoir of *libido*, both as the source and the destination of all its vicissitudes; therefore the term *libido* could either be dispensed with or serve to denote any psychic energy. Yet, as the older Freud revised his theory of the instincts, this fairly monistic view gave way to an even more radical dualism—that of *eros* and *thanatos*.

Eros, or love, now stood for both the sexual and the self-preservative instincts, united in a single concept; but even as such, *eros* was not the unique and overall principle. Opposing it was *thanatos*, the death-instinct, a consummate, self-referential aggression inherent in every organism and conflicting with its instinct for self-preservation. *Eros* seeks life, unity, and growing organization; *thanatos* seeks disorganization, inertia, and death. To avoid total self-destruction by the death-instinct we must turn part of our aggression outward, trying to destroy other persons or external objects; but since reality impedes our efforts, we are in many cases bound to re-interiorize the aggression with even greater damage to ourselves.[19]

A twentieth-century pre-Socratic, a modern Empedocles opposing universal love and hatred,[20] Freud in his revised theory of *libido* is at odds with Spinoza on two major counts. He opposes a radical dualism to Spinoza's monism of the *conatus*,[21] and he makes the death-instinct—the very opposite of *conatus*—a primal drive of the organism. That an entity should seek its own destruction—and not merely because of a special conjunction of causes, but as a built-in, fundamental drive—is unthinkable for Spinoza, who based his system on the opposite principle, namely, that "no thing contains in itself anything whereby it can be destroyed" and that "nothing can be destroyed except by causes *external* to itself."[22]

These major statements are made as part of the explication of the *conatus*; they make it understandably hard, if not outright impossible, for Spinoza to account for acts of suicide, and eventually they lead to his famous dictum that the free or rational man "thinks of death least of all things, and his wisdom is a meditation not of death, but of life."[23]

Spinoza, the cognitive rationalist, was bound to reduce all irrational actions and drives to faulty understanding and inadequate ideas. Freud, in his grimmer and more volcanic view of humanity, had perhaps a better appreciation of the dark recesses of desire (which, following Schopenhauer, he even excluded from the domain of time, space, and logic).[24] At any rate, on the issue of primal motivation, or *libido* and *conatus*, the distance between them is vast.

Yet Freud and Spinoza remain closely akin on the fundamental issue: understanding human beings as finite natural beings constituted by a principle of desire, whose vicissitudes and transformations underlie all forms of behavior, motivation, and higher culture. From this point of view we may agree with Hampshire's claim that the parallel of *libido* and *conatus* "is more than superficial."[25] Indeed, the resemblance exists *only* on the fundamental level, whereas a detailed examination must yield, as we have briefly sketched, important and even crucial disagreements.[26]

Self-Knowledge

Spinoza and the Third Kind of Knowledge

The affinity and the tension between Freud and Spinoza will become clearer if we concentrate on a central preoccupation common to both: self-knowledge. For Freud as for Spinoza this is the main road to emancipation; it is the cornerstone of Spinoza's ethics and of Freud's therapy. But the difference between the terms *ethics* and *therapy* already indicates the gap that separates them.

Self-knowledge for Spinoza must pass through knowledge of the world. I do not understand myself in direct awareness, or by simply concentrating on my own personal history, assisted (as in Freud) by a limited inventory of general hermeneutical codes. The road to self-knowledge is much longer and indirect. I do not start with myself but with the universe at large, which from the outset I have to grasp as a single totality identical with God. Then, equipped with the general knowledge of the laws and causal patterns governing the universe, I have to locate my own particular place and mode of activity within the totality. This presupposes the second kind of knowledge in which I engage in diversified scientific study, both of physics and physiology and of psychology and sociology. I must understand what particular things are; how the body is related to the mind; how bodies work and how affects arise; what the genesis of social contexts is; and how my own body, affects, and social links are determined by the causal environment. Thus I proceed to decipher my own being from without, that is, from the general patterns and laws governing the universe. However, in the third kind of knowledge, all this externally derived information fits together and coalesces into the specific "essence," or internal explication of the singular entity I am. At this (rather rare) point, having acquired a step-by-step scientific knowledge of myself from different causal points of view, I now perform an intuitive leap which, Spinoza believes, allows me to take a synoptic view of my singular existence as it inheres in God and follows internally from his eternal essence. The mediating causal links have been internalized and synthesized into a singular essence they are said to constitute and are equivalent to. There is no additional information here, only a new understanding and organization of the same cognitive ingredients.[27]

This is also the highest degree of self-knowledge, with its accompanying intellectual love of God which liberates and redeems. At first, my direct awareness of myself has been merely confused knowledge, *imaginatio*. To progress, I had to replace it with knowledge of the second kind, the scientific knowledge by which I approach my being from without. But knowledge of this kind lacks the affective power required to transform and liberate me. In order for it to produce such effects, scientific knowledge must fulfill two conditions. First, it must from the start be conceived and felt as explicating a basic metaphysical truth, namely, the identity of nature with God and of the individual's essence with the nature-God. Ultimately grounded in intellectual intuition, this truth underlies the scientific process throughout. Second, discursive scientific progress must eventually give way to the synthetic intuition described above, which generates sufficient affective power to take over one's life and to transform one's passions. Scientific knowledge is flanked, so to speak, on both sides by intuitive strata, one underlying the process from the start and the other taking it to its climax.

At the same time—and this is Spinoza's novelty—the high ethical objective can only be reached by way of a detailed mechanistic science. Metaphysical generalizations in themselves are worthless even when true. The more particular things we know, the more we know God; therefore, in knowing ourselves according to the detailed particular causes which determine us, we spell out our inherence in God in concrete empirical terms; and this is indispensable to the next, intuitive stage, where causal knowledge is internalized and our singular essence emerges as inhering in God through a chain of immediately grasped relations.

To reach this semimystical stage, we must therefore embark on a diversified program of study, aimed at knowing ourselves more and more as creatures of nature, having acquired the general knowledge described above. I must know my specific place within the chain of being; the actual circumstances of my being in the world; the causes which explain my bodily situation, my personal biography, my structure, and the mental and social forces active in me; the hidden causes of my fear; my errors; the ignorance of which I am victim; my suffering, my ambitions, my covert motives, the powers that make me waver between fear and hope, joy and grief, and other unstable emotions that hold my life in bondage. All this requires a thorough scientific study not only of the body—through physics and other sciences of "extension" (physiology, chemistry, climatology, etc.)—but also of psychology.

It is no accident that Spinoza devotes an entire book out of the five books of his *Ethics* to psychology. The science of psychology must replace and illuminate the direct awareness we have of our minds as a means to self-knowledge (and on the higher level, psychology should take the place of theology as a means to salvation). This undercuts the role not only of ordinary introspection, but also of the more refined techniques of mystical concentration, direct self-contemplation, and the like. All these must give way to a mediated body of science, using general laws and patterns, a "geometric" science, says Spinoza, explaining human follies and the most irrational passions through the clear and distinct power of reasoning.[28] The way from ourselves to ourselves—from the confused direct consciousness we have of our bodies and minds to the new, rational (and eventually redeeming) self-knowledge we gain at the end—thus passes through psychology as a universal natural science, a science, moreover, whose objects are *sui generis* and cannot be reduced to those of physics or any other science.

This not only confirms the autonomous status of psychology, which Descartes had already granted, but makes this purely natural science a necessary and privileged road to redemption. The same can no longer be said of Descartes, nor of any other philosopher who remained faithful to the religious and theological monopoly of salvation; and in this Spinoza took a further step toward Freud.

Freud, Self-Knowledge, and Repression

Freud's ambitions were far more modest than Spinoza's. He was not concerned with salvation but with therapy. Freud lacked Spinoza's semireligious pathos and was better acquainted with the depths of human irrationality. But like Spinoza he was motivated by the quest for human emancipation and believed that whatever liberation may be in store for humans must grow out of their self-knowledge. Overcoming the repressed, the neurotic, the abysmal burdens and complexes that shackle the mind and distort its functioning depends in large measure on some form of self-knowledge. So does the process by which consciousness extends its dominion over the seething volcano of the "id" and enables the individual to achieve stability or restore his or her capacity for a life of enjoyment and creativity—and also by which civilization, however fragile, is allowed to function and to persist.

Freud explicitly states that his goal in therapy is to bring the repressed to consciousness. Illuminating the hidden psychic forces that generate a neurosis is the principal means of overcoming it. Using a series of clues, associations, dreams, and the interpretation of other signs and symptoms, a kind of archaeology of the mind is carried out, which penetrates to its past, to childhood traumas, and to early psychological history. The repressed gradually returns to consciousness and the old psychic conflict is renewed, the one which originally had ended in repression, but which now is maneuvered toward a saner conclusion. The aim of therapy, according to Freud, is to dissolve the state of repression so that the energy arrested in it (which frequently has been spent on neurosis) will be diverted into new channels and, through sublimation and other means, will enhance the person's capacity for enjoyment, creativity, and mental stability.

The centrality of self-knowledge in Freud's system is also indicated by the crucial role he assigns to its opposite concept, repression. Freud leaves no room for doubt on this matter. "The theory of repression," he says, "is the cornerstone on which the whole structure of psycho-analysis rests."[29] Elsewhere he reiterates: "It is possible to take repression as a center and to bring all the elements of psycho-analytic theory into relation to it."[30] Repression and its uncovering become the systematizing concept of his theory. Freud elaborates:

> The theory of repression became the corner-stone of our understanding of neuroses. A different view had now to be taken of the task of therapy. Its aim was no longer to 'abreact' an affect which had got onto the wrong lines, but to uncover repressions and replace them by acts of judgment which might result either in the accepting or the condemning of what had formerly been repudiated. I showed my recognition of the new situation by no longer calling my method of investigation and treatment *catharsis* but *psycho-analysis*.[31]

It was thus the discovery of repression as the basis of neurosis—and, consequently, the discovery of the recall to consciousness as the road to therapy—which founded psychoanalysis.

The same emerges from Freud's account of his abandoning hypnosis as a method of therapy.[32] This, he says, was the crucial step that separated him from Josef Breuer and led to the founding of the psychoanalytic movement. The difference between the two methods is succinctly put by Freud: "Hypnotic treatment seeks to cover up and gloss over something in mental life; analytic treatment seeks to expose and get rid of something. The former acts like cosmetics; the latter like surgery."[33]

The shortcoming of hypnosis lies in its unconscious nature and the attempt at direct manipulation of the unconscious. It works by suggestion, not by understanding and interpretation. The hypnotist tries to get rid of the neurosis by direct intervention, as it were, in the psychic depths, bypassing consciousness. But in so doing, he reaches only the symptoms and misses the roots of the disturbance. For—and this was Freud's discovery—the disturbance springs from repression, namely, the self-induced clouding of consciousness and its conversion into the unconscious, as a result of powerful, unresolvable conflicts whose energy now feeds the neurosis. Repression does not merely screen off a disturbance that exists independently of it, but is the root of the disturbance, its very cause. Therefore, it must be completely dissolved in order for the process of healing to begin.

By using suggestion, hypnosis manipulates the patient's unconscious without letting his or her ego play an active role in the therapeutic process. But once it is discovered that the root of the neurosis lies in repression, the patient's active and conscious participation becomes essential to therapy. The old struggle of the instincts (fundamentally sexual ones) which repression cast into the depths of oblivion must be re-enacted in the patient, a process in which his or her consciousness plays a role of understanding and self-interpretation mediated by transference as a special emotive and intellectual relationship with the therapist.

> In order to resolve the symptoms, we must go back as far as their origin, we must renew the conflict from which they arose, and, with the help of motive forces which were not at the patient's disposal in the past, we must guide it to a different outcome.[34]

In order to renew the conflict it is necessary to bring its causes back to consciousness, while overcoming the resistances which created the repression and eliminating the latter. This is performed with the help of self-interpretation, which replaces the method of suggestion with the method proper to psychoanalysis, based upon the extension of consciousness.

The concept of repression, says Freud, makes psychoanalysis unique and distinguishes his own concept of the unconscious from what he calls rather disparagingly the "philosophical opinions about the unconscious," which existed in his day or before him (since Leibniz's "petites perceptions," or even since Spinoza).[35] The unconscious with which Freud (especially the early Freud) is concerned is primarily that which has *become* unconscious, that is, that which through repression has sunk into amnesia. On the other hand, this is also the reason why psychoanalysis cannot cure all mental ills, but, as Freud stresses, only those built upon the mutual relationship between the conscious and the repressed, especially neuroses and compulsion.

Conquering the Id: Enlightenment and Its Fragility

The centrality of repression implies the importance of its complement, the recall to consciousness and self-understanding. So vital is this concept for psychoanalysis that we may see Freud—this explorer of the dark realms of the mind, the philosopher of the unconscious, who stresses the chaotic, volcanic, and disorderly in human existence—as actually representing a modern strand of the Enlightenment (a movement of which Spinoza was a chief forerunner over two centuries before). Freud's ideal is the heightening of consciousness and the extension of its domain. His motto is "know thyself"; he aspires for lucidity, for demystified self-knowledge. This was the ideal of the Enlightenment, but now it is recognized as infinitely more difficult to attain because of the hitherto unimagined depths of the unconscious and its power of resistance. Self-knowledge now becomes a momentous task which can only be achieved on a limited scale. In addition, Freud (at least in his early work) focused more on the unconscious which results from repression than on the full extent of unconscious life. Thus the centrality of repression not only highlights the goal of self-awareness but also restricts its scope. Later, when Freud developed his metapsychological theory (and clearly defined repression as only part of the vast unconscious field),[36] he not only maintained the ideal of self-knowledge but further expanded it. In the following passage he rephrases the aims of psychoanalysis in terms of his new metapsychology (the ego, the id, and the superego):

> Its intention is, indeed, to strengthen the ego, to make it more independent of the super-ego, to widen its field of perception and enlarge its organization, so that it can appropriate fresh portions of the id.[37]

The recall to consciousness is retained but its role as a method of liberation is expanded. We are no longer concerned with the products of repression alone, but with the conquest of the id in general—the irrational and opaque principle that is the foundation of life and its energy. It is in this dark volcanic mass that the ego must conquer ever-increasing areas if the person is to experience a more stable and liberated personality. However, in order to succeed in this conquest the ego must already be significantly strong and liberated—and especially free of that unconscious form of self-oppression exercised by the superego with its guilt-feelings, conscience, and internalized self-destruction. Here lies another form of oblivion, or amnesia, parallel but not identical to repression in the classic sense. What the ego ignores here are its true relations with the superego, and the actual nature of many of the norms which, internalized, engender distressing conflicts within the individual and thereby make him or her suffer acute repressions and neuroses.

Freud's metapsychology thus expands the scope and emancipatory role of self-knowledge both within the individual and in the critique of culture and ideology. Here Freud comes close to Spinoza, since self-knowledge of this kind requires us to rely more on science and less on hermeneutics, that is, it presupposes that we understand mental and cultural mechanisms and their hidden action, and no longer concentrate on the interpretation of particular signs and clues from the individual biography.

At the same time, Freud's analysis of the repressive potential of the superego brings him close to Nietzsche, who also offered a critique of moral values, guilt, conscience, and the like (and their cultural effects and price) by analyzing their psychological genesis and mechanisms. But, in contrast to Nietzsche, Freud maintains that self-knowledge can have a solid basis in science as objective truth. Freud also sees lucidity—a demystified consciousness in various modes—as an end in itself and as a leading cultural value; and although he was aware of its weakness, limits, and fragility, he stressed the need to cultivate it as much as possible. Nietzsche would have seen in Freud a deviant Nietzschean who falls back upon a form of scientific rationalism. His principles of truth is a "perspective" which betrays his wish to impose illusory order on the world of chaos, though he is much better acquainted than others with its chaotic depths. From this point of view Freud stands midway between Nietzsche and Spinoza. Like Spinoza, he accepts the principle of intellectual self-knowledge and the value of truth as a nonrelative ideal; like Nietzsche, he acknowledges the limitations and the fragility of this ideal and the volcanic depths seething beneath it.

Major Differences: Therapy versus Salvation

The Road to Emancipation

There are, however, important differences between Freud and Spinoza. For if both see self-knowledge as a way to emancipation, they do not understand either the road or the emancipation in the same way.

In the first place, in Freud self-knowledge liberates from complexes and neuroses; it is therapy and not salvation. Freud sees science as a secular substitute for the highest spiritual value, but the latter cannot replace religion and its rich emotional scope. Science, as the enemy of illusion, should not become a new illusion; and this would happen if it claimed to achieve impossible goals. The enlightenment, the lucidity, and the emancipation which science bestows, are more limited in scope. They cannot alleviate or compensate for man's impotence and insignificance in the universe. This impotence must be recognized and accepted as such, an experience which accompanies man from first to last. Moreover, it is reinforced by self-knowledge; and the alleviation of anxiety enables this experience to become stabilized as man's authentic spiritual stance.

Second, self-knowledge in Freud is not mediated by much metaphysics and general science. A person need not go very far beyond himself or herself—she or he need not gain detailed knowledge of the universe, the laws of nature, God, and so on—in order to attain liberation. The Freudian patient is much more centered upon herself and her own personal psychological history.

This difference is also related to the therapeutic aims of the Freudian system as distinguished from the search for salvation that motivated Spinoza. Freud remains basically a physician. True, Spinoza saw his *Ethics* as a kind of "medicine for the soul" analogous to bodily medicine; but this was meant in a metaphoric and metaphysical sense, not in the pathological sense of modern psychoanalysis. The soul is in need of "cure" because of its bondage to the passions and the imagination. Its laws, in other words, are ethical, not medical. It is therefore quite possible for the Freudian treatment to produce a normal, fairly balanced personality which from every other point of view will remain a mediocre human being whom Spinoza will see as unfree and living by his or her "imagination." This reflects, indeed, a crucial difference: the goal of Freudian therapy is to produce a normal person; the goal of Spinoza's ethics is to produce a non-normal person—a rare human being of uncommon inner excellence.

Conatus *Reconsidered: Finitude and Salvation*

We may now return to the question of *conatus* versus *libido* and see a similar difference implied in it. Just as self-knowledge in Spinoza has a salvation perspective lacking in Freud, *conatus*, too, unlike *libido*, has a metaphysical dimension that is attached to the quest for salvation.

Conatus, says Spinoza, is the "actual essence" of finite things; it is not a property they possess but the principle of their very being. They all *exist as* this striving, which has a metaphysical significance translated into the more common forms of desire—physical, social, and intellectual. Or, to put it differently, *conatus* primarily seeks a "metaphysical utility" which then takes the form of more concrete utilities. Self-preservation, the declared object of the *conatus*, can also be understood (in metaphysical terms) as the quest to extend duration (*duratio*) indefinitely in an attempt to prevail over finitude. As finite beings, humans are bound to exist in the temporal domain of duration while at the same time endeavoring to attain the supratemporal existence Spinoza calls eternity.[38]

This paradox is resolved in that the striving to overcome duration is expressed in terms of duration itself—as its indefinite extension. True infinity (or eternity), which by nature is nontemporal and qualitative, inevitably becomes translated (and degraded) into a quantitative and temporal version of itself as the object of *conatus*, the form of indefinite duration.

Even in this form, however, the striving is doomed to failure. Particular things must pass away and die. The most they (or rather, a trifling number of them) can do is, through self-knowledge of the "third kind," become identified with God in the essential part of their minds; this realizes eternity *within* duration, that is, within the span of this life and as an event in the immanent world.[39] The true object of *conatus* (as it becomes *conatus intelligendi*, the striving for knowledge) thus turns out to be nothing less than salvation, the overcoming of finitude by realizing eternity-within-duration; and this gives the concept of self-preservation its deep, underlying meaning. The true final object of the natural striving which constitutes our being in Spinoza is infinity or salvation. *Conatus* in this sense is not very remote from the principle of *eros* in Plato.

Freud, however, does not burden his own theory with a metaphysics of salvation. This is a major difference between Freud and Spinoza which we encounter all along. We have seen it with regard to their views of self-knowledge, and now we see it expressed again in their respective anthropologies of desire.[40]

Hermeneutics and Nomological Science

A further difference has already been hinted at: self-knowledge in Freud is more the work of hermeneutics than of rigorous nomological science. It depends less on knowledge of lawlike patterns that govern natural phenomena (psychological and otherwise) than on deciphering signs and clues from one's personal psychic history; and its language, accordingly, is more tuned to the interpretation of symbols, metaphors, associations, and the like, within a given cultural and biographical context than toward the strict logical rigor of scientific discourse.

At the same time, hermeneutics is here put into the service of causal explanation. Its aim, like that of the police detective or the archaeologist, is to uncover a singular objective truth. (In Spinoza's words, it seeks to uncover the proximate cause or even the "genetic" definition of its object.) In this respect the weaker hermeneutical links serve an underlying model of rigorous causal determinism.

This introduces a major ambivalence into Freud's theory. Its methodological status wavers between alternatives that do not seem compatible. On the one hand, Freud insists that his doctrine is *Naturwissenschaft* (natural science). He believes in objective scientific truth and considers his theory to fall within it. Accordingly (and because of the dominant mechanistic idiom of natural science), Freud pictures the psychic life as a semimechanistic apparatus, where instinctual energy flows back and forth, invests itself in various objects, retreats, is being transformed and sublimated, and so on. All these movements are subject in principle to quantitatives analysis and occur under the rules of dynamic efficiency (also described as psychic "economics"). Yet, on the other hand, the actual causal links that determine psychic life as Freud describes it (especially in therapy, where it counts most) are determined by meaning and by meaning-carrying signs, their interpretation, and their interiorization. This is quite a different domain and type of discourse. The links between signs, meaning, and interpretation, on the one hand, and the vicissitudes of instinctual energy on the other hand, belong to two different methodological paradigms which Freud has taken great pains to reconcile. This is a major reason why psychoanalysis has always suffered from insufficient recognition and its scientific status is debated to this day.[41]

Self-Knowledge and Affect: The Imaginary Love of the Doctor

The most important difference between Freud and Spinoza concerns self-knowledge and affect. In Spinoza, self-knowledge of the "third," or highest kind, is supposed to produce a most powerful affect, the intellectual love of God, which dominates all others and transforms them from modes of bondage to modes of freedom. In other words, self-knowledge is the sufficient cause and lever of the psychic energy that revolutionizes the personality and imparts new quality to life.

Not so in Freud. Despite what Freud attributed to Leonardo (and, by implication, to Spinoza and to himself), these are rare cases. The ordinary person cannot attain self-knowledge first and a liberating affect later. He must have an affective support for the process of self-knowledge itself—and a very powerful support at that, since self-knowledge must struggle with stubborn repressions and resistance. The energy for this struggle is drawn from the process known as "transference," where the analyst becomes the object of the patient's intense emotions, usually of love and attachment, but sometimes also of hostility. Transference becomes a necessary middle term between the patient and himself or herself, and as such it is a cornerstone, almost a dogma of the Freudian system. The patient does not attempt to know himself or herself directly, but only by the mediation of his or her powerful emotive relationship with the therapist. This love is imaginary by nature. It is not built on a real relationship between two persons, but on an imaginary situation valid within the confines of the clinic and for the duration of the treatment (its charge of psychic energy is, of course, real and intense). As such it is capable of mobilizing sufficient libidinal power to break the patient's resistance and enable him or her to review the repressed experience and bring its underlying conflicts to a new, more stable resolution. The power by which the patient retrieves the drama of the past from the depths of self-incurred oblivion (repression), by which he or she reenacts the conflicts and struggles to resolve it differently, is not a cognitive force but an affective one. The displaced erotic power of transference mediates between the patient and himself and provides the indispensable ladder for the difficult ascent toward self-knowledge. This is not *amor dei intellectualis* but a kind of *amor medici imaginarius*—not the intellectual love of God, but the "imaginary love of the physician" which is converted into the powerful emotional lever that makes self-knowledge possible.

Self-Consciousness and the Other

Transference also implies that a person (here the patient) can gain self-consciousness only by relating to another consciousness, both in the mode of conflict and emotional confrontation and through intellectual intercourse. This Hegelian (and, in another sense, Socratic) principle absent in Spinoza takes a specific psychoanalytical shape in Freud.

In the doctor-patient situation, the analyst represents for me, the patient, the element of "otherness" in general, which I encounter as a limit and an opposition; the therapist thus embodies the "reality-principle" that stands in the way of my shapeless and unyielding drive for satisfaction.[42] But, in addition, otherness is here represented by another mind, a different person, with whom I enter a mind-to-mind relationship of conflict, love, and possibly even hatred. The analyst provokes me to draw from myself materials which he or she turns into clues and hermeneutical suggestions concerning my own psyche and life; and when, challenged by the therapist and spurred by our emotional relationship, I finally interiorize the interpretations thus produced, our conflict gives way to a kind of mental identification; my consciousness, by linking itself to that of the analyst, attains that *self-*consciousness which was the object of the process.

This may sound (and partly is) a Socratic principle made to fit the analyst's couch. But it has a closer and more modern source in Hegel's dialectical idealism. Unlike the analyst, the Socratic teacher can perform the role of "midwife" even if the disciple does not relate to him or her emotionally; and in Spinoza, no teacher is necessary at all. Given Spinoza's Cartesian doctrine of the "natural light," the mind is able to

produce *of itself* the clear and distinct ideas that determine its knowledge of the world and of itself. (Who indeed more than the solitary
Jewish heretic could testify to the mind's ability to be its own "midwife"?) That self-consciousness presupposes interpersonal desire and
conflict is a Hegelian principle which undermined the Cartesian tradition and which Freud, perhaps unwittingly, built into the psychoanalytic situation.[43]

Yet Freud renounces the idealist notion of the ego as subject, and
thus comes close to Spinoza's naturalist account of the mind. In Spinoza, the mind is but the nexus of complex ideas of the body. There is
no separate, unifying self which "holds" or "possesses" these ideas; in
other words, our mind does not *have* ideas but *is* these ideas. Similarly
in Freud, the ego is not the subject of "its" ideas, but the conscious,
outwardly oriented function of the stream of psychic life itself. The
ego, Freud insists, "is . . . only a portion of the *id*, a portion that has
been expediently modified by the proximity of the external world with
its threat of danger."[44] It puts the *id* in relation to the outer world and
screens it off from the world through the mechanism of repression and
other psychological transformations, all understood as determining
consciousness in a natural and quasi-automatic manner.

The ego in Freud has no connotation of a Kantian (or even Cartesian) subject,[45] not only because it is causally determined and lacks
transcendental status, but because it has no function of self-ascription,
whereby it imprints its identity upon "its" ideas and thus unifies them.
(One may even add that the idealist notion of the subject, with its connotations of "purity" and "autonomy," must seem to Freud a narcis-
sistic illusion.) Hence knowledge, in Freud no less than in Spinoza, is
more a mode of being than of having, not something we possess but
something we *are* or *become*. As Monique Schneider notes, in attaining
knowledge we do not gain an acquisition, as if something new were
added to the inventory of our possessions, but rather we exist differently, that is, our psychic being is modified.[46]

This reduces the scope of actual self-knowledge to the successfully
interiorized one. Mere understanding by the patient of hermeneutic
clues and explanations worked out with the analyst is not enough.
"Well, I have now understood—so what?" is a statement that analysts
keep hearing. Moreover, a superficial acceptance of the analyst may
serve as abnegation—a merely intellectual admission of the repressed
content that actually changes nothing in the repression (and the neurosis) itself and sometimes even serves to defend it. Self-knowledge
then has in Freud both a superficial and a genuine mode; the former is
only a change in our state of consciousness, while the latter entails a
change in our whole psychic being.

The Mind's Body

As Spinoza had maintained overtly, so Freud implies tacitly: psychic changes have their bodily correspondents. The early Freud was anxious to secure an autonomous scientific role for psychoanalysis, independent of anatomy and bodily medicine; hence he resorted to language that ignored the somatic parallels of psychic events. But the older Freud no longer hesitated to refer to the body as the locus of psychoanalytic structures and processes. The "*ego*," he says, "is first and foremost a bodily ego"; it has a spatial dimension even in the "anatomical" sense.[47] The *id* is "open at its end to somatic influence,"[48] a less emphatic statement which reveals Freud's vagueness on the details, yet stresses his principle of psychosomatic complementarity.

It follows both from the text and the logic of Freud's position, that some physiological substrate must exist to which psychoanalytic structures—and even particular processes—are attached. As in Spinoza, in order to maintain a strict philosophy of immanence while refusing to simply reduce mental phenomena to bodily states, some sort of mind-body parallelism must be admitted, whereby the psychic and the somatic aspects of the organism are two complementary expressions of the same. Or putting it differently: if the mind is to be the object of autonomous study and interpretation, without admitting a transcendent ground for it, then the mind must be both attached to a body and irreducible to the terms by which the body is studied. This is, fundamentally, also Spinoza's position.

Freud, it appears, tends to think of the somatic side of mental life in "anatomic" and even neurophysiological terms; but Freudians are not logically committed to this restrictive approach. Without contradiction, they may agree with Spinoza that the arena for mental processes is the whole bodily organism, down to its minutest functions and events. In today's terms, the somatic processes underlying psychoanalytic changes may have to do with metabolism, immunization, genetic modification, and other subtle biochemical processes, as well as with bodily functions for which the state of the science does not yet supply information. Implicitly, then—if only implicitly—Freud is here closer to Spinoza than his biology-shy idiom would suggest.

LOGOS AND ANANKE

There is a sense in which rational knowledge and disillusioned self-understanding replace religion in Freud, too, albeit in a low key with no suggestion of salvation. On several occasions Freud speaks, almost

Spinozistically, of the liberating power of the rational understanding of necessity. *Ananke* and *logos*, necessity and the rational intellect, are his twin gods.[49] *Ananke* is the old reality principle, now understood as harsh necessity;[50] as such it replaces the *moira* of ancient Greek tragedy and becomes the object of mature acceptance. *Ananke* has several connotations in Freud, ranging from the stringent impediments of daily life to a universal cosmic principle;[51] in the latter (major) role it stands for something like Spinoza's impersonal world of necessity, though without the latter's divine attributes and inherent rationality. *Ananke* reigns in a godless, anonymous universe, stripped of all the consoling features that human desire—especially, as Freud believes, our narcissism and infantile craving for a father figure—wove into it through illusion. Thus *ananke* comes closer to Nietzsche's *fatum* than to Spinoza's *natura*.

Here, indeed, Freud deals with the self-knowledge not of the patient but of man in general; and he links it to *logos*. *Logos* is the counterpart of *ananke*, never as a cosmic but as an educational principle, a human response to the reign of necessity. *Logos* does not inhere in reality itself (again unlike Spinoza) but only in man, where it helps him shed his illusory consolations, educate himself in the discipline of *ananke*, and learn to accept it with fortitude and maturity. This is wisdom, even a mode of freedom in Freud; but it is neither *amor dei* nor *amor fati*. Freud's calm acceptance of *ananke* involves no potent emotion or existential drama; there is no form of exaltation, no love for the totality of the universe, no proud and joyous defiance of nothingness. Freud's is a milder, more restrained, perhaps paler attitude, less metaphysical in mood and much more modest in its claims and expectations. Powered by the feeble if unremitting *logos*,[52] Freud's version of wisdom perhaps corresponds to Spinoza's second kind of knowledge but certainly not to the third.[53]

Ananke has, however, its own built-in form of consolation. Freud remarks that "it is easier to submit to a remorseless law of nature, to the sublime Ἀνάνκη, than to chance."[54] Thus, if we know that death is universal and inevitable, we can better accept our own death and that of our loved ones. Does this mean, Freud wonders in moments of self-suspicion, that the notion of natural necessity is yet another illusion we form in the quest for consolation? Had Freud persisted in this Nietzschean suspicion, he would have been led to a relativist theory rejecting the concepts of scientific truth and objective reality. Yet Freud ends up rejecting this "anarchist" view (as he calls it) with rigor. "No, our science is not an illusion," he declares. "But an illusion it would be to suppose that what science cannot give us we can get elsewhere."[55]

When using the idiom of *ananke* instead of the "reality principle," Freud tends to take the standpoint of the philosopher rather than that of the psychoanalytic therapist; at times, he speaks as the therapist of *culture*. (Attempting a psychoanalysis of culture may be a more proper task, or replacement, for philosophy which usually, according to Freud, is an expression of narcissism.[56]) Religion is analyzed as an infantile neurosis to which humanity must submit in its painstaking growth toward maturity, but from which, in the distant though not indefinite future, we shall be cured by science (and particularly, so it seems, by that scientific self-understanding that psychoanalysis will provide).[57] Freud here makes himself an heir to the philosophy of the Enlightenment and echoes its optimism, to which, however, on the basis of his own principles, he is not quite entitled. "The voice of the intellect is a soft one, but it does not rest until it has gained a hearing," Freud declares. "In the long run, nothing can withstand reason and experience."[58] Coming from a Diderot, a Kant, a Feuerbach—or even a Spinoza—such words would not have the dissonant ring they have in Freud, the great connoisseur of human irrationality, who had otherwise denied that by merely exposing an illusion or a neurosis we can abrogate and overcome the powers behind it. In the case of the individual patient, Freud saw the need to indicate (in his theory of transference) a source of libidinal energy by which resistance and repression can be removed. Where then, in parallel manner, do we find the auxiliary eros by which the intellect (*logos*) is to win its long-fought battle against religion and for the demystified acceptance of *ananke*?

Freud's failure to provide an adequate answer to this problem makes him, on this specific but important issue, more of a naive than a dark enlightener.[59] That Freud himself was capable of overcoming illusion and accepting the various aspects of *ananke* is unquestionable; it is attested to by both his intellectual stand and also by the quiet force and endurance he showed throughout his adult life, especially in the last sixteen years during which he suffered discomfort and daily pain and had to undergo thirty-two surgical operations (an average of one every six months)—without complaint, self-praise, or false consolations. He clung to life with stoic fortitude and vigor—working, writing, analyzing patients, and producing some of his most innovative theories and some of his best and most elegant pieces of literary style.

Yet, if Freud's life was to serve as an educational model, did it provide a realistic example? Is everyone capable of such a creative (or at least nondepressive) resignation to *ananke*? Why should the common person give up his or her consoling illusion, so deeply ingrained in his or her instinctual constitution? Freud thus faces the classic problem of the relation between the enlightened few and the multitude. Yet, whereas Spinoza had a special theory for the masses—and thereby a vehicle for historical change and progress—in Freud no such theory (or strategy) of progress is available.

It will not be surprising to discover that, on Freud's account, Leonardo, the link between himself and Spinoza, had also resigned himself to the wisdom of *ananke*.[60] Though Leonardo frequently expressed admiration for the Creator as the ultimate cause of nature, there is no indication "that he wished to maintain a personal relation with this divine power." Rather, "the reflections in which he recorded the deep wisdom of his last years breathe the resignation of the human being who subjects himself to ἀνάγκη, to the laws of nature, and who expects no alleviation from the goodness or grace of God."

A subtler, though perhaps even stronger threat unites Freud to Spinoza through Heine, the poet-philosopher whom Freud liked to quote with evident empathy. In *Future of an Illusion*, Freud has just declared his aim to be the educator of humanity to the painful maturity of *ananke*, painting this ideal in colors that are borrowed, at least in part, from the palettes of Spinoza and Nietzsche. Then, to sum up and highlight this experience of total this-worldliness, Freud joins his "brother in nonfaith" in the exclamation:

> *The heaven we shall leave*
> *To the angels and to the sparrows.*

This is, of course, the famous couplet in which Heine encapsulated his Spinozistic philosophy of immanence. In calling Heine a "brother in nonfaith" (*Unglaubensgenossen*) Freud is using a witticism that Heine himself had formed in reference to Spinoza; thus the three of them are consciously united by Freud. The subtlety of the appellation is even greater. The term "your *Glaubensgenossen*" (co-religionists) was used, for example, when speaking of other Jews to a Jew; thus Freud, in reversing it to *Unglaubensgenossen*, implies a congregation not only of heretics in general but, specifically of *Jewish* heretics—a distinct phenomenon in the history of European modernization. Moses Hess saw in Spinoza the archetype of this phenomenon—a Jew who transcended all historical religions to become the prophet of a secular and this-worldly religion of reason. This image may apply even more to Freud who, unlike the solitary and esoteric Spinoza, had the temperament and will-to-power of a leader and even a founder of a church.

It is noteworthy that while claiming that psychoanalysis is a science, Freud also calls it a "movement" (*Bewegung*), denouncing dissenters as secessionists.[61] To disagree with him was not so much to make false statements as to become a traitor. Equally important is the role of Freud's own life (both its reality and its mythological image) in establishing his movement. Freud's long struggle against resistance and prejudice, his perseverance, courage, honesty, and lucidity, his personal gentleness and lack of rancor—his moral no less than intellectual virtues—became important in spreading his word. Ernest Jones' life of Freud had in this respect not only a historical function but also an indirect apostolic one. No less central was the saga of Freud's intellectual journey (whose stages he made known to the world in several essays), in particular the years of his self analysis: Freud's concentrated struggle with himself and his dreams from which his new theoretical insights sprang may call to mind the lives of great mystics, prophets, and saints, their going to the "desert" for concentration and self-overcoming in the abyss of solitude. Like Jesus or Moses (who had always fascinated Freud) and like Socrates and Spinoza, Freud's own life has a mythical dimension inseparable from his message.

CONCLUSION

In conclusion, Freud and Spinoza are united by a naturalist determinism which includes the pathos of human emancipation by means of self-knowledge. But in Freud this is an emancipation from complexes and neurosis, it is therapy and not salvation. Freud is a prosaic atheist, without Spinoza's absolute and semimystical metaphysical aspirations.

The Freudian method is made to produce a normal person; Spinoza's way is meant to produce a *non-normal* person, a rare and exceptional human being. As Spinoza says in conclusion of his *Ethics*: "All things excellent are as difficult as they are rare."

Self-knowledge in Freud is not mediated, as in Spinoza, by metaphysics or by a detailed nomological knowledge of nature. Using a minimum of general codes and structures, it is essentially concerned with the interpretation of particular signs, utterances, dreams, slips, fragmented memories, and the like, drawn from the patient's personal biography. Thus it is more hermeneutics than science, or holds an ambivalent position between the two.

Spinoza and Freud both see man as a natural creature only, a principle of desire or reservoir of libido, who despite his being determined by natural agents strives for emancipation and is capable of achieving it. Both thus stress the tension between human bondage and the liberation of man by means of self-knowledge, which remains an intrinsic natural phenomenon and is no longer "God-given." Their humanism rejects religious and metaphysical illusions and offers a kind of dark enlightenment, which Spinoza's philosophy brightens up by making nature and reason the substitute for an absolute religion. Spinoza's world could horrify and outrage only those schooled in a theistic frame of mind; in fact, it is a world of order and absolute meaning, a world illuminated from within by the light of reason, which offers man the perspective of metaphysical salvation. Of the two thinkers, Freud is the more uncompromising atheist, who has internalized Kant's critique and raised it to its utmost consequentiality. Human liberation in Spinoza leads man to the infinite; in Freud, liberation leaves man in his impotent finitude in the universe.

A final word about the Jewish situation of Freud and Spinoza. Spinoza had no way of retaining his Jewish affiliation while rejecting the religious beliefs of the Jews and stepping outside their organized community. But for Freud, living after the structures of traditional Jewish life had been shattered, this was a viable possibility. Freud was a nonreligious Jew, a heretical Jew, but a Jew nevertheless, as he regarded himself[62] and was seen by the other Jews and by non-Jews as well (including the Nazis, who burnt his books and drove him in old age to exile).

Freud repeatedly stressed his Jewish origin. He even surmised that only a Jew could have conceived of psychoanalysis, because of his marginal position. Later he added that only a "Godless Jew" was capable of that.[63] For many years Freud was a member of *B'nei B'rith*, and on joining in 1897 he indicated the Jewishness of his colleagues as particularly welcome to him, since he too came from the same people. Both his sons had joined Zionist youth movements but Freud, who suspected nationalism, was not a Zionist. Above all he rejected religion. He reiterated his being a Jewish heretic, an "infidel Jew" as he once referred to himself in English; and Heine he considered his "brother in nonfaith." The bond which links him to Judaism, Freud wrote in 1926 to his *B'nei B'rith* colleagues, is neither faith nor national feelings, yet what remains is sufficient to make his attraction to Judaism irresistible, consisting of "many dark mental forces whose power is as great as they are unutterable, and yet a clear consciousness of an inner identity, which is the secret of this mental structure." Freud thus experienced his Jewishness even as it remained partly enigmatic to him (the kind of enigma one is tempted to say "only Freud" could solve). In his old age he wrote to an unknown addressee: "I hope you are not unaware that I have always remained faithful to our people, and have never pretended to be nothing else but what I am: A Jew from Moravia whose parents came from Austrian Galicia."

In the same vein he wrote in 1930 in a special preface to the Hebrew edition of *Totem and Taboo*:

> No reader of [the Hebrew version of] this book will find it easy to put himself in the emotional position of an author who is ignorant of the language of holy writ, who is completely estranged from the religion of his fathers—as well as from every other religion—and who cannot take a share in nationalist ideals, but who has yet never repudiated his people, who feels that he is in his essential nature a Jew and who has no desire to alter that nature. If the question were put to him: "Since you have abandoned all these common characteristics of your countrymen, what is there left to you that is Jewish?" he would reply: "A very great deal, and probably its very essence."

Freud says that he cannot clearly express this essence in words, and adds rather optimistically: "Some day no doubt it will become accessible to the scientific mind."

Yet even as he stressed his Jewishness with feeling and pride, the old Freud was not deterred from depriving his fellow Jews of their greatest prophet, Moses, whom he declared to have been an Egyptian.[64] Spinoza, too, had undercut Moses' role by declaring the Pentateuch to have been written by a later author, Ezra; but the same kind of heresies that made Spinoza submit to a ban and be decried a renegade did not prevent Freud from being accepted and recognized as a brother. This was a radical historical change, which Spinoza had prefigured and embodied while being deprived of it himself. In the twentieth century a Jew could live outside the organized community and hold heretical views without having to renounce his or her Jewish identity or be rejected as a traitor. What had been anticipated by Spinoza has meanwhile become a living concept and a social reality. Today one can debate what a "nonreligious Jew" means; one can polemicize with such a Jew, denounce or extol him, or try to make him "repent"; but one can no longer deny his existence. The gulf which separates Freud's Jewish situation from Spinoza's throws this major historical change into sharp relief.

CHAPTER 7

Epilogue:
Immanence and Finitude

Spinoza was not the first philosopher of immanence; pre-Socratics, Epicureans, and Stoics had preceded him in ancient times. But with Spinoza the idea of immanence, powerfully systematized, re-emerged after having been discredited and repressed by the overpowering weight of medieval Christianity. Of course, Christianity had extended and amplified a Jewish world-view, to which it added a theological structure derived from Greek philosophy; and Judaism itself has been affected by some of its Christian transformations. Yet originally, the Jewish Bible was very far from the transcendent outlook professed by later theologians.

The ideas of a purely transcendent God, of an afterlife and an after-world, of a divine domain ontologically separate from ours, are posterior to the Bible and partly foreign to it. The biblical God is awesome, remote, and unseen, but nonetheless immersed in this world and in human affairs. His punishments and rewards are purely of this world; there is no hell or paradise, except an earthly paradise, the Garden of Eden, long lost (and perhaps one day retrieved—also upon earth). Meanwhile the Old Testament offers a Promised Land as the supreme religious restoration. God controls the earthly lives of individuals, the destinies of peoples, the course of the stars, the seasons, the oceans—all aspects of the actual world. God even has a worldly image in which he created man, and though no human being (save Moses) can look at it and live, the image, a visual entity, literally exists. The attempts of Maimonides and other Jewish theologians to explain it away allegorically are posterior to the Bible by over a millennium and a half.

Thus the most abstract and lofty God of antiquity remains attached to this world in almost every respect. Though personified as a separate entity, God resides within the world, gives life and governance to it, rewards, sanctions, destroys, and resuscitates—all within the (enlarged) boundaries of immanence. He is the form, the order, the government, the morality of this world, personified (and thereby distinguished) as a single subject—the King of kings.[1]

The supernatural itself is part of the ancient Hebrew's *this-worldly* experience. God's entourage resembles that of a king; his "angels" (*mala'khim*, originally meaning: messengers) appear to constitute a humanlike, if superior, community within the same world system. Miracles, too, are experienced as wonderous worldly events, since a world that contains God as resident is likely to bear his marks. After all, if great worldly powers (the wind, the Leviathan, Emperor Cyrus) can effect things out of the ordinary, why should Jehovah, a still greater worldly power, not be capable of even greater exploits?

It was mostly in the normative domain that the ancient Hebrew experienced the transcendent brunt of his religion. God as an awesome father was also a ruler, a sovereign, a lawgiver; and his laws did not express the immanent, natural life of the people but an external will that is radically, even brutally, foreign to it. This opposition was not an ordinary civilizing effect, not simply "culture" sublimating "raw nature," but a revolution within culture itself. To overcome the dominant pagan culture, the laws of Jehovah had to cause an inner rupture within life, denaturate it, uproot its immediacy, and imbue everyday acts with a new, sacred dimension that transcends them. Moreover, it was obedience to the external legislation which constituted the Hebrew's very identity, his belonging to the people of the covenant and the source of what he was.

Thus, as opposed to the immanent tendency of his world picture, the ancient Hebrew experienced the moral universe as rooted in transcendence. The invisible, supranatural power of transcendence did hover over his life, not so much a metaphysical entity as a metaphysical *norm and authority*. Here lies a major difference between his worldexperience and Spinoza's. Another crucial difference is that in the Hebrew Bible, the immanent tendency of life was not complemented by naturalism but by its opposite, the attempt to sacralize life by effecting a rupture between it and nature.

This tendency became dominant in second temple Judaism, when an otherworldly dimension emerged and an elaborate system of oral law spread its dominion over life. However, with the Pharisees and later rabbis, the thrust against nature crystallized into a kind of thisworldly sacralism, whereas their revolutionary offspring, the Christians, turned this thrust toward heaven, to the pure spirituality of the world above. The duality of the earthly and the celestial, the temporal

and the eternal, salvation and damnation, the celebration of pure spirit
in conquest of the flesh, and the re-orientation of life's meaning from
this world and the beyond—this duality, although it had its origins in
second temple Judaism (Pharisees and Essenes)—went far beyond whatever the Jewish rabbis proclaimed, and reached its refinement and
glory—also its doctrinal systematization (and frequent ossification)—
in the theological work of the church. Talmudic, then Rabbinical Judaism remained much closer to earth, much more immanent in its religious concerns, although at the same time extremely opposed to naturalism.

Jews spent most of their religious energies worrying about the daily
observance of their laws, the hundreds of old precepts and new rulings
applying to almost every aspect of life: food, sex, marriage, business,
family, festivity, hygiene, and dozens of other concrete issues, sometimes minute and seemingly trivial, but, because of their embeddedness in the Law, they were invested with metaphysical sanctity. Yet if
Jewish religious life remained largely practical and earthbound, its
pragmatism was never utilitarian, but metaphysical. Jews were spend-
ing great effort and skill solving problems of ritual and observance
which to non-Jews will seem absolutely *useless*. This again is their peculiar kind of immanence, an antinaturalistic immanence: nature is replaced with its opposite, the network of transcendent-anchored
norms, as the stuff and substance of earthly life.

Spinoza, of course, rejected both the dualistic transcendence of the
Christians and the denaturized, transcendence-ridden this-worldliness
of his fellow Jews. A "Marrano of reason," he shed all historical religions (though not all religious concerns), and offered salvation neither
in Christ nor in the Law of Moses, but in his own kind of religion of
reason—naturalistic, monistic, and strictly immanent.

Though a solitary and revolutionary thinker, Spinoza did not spring
from a void. His uniqueness stands out in a rich historical tapestry: the
Dutch republic, with its precapitalist oligarchy and incipient worldly
outlook; the scientific revolution compounding the new learning of
the Renaissance; the emergence of political interests and ideas placing
sovereignty and state authority within man-made institutions—are all
indispensable, if insufficient, for explaining Spinoza. But perhaps even
more important are his Marrano roots. When at the age of twenty-
four, a loner and heretic, Spinoza was expelled from the Jewish community, he carried with him not only Maimonides and the Hebrew
Bible, Crescas and the Cabbalists, but, existentially and prior to all, he
carried over a special and unique experience, that of the Marranos and
their descendants, which had already affected his queries as a young

man and which, transformed and incorporated in his later work, Spinoza helped transport from a provincial Iberian subculture into the open arena of Western intellectual history.

This move has divided the present work in two. The *Marrano of Reason* situated Spinoza within the Marrano culture, comparing and contrasting him with other Marrano intellectuals and life-forms. Without trying to "reduce" Spinoza to this (or any other) dominant element in his background, we saw the idea of immanence emerging and recurring in the Marrano experience, not always an articulated philosophy but as a personal stand, a manner of life, an existential and aesthetic outlook.

Spinoza gave this idea its philosophical form and power. An outsider both by birth and choice, banned by the Jews while refusing to convert to Christianity, he became the first European of importance who transcended the universe of revealed religion while presenting it with a powerful systematic alternative. His move encapsulated the principle of modernity in a most radical form. While other rationalists, Descartes and Leibniz included, revived in their ontologies the theistic world-picture of Christianity, Spinoza allowed no vestige of the world beyond to survive, either as a metaphysical entity or as a source of normative value. Thereby Spinoza became the founder of modern philosophy of immanence, effecting an intellectual revolution no less momentous and consequential than Kant's, and which, having reached its main impact several generations after Spinoza, still has offspring which upset and unsettle traditional thinking today.

Spinoza's immanent revolution set the ground for later "heretical" thinkers, who sought to construe the philosophy of immanence either more coherently or still more radically, or to extend its basic ideas to new areas (economics, depth psychology, etc.). What they shared with Spinoza was not only a "climate of ideas," as Freud put it, but a systematic context: (1) immanence is the only and overall horizon of being; (2) it is equally the only source of value and normativity; and (3) absorbing this recognition into one's life is a prelude—and precondition—for whatever "salvation" (or emancipation) humans can attain.

Within this nuclear context one can further argue about the adequate way to construe the world of immanence (see Preface). (1) Is it nature, as in Spinoza, or spirit, history, *Wille*, *durée*, or some other such metaphysical construction? (2) Should it be individuated as a single, infinite totality? (3) Should it be deified? (4) What structure applies to it—mechanical causality, organic purposivity, dialectical logic, or a much more fluid and flexible model? (5) Does it have this structure eternally? Is our Spinozistic quest for fixed, eternal laws well founded or rather a prephilosophical bias, perhaps a vestige of theological thinking? (6) Should the human being (either as subject or as natural species) be assigned a special position within the world of immanence? If so, in what capacity? How is the role of human history affected by answering the former question? Finally, (7) should human liberation (which presupposes the immanent revolution) translate the religious view of salvation into an equally absolute secular eschatology, or should it (by its very secularity) be confined to a narrower, more modest vision, limited by critical boundaries?

These questions can be multiplied or arranged differently, and the list of philosophers to which they refer can be enlarged. But together they draw a logical map of alternatives by which a philosophy of immanence can be—and historically has been—construed.

We saw how various philosophers evolved their alternative versions in relation both to Spinoza and, through him, to others, thus taking part in a tacit multiple dialogue. And because in each case the comparison with Spinoza concerned the question of the adequate interpretation of immanence, it was an essential comparison, which also stresses a crucial dimension in the other philosopher's work. In other words, we do not only study the problem of immanence through these thinkers, we also take a fresh look at them from the perspective of this common problem.

Thus, to Spinoza's concept of nature, Hegel opposes his concept of spirit, Marx the idea of man-in-nature, Nietzsche the formless mass of will to power, and Freud a new concept of nature, stressing its unconscious and instinctual side.

These are not particular solutions only but general types, each related to a different structure attributed to the immanent world. Thus in Spinoza, immanence is structured by mechanistic causality conceived as a pure logical chain; in Hegel by the subjectlike logic of development he calls dialectic; in Marx by his own brand of dialectic, that of economic production and the man-made purposivity inscribed within objective reality; in Nietzsche by the constant flux and transiency of being coupled with the self-transcending of will to power;[2] and in Freud by a natural causality extended to depth psychology and the study of culture, which uses symbolic and semiotic relations as allegedly natural causes.

In Spinoza and Hegel, the structure of reality implies that the immanent world is inherently intelligible and rational throughout (albeit under different models of rationality); in Marx and Freud, no rational *causa sui* is implied. Scientific determinism falls within the world of finitude and bears no witness to the inherent meaningfulness of being;

Nietzsche (following Schopenhauer) rejects determinism as based on the illusion of causality, and construes the world of immanence as indeterminate flux subject to changing, man-made interpretations.

Dogmatic versus Critical Philosophy of Immanence

We could go on drawing parallels, oppositions, and logical links between the various ways of construing a philosophy of immanence. We would thereby refine the logical map and fill in its contours. But then a further question arises. Given the general coordinates of the above map, can one decide which is the more adequate approach to immanence?

I do not think any single doctrine will provide the answer. Inescapable and omnipresent, the context of immanence is bound by finitude, hence also by constant openness to change. Yet there is nothing external to change it; all we have is the evolving substance of our own life and culture as it becomes reflected in ideas. This is the ultimate context of existence, the world of immanence in which everything else inheres. (In this loose sense it is indeed our "substance.") And while nothing external to it can dictate rules, provide answers, or criticize and change the contents within this sphere of immanence, there is also nothing within it to guarantee absolute, eternal truth.

Immanence thus implies autonomy, albeit a limited, finite autonomy. It involves a self-structuring process whereby forms and constrains are produced by the same agents who assume them—humans in their collective experience. Thus we have moral values, logical and scientific procedures, and patterns of public debate and persuasion (and of social and economic organization) by which these norms and procedures are eventually modified. And though none of them can claim absolute or transcendent validity, they provide a gauge, a structure, a provisional solidification of the flux of life into meaningful patterns and constraints, all produced by the finite power of immanence while giving it form and impetus.

The dichotomy "either God or moral anarchy" (or its seemingly secular translation, "either absolute values or nihilism") are vestiges of the transcendent outlook. A critical philosophy of immanence rejects the timelessness of man-made norms as well as their dismissal as meaningless. Humans exist by placing value on things beyond their naturally given state. This is the way we transcend ourselves and give our lives structure, meaning, direction, and an identity for which it is worthwhile struggling and making sacrifices even in the absence of timeless absolutes. Self-transcendence, the existential drive to go beyond ourselves toward a value and a meaningful identity, is sufficient to explain both the genesis of value (with its embodiment in social life-forms and institutions) and the binding power it has over us, as long as we recognize ourselves in it or sense it as part of our own identity. As such, values are alive—they are "relevant" and worth fighting for even when lacking a transcendent halo and imprimatur.

A philosophy of immanence can be either critical or dogmatic. Spinoza's paradigm was critical with regard to the origin of normativity, but dogmatic in its metaphysics and theory of salvation, since it turned the immanent world into a new absolute and offered a theory of salvation which makes it possible to overcome finitude. Hegel, the early socialists, and even Marx adopted a semireligious view of human salvation. A critical philosophy of immanence, however, accepts finitude as the irremediable human condition. Kant was the first to stress the inner link between criticism and finitude, though in conceiving philosophy as a closed, timeless "science" he failed to give finitude its full (and disturbing) force. In like manner, immanence and finitude are twin concepts, each necessarily implied by the other. But what follows from this mutual implication?

Above all (and against Spinoza), it follows that immanence cannot be construed as *causa sui*, let alone deified. Nor can we expect it to provide a timeless, immutable system of truth or value (an objection applying to both Kant and Spinoza). Here it is Nietzsche who bears the critical banner: the immanent "world," as he claims, must be open to a variety of interpretations by which the stream of human life structures itself and its experience. But Nietzsche commits the opposite mistake in idealizing transitoriness, which is no less fallacious than deifying permanence. The quest for order and meaning in the world is a valid and authentic human enterprise, provided that its tentative nature is not objectified into a timeless truth or alleged to be grounded in one.

Moreover—and this may be the most delicate or controversial point—as finite beings we can neither affirm the transcendent domain nor rid ourselves completely of its empty yet meaningful horizon. By "empty" I mean that it cannot be filled with any positive contents or even be asserted to exist. Yet this empty horizon is meaningful as a memento of our own finitude and a critical barrier against turning the immanent world into an absolute or a kind of God.

For the same reason, a critical philosophy of immanence cannot lead to "salvation," if by that we understand a secular translation of the religious ideal in its plenitude. Humans may indeed attain a degree of freedom, of mental and physical emancipation and, when lucky and creative, endow their lives with a measure of authentic meaning. Even so, they remain irremediably finite, and salvation in the sense of overcoming finitude (which was also Spinoza's goal) cannot be claimed or envisaged except as an illusion.

In a word, *to be critical, a philosophy of immanence must also be a philosophy of finitude.* Let me now elaborate the implications of this condition in these six issues: (1) the status of transcendence; (2) monism and pantheism; (3) the origin of normativeness; (4) truth and interpretation; (5) the human role; (6) emancipation and salvation.

(1) The Status of Transcendence

We begin by considering Kant, from whom the terms *critical* and *dogmatic* are evidently borrowed. Kant's critical stand follows from his recognition of man's finitude. This implies that we have no access to the transcendent domain. God, the immortality of the soul, freedom from natural determination, and the properties of the world as one totality, are transcendent issues which inevitably provoke our rational interest, but also lure us into making vacuous statements about them. The critically rational attitude is to abstain from such claims and accept living with the queries as fundamentally unanswerable.

It must be stressed that concern with transcendent issues is a *rational* necessity according to Kant and an authentic human stance. What he denounces as uncritical is the attempt to answer these queries or supply them with positive objects. Because transcendent questions cannot be rationally answered, it does not follow that they are meaningless or that we may turn to irrational principles (religious, mystic, nationalistic, etc.) to fill the void. Critical rationality requires maintaining the mind's transcendent quest along with the recognition that it cannot be fulfilled. It thereby creates an unfulfilled gap, a void, a tension, which is the mark of human finitude and a distinctive feature of the critical philosopher.

Thus critical rationality can neither abolish the perspective of transcendence nor give it concrete content and substance. Transcendence hovers over the immanent domain as a question mark, a possibility that will always remain empty for us. Since transcendence, on this critical view, is neither an entity nor a straightforward fiction, we may refer to it as a "horizon" which our finitude projects over being but which we may not solidify or fill with any objects. Nor can we adequately talk about it except in a roundabout way, by metaphor which points to this horizon without fixing anything actual about or within it.[3]

Our awareness of this empty horizon provides no knowledge of an actual thing, only an indirect realization of our own finitude; it also keeps us from inflating the status of the immanent world—the only one we may admit, know, and act upon—into a new absolute, adorning it with semireligious properties. Thus pantheism, either in Spinoza's or Hegel's version, is excluded by a critical view of immanence.

At the same time, critical philosophy re-directs the transcendent drive back into the actual world, where it serves an immanent function. In Kant this takes the form of the "regulative idea"; but seen more broadly, Nietzsche's ideas of self-overcoming and will to power also translate this notion of transcendence-within-immanence, as does Heidegger's existential analysis of man. Without overstepping his finitude, man surpasses himself into what he is not yet, that is, he projects himself into his realm of possibilities.

In Spinoza, immanent self-transcendence is expressed in the *conatus* striving to overcome finitude and attain salvation within this world; meanwhile it leads the person to excel and stretch the boundaries of his or her humanity to the utmost. But because its aim is to abolish finitude, it is incompatible with a critical philosophy of immanence, where finitude and immanence go hand in hand.

(2) Monism and Pantheism

A critical philosophy of immanence can no longer view the world as a unique totality, and certainly not as God. Here again Kant's critical principle may serve as guideline. From the standpoint of finitude—the only one a critical philosopher may admit—all being is inherently contingent and the concept of a necessary being or *causa sui* is therefore incoherent. Also (and again, as in Kant), as finite rational creatures we can know or interpret "the world" (i.e., our own field of experience) in fragmentary sectors only, not as a single, overall totality. Even if all the fragments potentially belong to the unity of the same world (as they do in Kant), they remain fragments only, and what we know as "the world" is at every given point a jigsaw puzzle with many pieces missing and all horizons indefinitely open.[4]

This is Kant's way of saying that the critical standpoint of finitude is incompatible with the idea of the world as totality. It also means that there is no *natura naturans* in Spinoza's sense, no infinite substantive unity underlying finite things in the world and endowing them with inherent rationality. The immanent world, critically conceived, is a system of finitude and fragmentariness only; in Spinoza's terms it is *natura naturata* without a *natura naturans* supporting it either internally or from without. In this, Nietzsche, Marx, and Freud have taken the more critical position as against Spinoza and Hegel.

Another reason why the immanent world may not be seen as absolute is the residual horizon of transcendence discussed above. Because it cannot be validly eliminated, there remains necessarily a gap, a rupture, which leaves this world incomplete and, so to speak, "deficient" in its ontological status,[5] even though no other world may be affirmed beyond it. This gap or fissure humans can fill only with their own immanent work, producing themselves, their values, their environment, through their own agency, but without being able to close the ontological gap or to expect complete salvation. In other words, no *causa sui* can be admitted either beyond the world or within it, though its concept is inevitable for us as an ever-evasive ideal, a negative image that only highlights our own finitude and that of the immanent world.

(3) The Origin of Normativeness

Since no positive transcendent principle is admitted, all values, norms, and the like can stem only from humans in their actual life and culture, that is, immanently. But this also means that humans are marked by finitude and thereby by the lack of moral absolutes. Immanent normativeness is linked to evolutions in man's self-image, institutions, patterns of action and discourse, and the subconscious instincts and projects interacting with these cultural forces. Hence, there is no single set of binding norms and no unique procedure for declaring and testing them, which can be valid universally and for all times.

Claiming that universality itself is the test will beg the question, because there is no way to determine a priori what is universal. This limitation, the most embarrassing for a Kantian-like morality, is not simply due to problems of application but to the nature of finite human rationality. Unapplied, having no basis in actual human attitudes, action, and communication, a priori moral principles are empty. They enjoy no timeless status in themselves, from which they are then "applied" to actual life, incurring different degrees of "deviation" and "incompleteness." Rather, *their embeddedness in actual life is their initial and only way to exist.* Whatever impurity, vagueness, deviation, controversial interpretation, or faulty communication may affect the rational principles is not a secondary fact, a matter of mere application, but expresses an essential feature of human rationality as finite rationality. Whatever we possess as rational elements must necessarily exist as embedded in our immanent life and practice, and thus also be prone to disagreement and change.

Kant's belief that he could found morality on an absolute led him beyond the immanent and critical domain because he postulated (as in knowledge) a unique, timeless paradigm of human rationality, which history only serves to explicate but does not affect; and because he grounded morality (unlike knowledge) directly in the "noumenal" domain. Thereby Kant turned transcendence from an empty horizon into the constitutive ground of moral imperatives and their alleged timeless universality.[6]

On the question of normativeness then, it is Kant who represents the dogmatic view of immanence whereas Spinoza offers a critical one. Reason in Kant cannot be construed, as in Spinoza, as part of the actual world but constitutes a second, separate world over and above it, with man participating as "citizen" in both. This is a secular vestige of Christian dualism, endowing man with a divine faculty emanating from heaven.

A philosophy of immanence must place the source of all normativeness in the actual world. In Spinoza, moral norms derive (for the general public) from the forces of desire and consent, sanctioned by political power and legislation; and the philosopher's best way of life derives from his own reason, also construed as desire and as an integral part of nature. But Spinoza too adhered to a single paradigm of rationality, and his "higher" morality (of salvation), though implying no transcendent Ought, is nevertheless committed to a unique ethical good.

Here again the viewpoint of finitude may serve us as criticism. Although the immanent world is all there is, in itself it is inexplicable and lacks inherent meaning; it is not *causa sui*. Man, however, existing as self-transcendence within immanence, creates meanings for himself and the world around him; it is through his own works, desires, projects, and endeavors that morally significant meanings emerge in the world. No external, timeless guidance is available to him, whether he welcomes it as salvation or rejects it as bondage. And since human life is neither static nor repetitive, the ethical universe, too, assumes various faces and is open to change.

The vehicle of these changes is human desire, embodied in actual life and practice and structured by social habits and institutions in which tradition and change, orthodoxy and revolt both play their respective parts. (The stabilizing powers of routine and conformity, however, will usually carry a heavier weight except in times of crisis.) And the carrier of change is frequently the individual consciousness partly alienated from the mainstream of society, though sharing a good deal of its latent principles and incipient new self-image and desires. Marginal standpoints, like Spinoza's, may anticipate and even foster change when they are sufficiently representative of what is subconsciously felt as a lacuna by leading segments of the society—even when this feeling is not consciously admitted.

Besides material norms, there must be culturally sanctioned procedures for challenging or revising moral attitudes, whether they be rational or authoritarian. But even when they claim to have a transcendent basis in God's will, in effect they all have their source in immanence as human creations (and inverted self-projection).

Recognizing the natural basis and mutability of the moral universe, a critical philosophy of immanence is not, however, committed to moral anarchy or to any specific mode of accepting and changing norms. Of course, accepting a normative framework or modifying it requires social discourse and communication as an a priori principle, one which a philosopher must recognize as an inherent condition of rationality; and this makes a certain amount of rhetoric (in the broad sense) indispensable. Yet in their hard core, all such processes and debates must comply with rational constraints in order to be accepted as critical. One can violate these constraints only at the risk of being irrational, or of sinning against what the embedded fundamental values project as their further or better explication. (The latter element serves to avoid conservatism and allows for valid rational criticism of a society even when refusing the "transcendental" severance of value from its natural social habitat.)

To conclude, the fact of lacking absolute validity (like that of God's alleged commands) does not make moral precepts void or vacuous. Accepting this dichotomy is another vestige of the transcendent frame of mind, that of religious absolutism translated (incongruously) into the world of immanence and finitude. It is, among other ways, by projecting values and norms that humans overcome their natural state and give meaning and direction to their existence; and this remains true even if there is no disembodied, extrahistorical guide to direct their way from the viewpoint of eternity.

(4) Truth and Interpretation

A similar point applies to the cognitive domain. In Kant the fragments of experience belong in principle to the unity of a single world, because they are all governed a priori by the same set of fundamental categories. This is another way of saying that there is a single, immutable truth both for metaphysics and the natural sciences.

In Spinoza, truth is unique because it models itself on the structure of the unique world-substance, with its allegedly deductive laws. Rejecting this view as dogmatic, Kant models truth on the structure and unity of the human mind, whose a priori forms are said to provide the basic framework for the natural sciences and for nature itself. Thereby the human mind, though finite, assumes in Kant the role of God in providing the anchorage for a single, immutable system of knowledge.[7]

A critical philosophy of immanence cannot, however, be a priori committed to the postulate that human rationality is exhausted by a set of pure, immutable forms that can be captured once and for all. Human rationality is an activity, not a set of forms; it is also a self-structuring activity, which shapes its own patterns by using them, that is, by projecting meaning and order onto what it calls the "world," without being able—or entitled—to objectify it into a single, univocal entity.

Just as Kant's critique does away with the notion that the world is an actual totality, so his own unity of experience can no longer be guaranteed as the permanent and unique way in which to rationally experience the world. Beyond Spinoza's totality and Kant's unique system of reason, the "world" lends itself to several possible systems of interpretation, each with a claim to express some form of human rationality, that is, the activity of bringing meaning and tentative order to our being-in-the-world ("experience"). If transcendence is an empty horizon, the immanent "world" is a de-totalized agglomerate of possible horizons which can be filled with content and shaped through an interpretation.

Interpretations, however, are not all born equal. Some are preferable to others for reasons which can be defended rationally even when they lack a conclusive edge. Some interpretations make better sense than others, are more fundamental (as in a scientific paradigm relating to a specific hypothesis), fit better with what is taken as "facts" or with other, correlative interpretations, or are more akin to the cultural context in which they arise and the rest of the Zeitgeist. Hence there are and must be clues and rules for adopting, modifying, and uprooting interpretations. Yet none of these may claim a timeless status.

Nothing in the immanent world can help us pull ourselves by the hair outside it. Even Baron Münchhausen, an expert in this field, must fail us, because in this case there is nowhere to exit. But this is no reason to renounce rationality altogether, like an angry child who breaks his toys because he has not been given better ones. As finite rational beings, we can recognize the worth of coherence, reasonable argumentation, optimal universality, and other cross-cultural factors, even without committing ourselves to the idea that human rationality is a fixed, closed system or that the work of self-transcendence and interpretation can be achieved once and for all.

While the minimal features of rationality must address themselves to humanity at large (represented as a community of ideal interlocutors), in effect, they are merely regulative abstractions. Actual human communication, both within and between communities, is at best semirational; and though rational elements are embedded in all forms of life, this embeddedness, along with the "impurities" and "deviations" it entails, is their *natural* way to exist. Even the most universally alleged form cannot be applied outside a definite context, determined by previous life-forms and interpretations. This limitation is not accidental but inherent; we cannot dismiss it as a mere gap between an "ideal" and its "application" since it derives from the finitude which affects human rationality in its very essence.

The a priori elements in our experience are also subject to such limitations. Although indispensable to all meaningful discourse and perception, their content, shape, and application may vary and even conflict because of existential and historical conditions. Therefore, philosophers who bring these a priori elements to light—a worthwhile, time–honored project—are not unveiling the immutable structure of some pure intellect, either divine (Spinoza, Leibniz) or human (Kant). Rather, they unearth the deep layers of some human life form or universe of discourse. Within any such domain, there is room for argument and hierarchical judgment; but more than a single one can validly be admitted, and together they illuminate the "world" (or our being within it)—not as a fixed, monolithic entity but as an agglomerate of possible perspectives, some of which may complement others but which cannot add up to a closed and fully coherent system.

This view radicalizes Kant's refusal to see the world as a thing-in-itself-like totality. What Kant puts forward instead—his immutable unity of experience—should be met with similar reluctance, since all are "dogmatic" postulates, transcending the boundaries of human finitude. Human rationality cannot guarantee that the unity of experience is immutable and fully coherent, any more than it can vouch for the inherent necessity of its a priori forms or for any other transcendent principle. What we do have is actual human life, with rationality as an open-ended process by which this life structures and transcends itself and gives meaning to its environment, all the while remaining within the confines of the process itself.

Is this a skeptical view? If so, then only in the affirmative or constructive sense of skepticism started by Hume and further evolved by Nietzsche. What Hume has done for the inductive-positivistic model of knowledge, Nietzsche may help us do for a nonpositivistic (or hermeneutical) one: turn skepticism into an affirmative position. A scientific account may be valid and enlightening even when not linked to some unique picture of truth. By being open to culturally mutable interpretations, the world is no less real or immanent; it only escapes encapsulation by "eternal" forms, essences, and the like, either in Plato's or Spinoza's way. Nor must we postulate such timeless aids in order to be able to evaluate, select, and modify interpretations according to rationally justifiable clues. Just as our societies, social institutions, and cultural forms have meaningful and constraining patterns without being eternal, so human rationality, the self-structuring power of life that informs them all and externalizes itself in them, can assume meaningful forms and constraints even when its norms lack the transcendent support (and fanatic edge) of a single, immutable truth.

Nietzsche, therefore, was wrong in wishing to replace the cult of eternity with a worship of transitoriness and flux. There is no inauthenticity involved necessarily in the human drive to create order and meaning—even if the world "in itself" lacks them. We do the same in building houses, empires, cities, and other civilized forms of life. Chaos and flux are only one ingredient of the immanent world; there is also the human activity by which order and shape are injected into chaos and the cosmic flux is captured and solidified into tentative, yet significant and fairly stable structures. Doing this is the genuine activity of humans, the way we exist and project ourselves within being.[8]

(5) The Human Role

One of Spinoza's boldest moves was to expurge nature of humanlike features and to reduce man himself to nature at large. The human features he thereby banned from nature were primarily purposes and perfections (including generic forms). At the same time, he allowed causality and logical inference as objective features of the world, inherent in the very nature of things.

Nietzsche, as we saw, objected that causality is also a feature projected by man, by which he falsifies a world-in-flux which in itself has nothing inscribed on it. While Nietzsche meant this as criticism, Kant in his Copernican revolution, and the various idealist positions he engendered, took a different view. Yes, was the idealist position, all forms attributed to reality are formed or affected by the human mind. But this does not necessarily make them illusory or useless. Knowledge means the application of human-shaped categories to the raw, uninterpreted mass of being in which we live. There are no forms "in themselves," no inherent meanings inscribed on the book of nature which, as good copyists, we must reproduce in our minds. Spinoza himself unwittingly projected his concept of deductive causality upon nature, and then thought he was reading it off the eternal nature of the substance. If this inverted projection looks analogous to the way the critics of religion (including Spinoza) explain the genesis of God's transcendent image, this is no accident: we cannot rid nature of humanlike (or human-bred) features, because no nature would then be left, only an indefinite, meaningless mass of being in-itself.

In Spinoza, meanings-in-themselves are made possible by the logical substance in which they are said to inhere. But this view, as Kant and Nietzsche will agree, invites transcendent postulates in through the back door. If, instead, we construe the immanent world not as substance or totality but as a horizon open to multiple and partial interpretations, then the agent of such interpretation, the human race, cannot be simply reduced to a nature existing in-itself, but must be recognized as playing a constitutive ontological role. The immanent world incorporates man's activity of interpretation; and man's being-there enlightens and imparts meaning to what in itself is, at least for us finite creatures, opaque.

The act of interpretation, however, must not be understood as exclusively or even primarily intellectual. It expresses itself first as praxis, the activity whereby humans live, act, relate to things and to other people, fulfill roles, and so on, and by thus interacting with the world, they tacitly shape and give meaning to the various things in their experience. Of course, no individual does this as an isolated Cartesian ego. We already exist in a largely interpreted world, using language, tradition, social institutions, and the like, as our modes of relating to things and thus as the carriers of meaning which we interiorize, translate or revise, and project again. But what counts as primary are not the tools but the activity of life itself as it projects itself through them.

Reflection is a latecomer, the owl of Minerva spreading its wings once the day's work is done. Before we articulate our experience in ideas and other cultural images, we "live them out," so to speak, interpreting ourselves and the things in the world by our behavior, life-styles, work and production, by participating in social roles and relating to other persons, organisms, and inert things around us. Some of this substantive interpretation seems to be going on unconsciously, affected by such forces as the individual's psychic history, by social persuasion and propaganda, or by more latent social, economic, and demographic undercurrents announcing a cultural shift.

In other words, interpretation is the movement of life itself, not merely conscious reflection upon it. We interpret being, and thereby shape the world and ourselves, the way Monsieur Jourdain in Molière's comedy used to speak prose. Later on we can verbalize these modes of life, transform them into images, metaphors, myths, concepts, art, religious cult, social and political theories, and so on, and also into sophisticated scientific structures: but this intellectual production, as Hegel had noted before Marx, is posterior to the forms of life themselves and crystallizes itself from them ex post facto. When we reflect and verbalize, the substantive work of interpretation is already done.

This puts us, ontologically speaking, neither "in front" of being or "facing" it from the outside (Kant), nor submerged and effaced within it as simple modes (Spinoza), but rather existing in-the-world as constitutive participants of whatever "the immanent world" may mean or be. "The world is human" said Sartre, echoing what others from Kant to Marx to Heidegger had maintained. The immanent world is not merely an in-itself. Kant had already shown this view to be "dogmatic." Immanence is man's world, the complex of horizons and perspectives in which human life takes and gives shape. That this world should be ontologically related to some form of human activity or culture is a critical requirement. But what do we understand here by the "human being"?

Certainly not an isolated Cartesian individual, or a pure, transcendental Kantian subject. Nor is the human being primarily a knowing creature. Idealism went off mark by feigning a pure subject that constitutes the world through knowledge. Thus the actual human being and the viewpoint of immanence were lost. It is as an inner-worldly ("natural") entity, not as a transcendental subject, that the human race fulfills its role in being, and also as a social creature, functioning in historical collectives which individuals make work and also cause to modify. Human beings fulfill this role by their actual life and praxis, that is, by the embodied interpretation of being which precedes its explicit cultural images. In these respects, Marx makes his own contribution to a critical philosophy of immanence.[9]

To conclude, human agency is ontologically relevant to whatever shape and meaning the world acquires, because it is from humans alone that meaning can flow. Attributing meaning to being in itself is no less anthropomorphic than attributing purposes to it. If this sounds like *hubris*, we may remember it is, rather, an expression of human finitude. The inability to overstep immanence is a source of humility and ontological loneliness which also, as self-overcoming, breeds a sense of freedom and pride.

(6) Emancipation and Salvation

As we have seen throughout this book, a philosophy of immanence is characteristically a philosophy of emancipation. It assumes that the recognition of immanence as the overall substance of life, when interiorized by the individual and impregnating the dominant culture and society, is likely to become a major liberating force. We encountered this link between immanence and emancipation in all the preceding chapters. But we also noticed the varieties in which it has been interpreted. Two types of questions arise: (a) can emancipation affect the individual directly, as distinguished or even opposed to the rest of his or her social time and place? And (b) can it translate the religious ideal of salvation in its full force?

Spinoza answers both questions affirmatively. An esoteric thinker (and descendant of the Marranos), he saw the attainment of truth as independent of the political and cultural situation. Although improved political conditions enhance the chances of philosophical life, they are not a necessary condition for it. The sage can attain the highest philosophical degree in isolation, even when the general multitude is far from its path.

This Marranesque outlook is not, I think, as dogmatic as it is naive. The historicality of human life and advancement was not sufficiently recognized in Spinoza's time. Nature and reason "as such" were the objects of concern, while history, as in Descartes, was merely the accumulated burden of past errors and prejudices from which the philosopher had to tear himself away as he took the standpoint of pure reason. It was Kant who, first among the major philosophers, maintained that reason itself depended upon history for its self-explication and implementation in the world. This idea Hegel elaborated into a global and semireligious philosophy of history, while Marx transposed it to a naturalistic, economico-social context and imprisoned it within the confines of rigid historical determinism.

Thereby naiveté has turned into dogmatism. A critical concept of immanence, while recognizing the interdependence of the individual and the historical situation, will not see it as deterministic. Existentially, individuals escape full rational definition; and human individuals, as self-transcending beings, cannot even be defined by what they have themselves been or done. There always remains an irreducible factor that defies scientific, historical, or rational determination even while admitting a statistically predictable situation when larger social entities are concerned (groups, periods, subcultures, etc.).

As finite, the individual's position is ambivalent at its very core; he or she is both determinable within a larger context and indeterminable in his or her most intimate individuality. Moreover, he or she is necessarily a constitutive agent of the broader social structure which affects him or her, because this structure cannot exist other than by being interiorized and re-enacted by concrete individuals who, as such, reiterate and color their roles in their own, idiosyncratic ways.

In any context, in any society, individuals as such represent the principle of deviation, the unpredictable existential factor escaping full determination; yet it is only through them that global historical forms exist. Hence the power which builds and maintains these forms (and is largely harnessed by them) is also what undermines their solidity and keeps them in constant movement and openness to change. As Spinoza's own case illustrates, it is often the alienated marginal individual, falling out of tune with mainstream society (though still sharing part of its underlying goals and incipient aspirations) who serves as the catalyst of social and cultural change.

It is therefore not *from* history that humans become emancipated, but *through* and *within* it. Whatever liberation we may expect must occur through its medium. This implies, against what Hegel and Marx seem to believe, that there can be no end of history, no transhistorical state announcing full human liberation. Secular messianism is a contradiction in terms. If it translates the religious idea of salvation in its absolute force and plenitude, then it is neither secular nor truly immanent, but remains attached to a transcendent religious ideal. From the critical standpoint of finitude, the messianic "kingdom of God upon earth" is at best a regulative transcendent dream. To view human history as leading to it—either necessarily or even as a plausible outcome—is to maintain the dogmatic import of transcendent religion within what purports to be a philosophy of immanence.

Secular illusions are frequently worse and may have more ominous consequences than religious ones; and as the last century has demonstrated dramatically, secular eschatology is not merely a philosophical fallacy but a major source of human suffering and inhuman atrocities.

Equally uncritical is Spinoza's view of individual salvation, because it is supposed to provide a way for the *individual* to overcome his or her finitude. A critical view of immanence recognizes that humans are irremediably finite and nothing, not even this recognition, can redeem them of it. The emancipating power of immanence, in other words, cannot match the absolute rewards that religion promises; and since it is by demystifying such promises that the idea of immanence has its liberating effect, it will be ironically self-defeating to replace a religious illusion by a secular one. Emancipation from religious illusion excludes all absolute claims; it shrinks the horizon of human emancipation to much more limited dimensions, as befits a critical and immanent outlook. And this means above all: finitude is never abolished; whatever liberation we can attain must remain within its pervasive boundaries.

The opposite danger also exists. Recognizing that man is irremediably finite gave the early Sartre a sense of redemption as strong as that of religious believers; later he confessed this had been one of his greatest mistakes, an inverted form of theism. It is still a dogmatic religious temperament that interprets human finitude and contingency as "lost" or "condemned," a "useless passion" as Sartre called it; it is equally a transcendent religious impulse that seeks, dialectically, to find an "atheist redemption" in this very "damnation." Critical immanence is more sober, though no less intense; as in Freud, it takes a calmer tone, avoiding the great drama and semireligious heroism frequently associated with the acceptance of finitude. And this may be even harder to do.

In recognizing finitude—and finite rationality—as the foremost human mark, we assume both its potential and limitations, its promise and burden, as specifically *ours*. We accept finite rationality as the overall context of immanence, from which nothing can lift or "save" us, but within which human life can give structure and meaning to itself, always prone to transcendent illusion and self-deception, and constantly in need of restraining mementos. Interiorizing this recognition may provide the kind of philosophical self-knowledge, perhaps even wisdom, which leads to emancipation, not from finitude, as in Spinoza, but from its allegedly intolerable burden. Accepting a *natura naturata* without God may prove to be more difficult than partaking in the exuberance of *amor dei intellectualis*, but it is also a more critical and authentic human stance.

The preceding points are meant to delineate only the general contours of a critical philosophy of immanence. Many ways still exist to construe it. But Spinoza and the other "heretics" he engendered, with their quarrels, adventures, insights, and mistakes, add up to a worthwhile, if partial and open-ended, philosophical enterprise. The search for lucidity and disillusionment may never attain a final goal or provide more than partial emancipation; yet it will always accept the immanent world, with its finitude and inherent uncertainties, as the overall domain of being and value, neither hell nor paradise but man's metaphysical homeland, a creative, even joyful vale of tears where suffering and perseverance, finitude and autonomy inform one another.

Notes

Chapter 1

1. Retaining only the *Theologico-Political Treatise* and some earlier works, like *Descartes' Principles*, with the appended *Metaphysical Thoughts*, which do not necessarily express the author's intent.

2. Yirmiyahu Yovel, *Kant and the Philosophy of History* (Princeton: Princeton University Press, 1980), esp. pp. 88ff.

3. Lucretius, *De rerum natura* 1.101; quoted by Kant in his *Religion Within the Limits of Reason Alone*, tr. T. M. Greene and H. H. Hudson (New York: Harper & Row, 1950), p. 122; *Kants Werke*, Akademie Textausgabe (Berlin: Walter de Gruyter, 1968), 6: 131.

4. Julius Guttmann, *Mendelssohns Jerusalem und Spinozas Theologisch-Politischer Traktat* (48. Bericht der Hochschule für die Wissenschaft des Judentums, Berlin, 1931), p. 36 n. See also idem., *Religion and Science* (Hebrew; Jerusalem: Magnes Press, 1955).

5. For other and different aspects of the Spinoza–Kant relation, see Henry Allison, "Kant's Critique of Spinoza," in Richard Kennington (ed.), *The Philosophy of Baruch Spinoza* (Washington: Catholic University of America Press, 1980), pp. 199–228; cf. José Castaing, *Kant et Spinoza* (mimeograph, Paris, 1988).

6. See Carl Gebhardt, *Spinoza* (Leipzig: Reclam Verlag, 1932), p. 65.

7. Leo Strauss, *Persecution and the Art of Writing* (Glencoe, Ill.: Free Press, 1952). This involves hiding the esoteric meaning under a cover of intentional ambiguities, sometimes even contradictions, and extensive use of pious phraseology and quotations. When Spinoza in his *Theologico-Political Treatise* (p. 182, *Opera* 3: 173) quotes ironically the Dutch saying *keen ketter sonder letter* (there is no heretic without a [biblical] verse), he scores another masterly coup, since the irony lies on a higher level and the saying applies to the author as well. The need for prudence is explicitly declared when Spinoza, following Descartes (*Discourse on Method*, pt. 3), lays down the rule of conforming to the ways of speech of the masses (see *Treatise on the Intellect* 17); and when Spinoza

writes to Oldenburg (letter 73, 2: 298, *Opera* 4: 306–8) that in his *Theologico-Political Treatise* he tried to clear himself of the charge of atheism.

8. On Kant's relationship with contemporary censorship Emil Fromm offers a detailed analysis, based on the Royal Archives of Berlin (see *Kant und die preussische Censur* [nach den Akten im Königl. geheimen Staatsarchiv, Hamburg & Leipzig: Voss, 1894]). Other signs of this conflict are Kant's prudent discussions of political authority (see *Theory and Practice in Werke*, Akademie Textausgabe 8: 273–313; *Metaphysics of Morals*, pt. 1: *The Metaphysical Elements of Justice*, tr. J. Ladd [New York: Library of Liberal Arts, 1965], *Werke* 6: 203–356); his apparent ambivalence concerning revolutions in general and the French Revolution in particular (cf., e.g., the concluding chapter of *Theory and Practice* to par. 6 in *Der Streit der Fakultäten* [*Werke* 7]; and the attempt he made in *Religion*, pp. 112–13 [*Werke* 6: 121–22]) to find a place, even if far-fetched, to counter rational principles of theology. It is clear that Kant was motivated by a desire to avoid open conflict with the religious public (see *Kant and the Philosophy of History*, pp. 215ff).

9. A major device which both Spinoza and Kant use is to declare the compatibility of reason with Scripture (or with theology; see *Metaphysical Thoughts*, chap. 8; *Theologico-Political Treatise*, chap. 15; *Religion*, p. 11 [*Werke* 6: 13]). However, this is mere lip service to an idea that both philosophers actually refute in their books.

10. This is indicated in the *Ethics* (pt. 4, prop. 37): "Whatsoever we desire or do, whereof we are the cause in so far as we possess the idea of God or know God, I set down to *religion*." This description refers neither to historical religion nor to purified *religio catholica*, but to the highest metaphysical stage. The man who understands, through an articulated system, the identity of God with the totality of the world and his own place within this totality, has attained liberation and a new emotional status, dominated by joy and the love of God and marked by "active" (free) desires and motivations. In line with this, Spinoza in the same proposition gives the concept of piety (*pietas*) a philosophical definition par excellence, as distinguished from the popular meaning of this concept in his *Theologico-Political Treatise*.

11. This idea may partly invoke Aristotle's concept of practical reason.

12. Spinoza employs what he calls the "common" definition of (distributive) justice, i.e., "the constant and perpetual will to render every man his due" (*TTP*, chap. 4, *Opera* 3: 59).

13. Spinoza does formulate such a transition in his treatment of *notiones communes* (see *Ethics*, pt. 2, props. 37–39, and note 6 to the *TTP*).

14. The idea is that the man who falls short of philosophical reason can in the meantime rearrange his lower powers of imagination and association (memory) in a way that is conducive to semirational behavior. This behavior will have all the outer features and social benefits of rational conduct, only it will be less stable and, most important, it will lack power to liberate the agent and transform his inner life and personality.

15. I refer to all modes of mediation between spontaneity and receptivity, as

expressed in the fields of action, volition, natural teleology, etc., and not only in the field of knowledge.

16. Such as the "typics," the historical process, or the postulate of God's existence.

17. "If men were so constituted by nature that they desired nothing but what is designated by true reason, society would obviously have no need of laws; it would be sufficient to inculcate true moral doctrines; and men would freely, without hesitation, act in accordance with their true interests" (*TTP*, p. 73, *Opera* 3: 73).

18. See Strauss, *Persecution and the Art of Writing*, p. 46.

19. Spinoza's critical attitude toward literal meaning is similar to the critical attitude required in his and Descartes' science to sensations and empirical data. They serve as a starting point for knowledge and present the investigator with his questions; but in order to understand and define them he needs additional data and principles.

20. Spinoza does not use this terminology, but a perusal of chapter 7 of the *Theologico-Political Treatise* will show a strong analogy.

21. One such presupposition was that the Bible uses language *ad captum vulgi* (according to the comprehension of the multitude). Spinoza, who also knew the Talmudic equivalent ("Torah spoke the language of men" [Babylonian Talmud, *Brakhot* 31b; *Yebamot* 71a]) and the ways in which the idea was formerly interpreted, differed radically in his own interpretation. He denies that the Bible transmits higher knowledge in popular language, or that it is composed of two levels, esoteric and exoteric. For him both the significance and the wording of the Bible belong to the same level of *imaginatio*; and therefore it is futile to look for any hidden meaning that transcends the comprehension of the vulgar. This view is clearly derived from Spinoza's own scientific account of the nature of prophecy; and although he attempts to find support for it in the Bible itself, in fact this is a general rationalistic presupposition derived from his philosophy and then superimposed on the text.

22. P. F. Moreau, "La méthode d'interprétation de l'Ecriture Sainte," in *Spinoza, science et religion*, ed. R. Bouveresse, Actes du Colloque, Cerisy-la-Salle, 1982 (Paris: Vrin, 1988), pp. 109–14.

23. *Rel.*, pp. 100–105; *Werke* 6: 109–14.

24. *Ibid.*, p. 100, *Werke* 6: 110: "If such an empirical faith, which chance, it would seem, has tossed into our hands, is to be united with the basis of a moral faith . . . an exposition of the revelation which has come into our possession is required, that is, a thoroughgoing interpretation of it in a sense agreeing with the universal practical rules of a religion of pure reason. For the theoretical part of ecclesiastical faith cannot interest us morally if it does not conduce to the performance of all human duties as divine commands (that which constitutes the essence of all religion)."

25. *Rel.*, p. 101, *Werke* 6: 110: "This interpretation may, in the light of the text [of the revelation], appear forced—it *may often really be forced*; and yet if the text can possibly support it, it must be preferred to a literal interpretation

which either contains nothing at all [helpful] to morality or else actually works counter to moral incentives" (emphasis added).

26. Johann David Michaelis (1717–1791). Kant contends with Michaelis's posthumous essay, published in 1792 (a year prior to the publication of the *Religion*), where Michaelis accepts the literal meaning of Psalm 59:11–16, in which the poet prays for a cruel revenge on his enemies ("Consume them in wrath . . .").

27. See *Der Streit der Fakultäten*, *Werke* 7: 38–47.

28. In the *Religion*, Kant gives a series of doubtful reasons: (1) that it is traditional in all religions to twist a text for desirable purposes; (2) that his method does not violate the literal meaning to a great extent, since ancient mythologies share a hidden disposition to morality; (3) that the author might have meant what Kant attributes to him. Yet these arguments sound rather like excuses: (1) A prevalent custom is clearly not ipso facto justified. (2) What about cases in which the violation does occur? And even where there is a hidden moral implication, it is certainly not identical with the literal meaning. (3) The probability of such a case is very low (cf. Psalm 59:11–16). It is just as probable (and even more so), that the poet meant what he actually said.

29. See *Kant and the Philosophy of History*, esp. chap. 6.

30. Sylvain Zac, *Spinoza et l'interprétation de l'Ecriture* (Paris: Presses Universitaires de France, 1965).

31. Gershom Scholem, *Sabbatai Sevi—The Mystical Messiah, 1626–1676* (Princeton: Princeton University Press, 1973).

32. Noncontradiction is maintained by violating the literal meaning of the Bible, especially of those verses that have to do with the nature of reason and rationality. Typical examples are his comments on King Solomon (*TTP*, p. 44, *Opera* 3: 45); his casuistic arguments about the prohibition to eat from the tree of knowledge (*TTP*, pp. 63ff., *Opera* 3: 63ff.); or the allegorical and rather twisted interpretation of the critical dictum, "he that increaseth knowledge increaseth sorrow," which flatly contradicts the crux of Spinoza's ethics and anthropology (*Ethics*, pt. 4, prop. 17S).

33. See my detailed criticism of this doctrine in *Kant and the Philosophy of History*, pp. 287–98.

34. In saying this I do not mean to uphold Spinoza's scientific method in detail. Reducing the Bible to mere philological and historical factors cannot provide an exhaustive understanding of the phenomenon and even misses the central point. Biblical science must undoubtedly use genuine religious categories and treat the Bible as a religious document.

CHAPTER 2

1. Hegel, *Wissenschaft der Logik*, ed. G. Lasson (Hamburg: Meiner, 1963), 2: 217, my translation; cf. *Hegel's Science of Logic*, tr. A. V. Miller (London: Allen & Unwin, 1969), p. 580.

2. Ibid., p. 218 / p. 581; my translation.

3. *Critique of Pure Reason*, tr. Norman Kemp Smith (London: Macmillan, 1929, 1970), B xxxvi.

4. "Wenn man anfängt zu philosophieren, so muss man zuerst Spinozist sein" (*Geschichte der Philosophie*, in *Werke* [Frankfurt: Suhrkamp, 1971] 20: 165); Eng.: *Lectures on the History of Philosophy*, tr. E. S. Haldane & F. H. Simson (London: Routledge & Kegan Paul, 1955), 3: 257 (my translation).

5. *Phänomenologie des Geistes*, ed. J. Hoffmeister (Hamburg: Meiner, 1952), p. 19.

6. By "all relevant sources" I mean both explicit and implicit sources. The first includes, of course, Hegel's overt references to Spinoza in his *Lectures on the History of Philosophy* and in specific notes in the *Logic* and elsewhere. But in addition—and taking Hegel's own advice—I shall draw from the actual discussion of the *Logic*, where an implicit critique of Spinoza is being carried out in the reworking of such categories as Substance and Absolute, and in the crucial transition from the Objective Logic to the Subjective Logic.

7. *History of Philosophy*, 3: 282.

8. See Kant, *Critique of Pure Reason*, A 725–737/B 752–766; also, Yirmiyahu Yovel, *Kant and the Renewal of Metaphysics* (Hebrew; Jerusalem: Bialik Institute, 1973), chap. 8.

9. *History of Philosophy*, 3: 287.

10. There is indeed a reflective idea (*Idea ideae*) mounted over any particular idea, but there is no single divine *ego cogito* which unites them by ascribing them all to his singular subjective identity.

11. For a further analysis of Hegel's "becoming God" and the "truly revolutionary rupture it makes with the tradition of theology as a whole," see L. Œing-Hanhoff, "La nécessité historique du concept hégélien de Dieu," in Guy Planty-Bonjour (ed.), *Hegel et la Religion* (Paris: PUF, 1982), pp. 78–100.

12. Emil Fackenheim has stressed this in his *Religious Dimension in Hegel's Thought* (Boston: Beacon Press, 1967). It must be added that this is only a dimension, a moment of the Hegelian synthesis and not its totality. Social, political, and cultural processes are equally present; and by giving history a semireligious dimension they are elevated in their ontological status. The importance of social praxis in Hegel is not diminished, but rather emphasized by recognizing its semireligious context.

13. See Œing-Hanhoff, "La nécessité historique"; and: "The realization of freedom is the realization of the unity of the divine and human nature. . . . Hegel recognizes, of course, that this historical development toward the full consciousness of man's rational freedom involves a *reciprocal* action on the part of God and man, a 'cooperation' which is one of the truths manifest in the Lutheran conception of the Eucharistic celebration" (James Yerkes, *The Christology of Hegel* [Albany, N.Y.: SUNY, 1983], pp. 156, 158).

14. See Pierre Macherey, *Hegel ou Spinoza* (Paris: Maspero, 1979), p. 32.

15. *History of Philosophy*, 3: 252; *Hegel's Logic* (tr. from the *Encyclopaedia*, part 1, 1830), by William Wallace (Oxford: Clarendon, 1975), par. 151.

16. In speaking of Spinoza as "oriental," Hegel avoids a problem. The nov-

elty of Judaism, for Hegel, is that the former, merely naturalistic God has been personified. This does not fit very well with Spinoza, so Hegel sees him as retreating from Judaism to some oriental paganism.

17. See Hegel's *Early Theological Writings*, tr. T. M. Knox (Chicago: Chicago University Press, 1948), pp. 68–69; see also *Vorlesungen über die Philosophie der Religion*, the section on "Die Religion der Erhabenheit"; also the section in the *Phänomenologie* where Judaism is analyzed as alienation without expressly naming it (pp. 158–60). I have dealt with this problem in my "Hegels Begriff der Religion und die Religion der Erhabenheit," *Theologie und Philosophie* 51 (1976): 512–37; French version in *Hegel et la Religion*, ed. G. Planty-Bonjour (Paris: PUF, 1982), pp. 151–75.

18. Ironically, it is Spinoza—mediated by Mendelssohn and Kant—who strengthened Hegel's one-sided view of Judaism as pure "legalism," in which the servitude of man to God (the essence of Judaism for Spinoza) was expressed. In Spinoza, however, this "fear and trembling" posture is not dominant or specific for Judaism.

19. Spinoza rejects the idea of the incarnated "son of God" as he does all miracles. Even in his most sympathetic words concerning Jesus, Spinoza presents him as a man who had attained perfection, not as God—a notion which Spinoza clearly says he does not understand. Moreover, even the flattering things he says about Jesus as a man are attributed not to Jesus himself, but to the Scripture. Even on the basis of the Bible itself, if we avoid the additional burden of church dogmata, all we can infer is the superiority of Jesus over all other prophets, but only as a man.

20. In the *Phänomenologie [of Spirit]*, Hegel even seems to insist on the incarnation as a real and particular historical event, Absolute Spirit embodied in the particular person of Jesus. This is a bizarre idea, incoherent in Hegel's system, which—as Charles Taylor suggests—must see incarnation as a universal phenomenon, carried equally by all men and women in their history, and who viewed Jesus as an exemplary man, not God. The statement in Phänomenologie, if it is not made in the language of metaphoric *Vorstellung*, either stands unexplained or is to be taken as a critique of Catholic fetishism, ending in the absurdity of the Crusades. See Charles Taylor, *Hegel* (Cambridge: Cambridge University Press, 1975), pp. 489–94; see also Emil Fackenheim, *The Religious Dimension in Hegel's Thought* (Boston: Beacon Press, 1967), esp. chap. 5. In this section I adhere more closely to the letter of Hegel's interpretations of Christian dogma in the narrow sense (which, however, as we see from the literature, are also a matter of some debate). In my foregoing discussion I went beyond this narrow sense to expose the theological allegory embodied in the broader contours of Hegel's system—especially his philosophy of history, in which I found a heterodox Protestant deep-structure which provides a broader philosophical interpretation of incarnation. D. F. Strauss has brought out this idea in his *Das Leben Jesu* (1839), esp. vol. 2, par. 149. I certainly concur with Karl Löwith, who says that Strauss' reading is implied in Hegel himself (*From*

Hegel to Nietzsche [New York: Anchor Books, 1967], p. 330). See also Œing-Hanhoff, "La nécessité historique."

21. It can be argued that Hegel also secularizes "divine history," but this is true only in form, not in content. Hegel retains the substance of this idea and only translates it from the metaphor of religion to the conceptual language of philosophy. His secularization is also *sacralization*, whereas Spinoza desacralizes history altogether and under whatever form it may take.

22. If this view is true, how can we explain that there is for Spinoza an infinity of attributes which the human mind cannot know? What sense is there in a subjective projection of the mind to which the mind itself has no access? The limitation of our knowledge of the attributes will make sense only if the attributes are understood as real aspects of God—as Spinoza indeed intends them to be. It is true that Spinoza has problems deriving the material qualities of the attributes ("extension," "thought") by sheer analysis of the concept of substances. Therefore, he must appeal to the actual experiencing of the mind (as *intellectus*, not as *imaginatio*) to fill in the undeducible contents. To what extent this is incongruent with the rest of Spinoza's system depends on how strict an a priorist we construe him to be. But the problem concerns in any case the method of knowledge and not its outcome. There is no doubt that what the intellect thus attributes to the substance is considered by Spinoza to be two real and objective aspects of the universe. Only this enables us to have objective knowledge at all, for such knowledge takes place only by laws and causal explanations that necessarily presuppose either "extension" or "thought" as their fundamental category. Denying natural entities any one of these characteristics as real will make objective knowledge impossible, just as their underlying presence is a necessary condition for it. The attributes are "lower" epistemologically than the substance in that they are necessary only for knowing particular things in the universe, which must fall within some qualified range of phenomena and under specific natural laws, but they are not necessary for knowing a priori the substance-God as such. In this sense, the attributes are the aspects in which God opens up toward the realm of particularity; they are the material substrate of the *natura naturata*—but as such, precisely, they are real and objective.

Similarly, there is no doubt that Spinoza considered the particular modes as real entities, enjoying individuality and their own mode of existence (even of necessary existence). All existence is necessary in Spinoza, but there are two different kinds of existence (and of necessity). Existence can flow, necessarily, either from the essence of an entity or from something else, considered as its cause. The first kind of existence is eternal (in the sense of supratemporal), belonging to God or substance alone; the second kind is finite existence, belonging to the particular modes and expressed in their *duratio*. This term does not signify time in Spinoza, but a certain mode of being, the kind which must eventually pass away—a mode of existence which is proper to finite (and therefore perishable) things. They are real; but they merely endure.

The endeavor (*conatus*) to so endure also gives finite things their singular individuality (another sign of their actuality). *Conatus* is defined as the very being of the finite mode, not as a special activity on its part. *Duratio* and *conatus*, the specific mode of being of finite things and what makes them separate individuals, are thus, not surprisingly, linked together in Spinoza.

The only reality that finite modes seem to lack is the eternal kind; but this statement, too, must be qualified. In a series of concise and connected passages, the most speculative in his work, Spinoza makes clear that finite modes, too, when grasped from the highest standpoint of knowledge (*scientia intuitiva*) are conceived as "true and real" even in the sense of eternity (*Ethics*, pt. 5, prop. 29S). Existence is then attributed to them not merely as duration but also in terms of "the very nature of existence, which is assigned to particular things because they follow . . . from the eternal necessity of God's nature" (pt. 2, prop. 45S). This is based on the crucial principle of particularization (pt. 1, prop. 16) which states that an infinite range of particulars must ensue necessarily from God in a logical-eternal order.

This conclusion is taken a step forward if we consider that *scientia intuitiva*, the highest degree of knowledge, involves grasping a particular mode through its inherence in God, and thereby also views God through his finite expression in particular things. This reciprocity is essential to Spinoza and what gives it power and depth also provides the deepest grasp of reality, applicable not only to individual things but to the totality as such. Equipped with this higher viewpoint, we can come back, as it were, from book 5 to book 1 of the *Ethics* and gain a deeper insight into God and his ontological structure. What Spinoza says is that God too is grasped and exists in his true reality only as particularized; and, therefore, his particularization, according to proposition 1.16, is not an additional act of the absolute but one which is constitutive of it. In other words, from the standpoint of *scientia intuitiva*, the finite and the infinite sides of the totality are mutually dependent; God in the aspect of infinity, as *natura naturans*, is cause of himself only by being the cause of his own finite aspect, as *natura naturata*.

23. Recently there has been a trend to bring Spinoza and Hegel much closer than can be, I think, admitted. Errol Harris criticizes Hegel for not having seen that Spinoza is already himself almost a Hegelian. This seems to take matters too far—and much beyond the hard core of difference which I maintain remains. Pierre Macherey, in a more restricted move, also leads Spinoza a long way toward Hegel while taking, on the remaining issues, the Spinozistic alternative against Hegel and seeking, without pretending to find, another dialectic than Hegel's (possibly a materialistic one) to do the job that, Macherey feels, Spinoza was groping for and Hegel performed with a wrong kind of dialectic (see his *Hegel ou Spinoza*, note 14, above). Apart from my scepticism about the conceptual possibility of a materialistic dialectic (dialectical logic requires a subject-matter capable of interiorization and a kind of "memory," otherwise dual negation will not result in something new but will, as in formal logic, merely return to the point of departure), I am more at peace than Macherey with the current view that in Spinoza an actual breach occurs between the finite

and the infinite, even if this comes as a result of criticism and is opposed to Spinoza's own intention.

24. Macherey tries to minimize this result, but with little conviction. See his *Hegel ou Spinoza* (note 14).

25. I mean his theory that God as infinite comprises no negation (*Ethics*, pt. 1, ax. 6, exp., pt. 1, prop. 8S)—while determinate items involve it necessarily (*determinatio negatio est*). The latter principle is highly praised by Hegel as a predialectical intuition, which it is not. Spinoza did see, of course, that negation is constitutive of any specification; but precisely for this reason he denied negation from God as totality and arrived at his basically undialectical system.

26. I stress the word *ultimately*; for this is true only in global contours and in the final analysis, not in the detailed texture of Hegel's work, which pays deep dialectical tribute to the forces of the irrational and the "cunning of reason."

CHAPTER 3

1. "Die romantiche Schule," *Sämtliche Werke* (Munich: Kindler Taschenbücher, 1964), 9: 84.

2. *Confessions* in Heine's *Prose Writings*, tr. Havelock Ellis (London, 1877; repr. New York: Arno Press, 1974), pp. 294–95.

3. Quoted by Ludwig Marcuse in his biography of *Heinrich Heine* from a letter by Marx's daughter to Karl Kautsky. Marx, a failed poet, wrote verses with Heine and loved him, but declared him politically unreliable.

4. See Eugen Biser, *Gottsucher oder Anti-Christ?* (Salzburg: Otto Miller, 1982), pp. 63–64. See also Hanna Spencer, "Heine und Nietzsche," *Heine-Jahrbuch* 11 (1972): 126–61.

5. "Zur Geschichte der Religion und Philosophie in Deutschland (1834–35)," *Sämtliche Werke* 9: 250. A partial English translation can be found in *Prose Writings,* "Religion and Philosophy," pp. 142–78.

6. "Geschichte," p. 237.

7. *Reisebilder*, in *Prose Writings*, p. 8.

8. *Germany: A Winter's Tale 1844*, tr. Hal Draper, in *The Complete Poems of Heinrich Heine* (Boston: Suhrkamp/Insel, 1982), caput 1.

9. Ibid. Draper translated *Zuckererbse* (see *Sämtliche Werke* 2: 150) as "sugar peas," which I modified into "green peas" to make clear the term refers to a vegetable, not a candy. "Green peas" is also the rendering in the older translation by Herman Salinger (New York: L. B. Fischer, 1944, p. 21). Incidentally, in defining *Zuckererbse* as "a kind of tasty peas savored in their shells" the classic *Deutsches Wörterbuch* of Jacob Grimm and Wilhelm Grimm (revised by Dr. G. Rosenhagen, Leipzig, 1914, 1954) actually quotes the same line from Heine as illustration.

10. See volume 1, chap. 4.

11. *Germany: Winter's Tale*, caput 2.

12. Ibid., caput 5.

13. But also very probably, of his academic rival Victor Cousin. On their

relationship see Joseph Dresch, "Heine et Victor Cousin," *Etudes germaniques* 11 (1956): 122–32.

14. Heine picked the same name for the French version of his history of German literature (English title, *The Romantic School*) as Mme de Staël's book *De l'Allemagne*, on which he commented: "Mme de Staël, of glorious memory, here opened, in the form of a book, a salon in which she received German authors and gave them an opportunity to make themselves known to the civilized world of France" (*Prose Writings*, p. 69; *Sämtliche Werke* 9: 13–14). Heine was clearly no feminist.

15. "Geschichte," p. 201. This idea too is of Hegelian origin, but in Heine it acquires a touch of paradox in that Hegel is seen as a pantheist and atheist. There is also, I think, a deeper personal reason for this. Heine, perhaps unwittingly, seeks to vindicate his assumed Protestantism to himself—and what is better than to see it as the root of its own *Aufhebung* leading to the new ideas of freedom, the vanguard of humanity at which Heine places himself?

16. "Geschichte," pp. 236–37; *History*, p. 170.

17. "Geschichte," p. 242; *History*, p. 173.

18. "Geschichte," p. 256.

19. Ibid., p. 275.

20. Ibid., p. 265; *History*, p. 174.

21. Ibid., p. 264.

22. Ibid., p. 280. Heine devotes surprisingly little attention to Hegel. In later years he prepared (so he reported) a special monograph on Hegel that he destroyed after his conversion (see *Prose Writings*, p. 306).

23. "Geschichte," pp. 209–18.

24. Ibid., pp. 209–10.

25. Ibid., p. 210.

26. Especially the brothers Rodrigues, the brothers Pereira, the poet Léon Halévy, Felicien David, and others. On this phenomenon, see J. L. Talmon, *Political Messianism: The Romantic Phase* (London: Sacker & Warburg, 1960), esp. pp. 77ff; see also the epilogue in volume 1.

27. "Geschichte," p. 213; *History*, p. 166 (my translation).

28. Ibid.

29. Ibid., p. 218.

30. Ibid., p. 217.

31. Ibid., p. 216.

32. Ibid., p. 213.

33. *The Romantic School*, in *Prose Writings*, p. 72; *Sämtliche Werke* 9: 16.

34. *Jüdische Kammerknechte* ("Geschichte," p. 214). The French translation reads "the Talmudic bankers."

35. Ibid., p. 217.

36. Ibid.

37. Heine's biographer, Ludwig Marcuse, rejects the word *conversion*. But he, too, paints a picture of a wavering skeptic, no longer a stout atheist.

38. *Confessions*, in *Prose Writings*, p. 306.

39. Ibid., p. 310.

40. Heine, as a young man, was a founder of the epoch-making Association for Jewish Culture and Scholarship (*Verein für Kultur und Wissenschaft der Juden*). This was for him a modern, nonreligious form of attachment to one's Jewish origins—which he did not quite renounce by his insincere conversion to Lutheranism. He saw Judaism as an ethnic and historical partnership which should continue as such.

41. This is customary: how Protestant theologians tend to relate to Luther, Christian philosophers (the young Hegel) relate to Christ, and all philosophers relate to Socrates.

42. See Kant's letter to Jacobi of August 30, 1789, in *Philosophical Correspondence*, ed. and tr. Arnulf Zweig (Chicago: University of Chicago Press, 1967), p. 158. Kant here misunderstands Spinoza who, he says, sought "a teleological [*sic*] road to theology."

43. As for Mendelssohn, who equally lost the war because he was a theistic metaphysician, Heine nevertheless praises him for his reform of Judaism. This was, for Heine as historian, another phase in the evolution of religion in Germany: Mendelssohn did for the Jews what Luther did for the Christians—restoring the Bible in face of the Talmud, which is the "Catholic" element in Judaism. Heine oversimplifies the fact that Mendelssohn was, indeed, a major figure in Jewish history, leading to secular learning and through it to religious skepticism (this against Mendelssohn's wish). Mendelssohn, dialectically, encouraged a "Spinozistic" phenomenon among later Jewish generations.

44. Jews wrote much more about this-worldly affairs and their sanctified meaning, though they did so in a clearly defined and regimented way. This is what hostile critics viewed as the "mere" legalism of the Jews. In this respect, Hess had a more adequate view of Judaism (see discussion below), viewing its difference from Christian mortification not as quantitative, as did Heine, but as a difference in kind.

45. Jean-Pierre Lefebvre, "Heine, Hegel et Spinoza," *Cahiers Spinoza* 4 (1982–1983): 212.

46. *Die heilige Geschichte der Menschheit* von einem Jünger Spinozas, 1837. For a more detailed account of this work see S. Avineri, *Moses Hess* (New York: New York University Press, 1985), pp. 21–46. See also J. L. Talmon, *Political Messianism*, p. 211. Moses Hess's works have been recently edited by Wolfgang Mönke, *Moses Hess: Philosophische und sozialistische Schriften, 1837–1850*, 2d ed. (Ruggell [Liechtenstein]: Topos, 1980).

47. For detailed accounts of Hess, consult Edmund Silberner, *Moses Hess—Geschichte seines Lebens* (Leiden: Brill, 1966); Auguste Cornu, *Moses Hess et la gauche hégélienne* (Paris: Alcan, 1931); Shlomo Na'aman, *Emanzipation und Messianismus: Leben und Werk des Moses Hess* (Frankfurt: Campus, 1982); Zvi Rosen, "Der Einfluss von Moses Hess auf die Frühschriften von Karl Marx," *Jahrbuch des Instituts für deutsche Geschichte*, ed. W. Grab (Tel-Aviv: Tel-Aviv University, 1979), 8: 143–74. English works include Avineri's book cited in note 46 and essays or book chapters by Isaiah Berlin, "The Life and Opinions

of Moses Hess," repr. in *Against the Current* (New York: Viking, 1980), Sidney Hook (repr. in *From Hegel to Marx* [Ann Arbor, University of Michigan Press, 1962]), and Georg Lukács (repr. as "Moses Hess and the Problem of Idealist Dialectics," *Telos* 10 [1971]: 3–34), among others. On Hess and Spinoza see Michel Espagne, "Le Spinozisme de Moses Hess," in *Spinoza entre Lumière et Romantisme, Les Cahiers de Fontenay*, 1985, pp. 143–55.

48. G. D. Cole, *A History of Social Thought* (London: Macmillan, 1955), 1: 240.

49. On this I concur with Avineri. However, Avineri (*Moses Hess*, p. 44) sees in the socialist synthesis "a new synthesis of Judaism and Christianity" whereas I maintain that it transcends both Judaism and Christianity and moves toward a new secular universe which negates all historical religions yet preserves and elevates their vision of redemption to a universal level. Still, the universal vision had itself issued from a Jewish nucleus.

50. "Kommunistisches Bekenntnis in Fragen und Antworten" §6, in *Rheinische Jahrbücher zur gesellschaftlichen Reform* (Constanz, 1846), pp. 166ff.

51. Recently discovered by Michel Espagne in the archives of the Amsterdam International Institute for Social History. See his "Le Spinozisme de Moses Hess" (cited in note 47), pp. 146–47.

52. Sometimes Hess uses far-reaching terms, as in stating that the future all-German state cannot but be religious, because religion has so deeply penetrated the blood of the German nation which this state is about to express "as its most authentic and free creation" (*Die Europäische Triarchie*, in Hess, *Philosophische und sozialistische Schriften, 1837–1850*, p. 144). Espagne points out that even with respect to the French imperial state Hess showed manifest weaknesses (Espagne, p. 152).

53. Silberner, *Moses Hess*, p. 443.

54. Feuerbach began by defending Hegel against a book by C. F. von Bachmann entitled *Antihegel* (see Ludwig Feuerbach, *Kleine Schriften* [Frankfurt: Suhrkamp, 1966], pp. 14–77); and Karl Löwith, *From Hegel to Nietzsche* (New York: Doubleday, 1967), p. 70 and note 64. On Feuerbach generally, see Marx W. Wartofsky, *Feuerbach* (Cambridge: Cambridge University Press, 1977); and Eugene Kamenka, *The Philosophy of Ludwig Feuerbach* (London: Routledge and Kegan Paul, 1970).

55. Starting in 1839 with an article, "On the criticism of Hegelian Philosophy," and following up in *On Theses Toward a Reform in Philosophy*, *Principles of the Philosophy of the Future*, and *Essence of Christianity*.

56. In a fragment on Spinoza published in 1978 by W. Schuffenhauer, "Aut deus aut natura," in *Archivio di Filosofia: Lo Spinozismo ieri e oggi* (Padova, 1978); repr. in *Cahiers Spinoza*, tr. J.-P. Osier (4 [1982–1983]: 205–10). As it turns out, Feuerbach adapts Spinoza's parallelism to his sensualist principle: a given truth can be either expressed as thought or as a sensual, extended picture. Both are identical and the latter, in its sensibility, captures the whole content of the conceptual thought; it is a full, synonymous translation of it. This revokes the Kantian idea of schematism, but also Hegel's belief that conceptual and imaginative thought differ in form but not in content, with the former

being higher than the latter. Feuerbach reverses this order and, it seems, attributes this theory to Spinoza himself.

57. *The Essence of Christianity*, tr. George Eliot (New York: Harper Torchbooks, 1957), pp. 12–13.

58. Ibid., p. 197.

59. *Die Phänomenologie des Geistes*, ed. J. Hoffmeister (Hamburg: Meiner, 1952), esp. pp. 158–62. Without mentioning Judaism by name, the analysis here fits the account of Judaism by the young Hegel. See *Hegels theologische Jugendschriften*, ed. H. Nohl (Tübingen: Mohr [Siebeck], 1907) and elsewhere; and the more mature but fundamentally similar analysis of Judaism as a religion of sublimity in Hegel's *Lectures on the Philosophy of Religion*. I have dealt with this topic in "Hegels Begriff der Religion und die Religion der Erhabenheit," *Theologie und Philosophie* 51 (1976): 512–37 (partly reprinted in *Hegel et la Religion*, ed. G. Planty-Bonjour [Paris: PUF, 1982], pp. 151–75).

60. See my essay on Hegel's concept of the religion of sublimity, mentioned in note 59.

61. *Essence of Christianity*, pp. 532–35.

62. Ibid., p. 231.

63. *Grundsätze der Philosophie der Zukunft*, par. 53, in *Werke* 2: 315ff; Eng. tr.: *Principles of the Philosophy of the Future* (Indianapolis: Bobbs-Merrill, 1966), p. 69.

64. Even though this is an odd theory, I was not persuaded by Wartofsky's attempt to construe it as naive realism and a direct sequel to French eighteenth-century materialism. Wartofsky is led by this interpretation to dismiss as merely "careless" or confused the attempt Feuerbach makes to say something less ordinary and indeed original—if certainly incoherent. The theory (of the senses) Feuerbach suggests is a kind of inverted Hegelianism, or rather a "Hegelianism of the senses": actual reality (*Wiklichkeit*) is attained by sense perception rather than reason, but in such a way that the subject side of perception is united with its object side (just as was the case with reason in Hegel). Or, comparing this theory with Kant: the subject's perception is necessary (though not sufficient) for the object to be actual, but (1) this is a sensual rather than intellectual perception; and (2) it gives us the thing itself and not a mere phenomenon. This peculiar epistemology, despite its flaws, distinguishes Feuerbach's intent from naive realism and the French materialists as well as from idealism of Kant and Hegel.

65. I say "rather Hegelian," because sensibility to Feuerbach is both subject and object, both the sensing activity and its corporeal counterpart.

66. From this standpoint, I cannot agree with Marx's statement in his famous Second Thesis on Feuerbach, that Feuerbach lacked the principle of subjectivity. He lacked it only in the practical sense used by Marx, that of humanity shaping its world (and itself) through work.

CHAPTER 4

1. Maximilien Rubel, "Marx à la rencontre de Spinoza," *Cahiers Spinoza* 1 (1977): 14. For Marx's Spinoza excerpts and the slight departures from the

original, see Alexandre Matheron, "Le *Traité Théologico-Politique* vu par le jeune Marx," *Cahiers Spinoza* 1 (1977): 159–212.

2. "Towards the Critique of Hegel's Philosophy of Law [sc. Right]: Introduction," in *Writings of the Young Marx on Philosophy and Society*, tr. and ed. Loyd D. Easton and Kurt H. Guddat (New York: Doubleday, 1967), p. 249 (henceforth: "Towards the Critique").

3. The severance of man from nature under economic alienation is itself partly real—but as a historical, not a fundamental, state. The "false reflection of reality" is here in part a true reflection of false (alienated) reality.

4. Rubel, "Marx à la rencontre de Spinoza," p. 14; see also his "Marx à l'école de Spinoza," in *Proceedings of the First Italian International Congress on Spinoza*, ed. E. Giancotti (Naples: Bibliopolis, 1985), pp. 381–400. Cf. Rainer Bieling in his doctoral dissertation, "Spinoza im Urteil von Marx und Engels," Ph.D. diss. (Berlin, 1979). Although Bieling, in a curious and unwarranted way, dismisses Rubel's work as "quantité négligeable," he takes more or less the same stance. His main topic is the judgment passed by Marx and Engels on Spinoza at different times and not so much the underlying presence of Spinoza's ideas in Marx's thought. Bieling's conclusion—that Spinoza's image varies as a function of Marx's attitude toward Hegel (and Feuerbach)—may be true concerning Feuerbach, but is not convincing with regard to Marx. For, if we follow a thematic analysis (as attempted in this chapter), we will see how Spinoza underlies the texture of Marx's thought, whatever his express judgment of Spinoza.

5. Neither Marx nor Spinoza takes this to be mere propaganda, though, as we shall see, the manipulative element is stronger in Spinoza. Marx, in transforming the "multitude" into the "proletariat," postulates that its consciousness is essentially the same as that of the philosopher, and admitting only simpler expression, not inferior content. At the same time, he subjects the philosopher, too, to the constraints and limitations of his historical situation, thus achieving an essential par between "philosopher" and "multitude" and fusing them together in the form of the action and class-consciousness of the organized proletariat.

6. "Towards the Critique," in *Writings of the Young Marx*, p. 249.

7. Ibid., p. 259.

8. Ibid., opening sentence.

9. Marx has even been credited with the enthusiastic pun that henceforth, "there is no other road to truth and freedom except that leading through the stream of fire (*Feuer-Bach*)" (lately quoted in Easton and Guddat, *Writings of the Young Marx*, p. 95). But it has been shown that actually Feuerbach himself was the originator of the pun. See Hans Martin Sass, "Feuerbach statt Marx," *International Review of Social History* 12 (1964): 118.

10. In the *Holy Family* (London, 1957), p. 186, Marx lists Spinoza, Descartes, and others as a group of "seventeenth-century metaphysicians," a term he uses in the negative sense (but also dialectically; at the time he could not do

otherwise). French materialism is seen in this text as a higher stage, correcting this metaphysical bias.

11. This thesis criticizes previous materialism, including Feuerbach's, for being merely cognitive and not practical. Marx defines this as a lack of "subjective" approach, and sees praxis as the proper subjectivation of reality. Idealism was in this sense superior to inert, perceptual materialism, for (in Kant and Hegel) it stressed the activity proper to the subject yet still conceived of this subjectivation as cognitive and therefore abstract. The true subjectivation of reality is practical; this is Marx's own practical, or "materialist," version of the Copernican revolution referred to above.

I should add that the primacy of praxis in Marx, both in the social and the ontological sense, is the first and foremost meaning of "materialism." On this general issue, see also S. Avineri, *The Social and Political Thought of Karl Marx* (Cambridge: Cambridge University Press, 1970), chap. 3; and N. Rotenstreich's analysis of Marx's theses on Feuerbach (*Basic Problems of Marx's Philosophy* [Indianapolis: Bobbs-Merrill, 1965]). Avineri misrepresents *Hegel's* ontology, which he reads through Marx's allegations while accepting Marx's charges and characterizations of Hegel at face value; but I fully concur with the thesis of this chapter, namely, that "the pre-eminence in Marx's discussion of economic activity does not derive from the pre-eminence of material economic values, but from Marx's view of man as *homo faber*" (p. 77). Rotenstreich, while criticizing Marx's placing *homo faber* over *homo sapiens* (p. 46), recognizes the primacy of praxis as the crucial materialist issue in Marx, and states that "Marx's concept of practice is parallel to Hegel's concept of Spirit and was developed to replace it" (p. 41)—a correct observation that also underscores Marx's Spinozistic departure from Hegel. Since I had the opportunity of reading these two works in earlier Hebrew versions, let me add still another—not yet translated from the Hebrew—which I found inspiring: Meshulam Groll, "Marx's Anthropology," in his *Selected Writings* (Hebrew), ed. M. Brinker, 2 vols. (Tel Aviv: Tel Aviv University, 1969), 2: 9–78.

12. A systematic reconstruction is based upon the texts not as sources for quotation, but as a basis for construing an argument or a train of thought; it aims at tracing the inner logic and commitments of a philosophical position even when they are not spelled out explicitly; and at times it may even overrule an explicit thrust of their implications. Such a reconstruction must be made from a certain systematic point of view; and it must draw a line between fundamental incongruities which must be brought to light, and minor ones which may be overlooked. In this chapter, my point of view is that of the problem of a philosophy of immanence without inherent teleology, which underlies this part of the book.

13. E.g., "the worker can create nothing without nature, without the *sensuous external world*. The latter is the material in which our labor is realized" (*Economic and Philosophical Manuscripts*, "Alienated Labor," in *Marx's Early Writings*, ed. T. B. Bottomore [New York: McGraw Hill, 1964], p. 123). Or: "Man has not created matter itself. And he cannot even create any productive

capacity if the matter does not exist beforehand" (*Holy Family*, p. 65). In the former (and similar) texts Marx speaks of "inorganic" nature as the given substrate of work, using the term *inorganic* in an ontological rather than biological or chemical sense. It is the raw stuff of nature upon which the humanizing activity exercises itself. (See also A. Schmidt's rephrasing of Marx's concept of nature in *The Concept of Nature in Marx* [London: N.L.B., 1971], pp. 63–64.) The idea of an "interchange" between nature and man in this raw or "inorganic" sense is constant in Marx, going from the *Manuscripts* to the *Capital*, where it is sometimes reformulated as "the metabolism between man and nature"—equivalent to "human life itself" (*Capital*, tr. Ben Fowkes [Penguin, 1976], 1: 133. Also: "Labour is first of all a process between man and nature; in this process man, through his own actions, regulates and controls the metabolism between himself and nature" (ibid., p. 283).

14. As in his remark in *German Ideology* that raw nature exists nowhere "except perhaps on a few Australian islands" (*Writings of the Young Marx*, p. 418). Ironically, Marx does not notice that in calling these islands "Australian" he already puts them in a human context and undermines his own statement. From another angle, this view is reinforced by the claim that the senses themselves are historically determined. Living after the era of the great discoveries in astronomy, geography, and the like, and prior to our own space era, Marx, his thinking immersed in social and historical matters, seems to have been insensitive to the cosmos as such, which he observed only through the prism of culture and history, and of natural science as a historical entity. While Kant had experienced "the starry heavens above me" and "the moral law within me" as two independent domains, of equal infinity and sublimity, Marx from the outset views the former through the latter. The cosmos is seen through its role in human affairs, as a moment of history and praxis and the object studied by the natural sciences, which are human-historical products themselves.

15. The ambiguity gave place, on the one hand, to the crude materialism of Engels and the Soviet physicalism, and on the other hand to the analyses of the *en soi*, the *pratico-inerte* (Sartre), or the distinction between *vorhanden* and *zuhanden* (Heidegger).

16. Even natural science, the medium by which such "raw" nature can be addressed is a historical phenomenon and thus the product of the practical relation of man-in-nature, falling within its context.

17. *Manuscripts*, "Private Property and Communism," in *Early Writings*, 165.

18. *Manuscripts*, "Critique of Hegel's Dialectic," in *Early Writings*, p. 207. In Spinoza, of course, this rule applies only to particular things, whereas the totality—God—has its nature (or essence) within itself and still is natural (it is *nature* itself).

19. If so, then the contemporary Marxist philosopher, Karel Kosik, notwithstanding (see *Dialektik des Konkreten* [Frankfurt a. M.: Suhrkamp, 1971], pp. 34–35), Spinoza serves as prime model for Marxist philosophy not in his original unity of *natura naturans* and *natura naturata*, but in making the latter the new *causa sui* (see also n. 21).

20. The concept of "production" provides the categorical link between the "economic" and the "philosophical" aspects of Marx's deliberation in the *Manuscripts* and elsewhere. This is a systematic structure that is retained throughout. In the *Capital* it is called "the metabolism [*Stoffwechsel*] between nature and man" (see note 13 above). And in the *Grundrisse* for the *Capital*, Marx speaks explicitly of production and reproduction as changing the producers themselves along with the objective conditions.

21. This is approached from a different angle by Kosik. He sees Spinoza's unity of *natura naturans* and *natura naturata* as the prime model of "concrete totality," which is primary to materialistic (Marxist) philosophy and constitutes its answer to the question, What is actuality? That this concrete totality has fundamental economic categories is Marx's innovation, his contribution to ontology no less than to social analysis. Kosik himself explicitly speaks of economic categories as "forms of being" and "existential determinations" of the subject, and of their complete set as providing an analysis of "social being" (*Dialektik des Konkreten*, pp. 184ff.). But, we may add, since social being is mediated in Marx by the relations of persons to things and encompasses all modes of approaching being in general, the economic categories have even more fundamental ontological significance. For another way of linking Marx's ontology to his concept of activity (and work), consult Guy Haarscher, *L'ontologie de Marx* (Ed. de'Université de Bruxelles, 1980).

22. The mature Marx may have gone beyond this ethics to a less teleological standpoint—perhaps the single most important shift between his so-called "two periods." See Myriam Bienenstock, "On the Problem of Abstraction in *Capital*" (Hebrew) *Iyyun* 30 (1981): 75–91.

23. This mode of production must not be viewed simply as reproduction of the physical existence of individuals. Rather, it is a definite form of activity, a definite form of expressing their lives.

24. On the other hand, this was lost on many Soviet Spinoza scholars. Spinoza, as George Kline tells us, was a favorite with Russian Marxists: "Spinoza has received more attention from Soviet writers than any other pre-Marxian philosopher with the possible exception of Hegel" (*Spinoza in Soviet Philosophy* [London: Routledge and Kegan Paul, 1952], p. 1). Even before the revolution, Plechanov, a founding father of Russian Marxism and of the Russian Social-Democratic party, took to Spinoza, considering that Marxism itself was a variety of Spinozism, or, a Spinozism stripped of its theological attire. See also A. M. Deborin, who quotes Plechanov on this point in his essay in Kline's collection, and also his contribution, "Spinozismus und Marxismus," in *Chronicon Spinozanum* 5 (1927), where he further quotes Plechanov (p. 153), and declares that "Marxism, the leading revolutionary doctrine of the present, which is materialistic through and through, stems in its philosophical worldview from Spinozism" (p. 152). Deborin founded a whole school around this notion, and one of his colleagues even called Spinoza "Marx without a beard" (*Spinoza in Soviet Philosophy*, p. 15). Stalin later denounced this school—an *ultima ratio* in Soviet intellectual life—and it declined. (*note continued*)

That Deborin (like Marx and Spinoza himself) was of Jewish origin (his former name was Iofe), is a minor, though not an irrelevant, fact. We have seen how assimilated Jews in search of a universal human message have used Spinoza as a vehicle for thought. But even among the non-Jewish Soviet philosophers, their attitude to Spinoza was, indeed, ideological appropriation rather than balanced scholarship. For this reason, neither their embrace nor Stalin's rebuke can serve our analytic purposes here. They did indicate some important particular points, but their *vu d'ensemble* is usually unacceptably biased—not only with respect to Spinoza but also with respect to Marx himself. Their Marx is a rigid ontological realist, worked out by Engels and shrunk by Plechanov to an official doctrine of "historical materialism" in the most rigid ideological sense; and their Spinoza is an atheist and a "materialist" in a one-sided sense. They fail to realize the spiritual significance of Spinoza's identity of thought and extension, and view the divinity of the nature-God as spurious and the personal salvation perspective in Spinoza as irrelevant. One may think this a better philosophy than Spinoza's—but it certainly is very different from his.

25. Of course it is not the *actual* product which the worker in capitalist society makes that should have enhanced his or her subjectivity—not the bolt he or she screws or the electronic chip he or she welds. This product is already affected or determined by the current "alienated" system, its division of labor, mode of production, and distribution. Therefore, the "product that opposes and dehumanizes its creator" has to be understood in Marx in terms of the *system* it creates and underlies (i.e., capitalism); whereas the liberating mode of production must equally involve a new system of production and distribution (for Marx, communism).

26. The so-called "reflective judgment" of purpose that Kant devised for the field of knowledge (in the *Critique of Judgment*) has no bearing on reality—not even in its new, Copernican sense. It is not an object-shaping category. When studying certain types of phenomena, such as living organisms or empirical history, this principle calls for using the form of purpose as a pure methodological device, necessary from the standpoint of all rational investigators but unable to determine the ontic features of the object as a real entity in nature. Thus by Kant's own construal the cognitive form of purpose is insufficient and neither reaches nor affects the actual texture of reality.

27. I have dealt with these questions in *Kant and the Philosophy of History* (Princeton: Princeton University Press, 1980), esp. chaps. 3 and 4.

28. I say "meta-economic," for I mean the anthropological and ontological significance of material production which underlies Marx's concept of economics.

29. Marx himself used the term *practical materialism* to distinguish his views from Feuerbach's (see *The German Ideology*, in *Writings of the Young Marx*, p. 416). Engels and Lenin—and most of the Soviet Marxists—blurred the issue by ascribing to Marx an ontological realism (or materialism) he never asserted. Many other scholars, since Lukacs and even before him, rightly contested this

view. Recent analyses can be found in Schmidt (*The Concept of Nature in Marx*) and in Kline (*Spinoza in Soviet Philosophy*). Kline calls Marx's materialism "economic," but I prefer Marx's own term (*practical materialism*) because it hints at the broader context of economics.

30. The constitution of this substrate includes, of course, the social relations between humans, which both mediate and are mediated by the man-nature relation. But this dimension, important in itself, need not be spelled out in the present discussion, which centers on the origin of teleology and the natural-in-itself.

31. Alienation is central in Marx's work throughout; in his mature years he renounces the word, but not the issue.

32. A Frenchman who Marx frequently visited described him, with some simplification but also with some justice, as "the powerful investigator who had applied Spinoza's method to social science." More importantly, Marx himself struggled with Spinoza's method, writing to Lassale (May 31, 1858), that the inner structure of Spinoza's system was quite different from its overt and conscious exposition—and Marx later makes the same remark about his own *Capital*, in an afterword to the second edition of 1873. M. Rubel, who quotes these two facts, concludes that "the wish to make of his 'Economics' a work comparable to a construction *more geometrico* was certainly not foreign to the author of the *Capital*" ("Marx à la rencontre de Spinoza," p. 25). But, perhaps, what Marx sought was not the same method but another, as strictly scientific but better suited to its subject matter.

33. Allen Wood claimed that Marx's critical analysis of capitalism was not motivated by concepts of justice but by a scientific approach. (The American Marx debate is echoed in *Marx, Justice and History*, a Philosophy and Public Affairs Reader [Princeton: Princeton University Press, 1980], where Wood's original essay is republished.) As I see it, both motivations are equally present in Marx, who offers in the *Capital* "a science of redemption" and inevitably ends with providential teleology.

34. This, of course, is both following Hegel's method and demystifying it, as Marx claims he does. See Joseph J. O'Malley, "Marx, Marxism and Method," in *Varieties of Marxism*, ed. S. Avineri (The Hague: Nijhoff, 1977), pp. 7–42. Whether Marx can consistently hold to both is another question. But, interestingly, in both ways he opposed Spinoza: in opting for dialectics instead of deduction, and in criticizing Hegel's "mystified" dialectics because it deifies the rational totality. The latter move had already been taken by Spinoza, albeit without historical teleology. Marx's dialectics opposes both Spinoza and Hegel in that it cannot allow for any divine connotations; to be consistent, it must be construed as a dialectic of pure finitude (or of the *natura naturata* taken as the whole totality). In this sense, Sartre's attempts in the *Critique of Dialectical Reason* were, at least programmatically, a consistent offshoot of Marx's dialectic of finitude, in its opposition to both the deductive and the dialectical explications of the absolute offered by Spinoza and Hegel, respectively.

35. Spinoza confirms this almost literally in a letter (no. 78) to Oldenburg, and the conclusion follows from the logic of his theory. There are various attempts to resolve this problem; but my aim here is not to discuss it in itself, but to trace a structural similarity with Marx.

36. See his *Critique de la Raison Dialectique*, where this became a major problem in the philosophy of history. See also the epilogue to vol. 1 and my articles: "Existentialism and Historical Dialectic," *Philosophy and Phenomenological Research* 39 (1979): 480–97; "Dialectic Without Mediation," in *Varieties of Marxism*, ed. S. Avineri, pp. 175–94.

37. I concur here with Schmidt (reviewing E. Bloch's Marxian analyses in *Das Prinzip Hoffnung*); see his *Concept of Nature in Marx*, pp. 127–28. Karel Kosik (*Dialektik des Konkreten*, pp. 189–90) dismisses those who see in the *Capital* a "messianic" or "Hegelianizing" drive as "bourgeois" and "reformist," meaning, probably, all four terms as derogatory, but offering little more than verbal confusion to support his objections.

38. This paradox may well affect Marx's very materialism, if the essence of the latter consists, as Balibar suggests, in a critique of mystifying images and speculative ideologies, rather than in some substantive philosophy of history (Etienne Balibar, "La vacillation de l'idéologie dans le Marxisme, Part 1," in *Raison Présente* 66 [1983]. I quote from a mimeograph of the manuscript, p. 8.) Balibar, a distinguished proponent (since *Lire Marx*, in which he collaborated with Louis Althusser) of the so-called "structuralist" reading of Marx, adds in the present essay that eliminating speculation (the prime meaning of materialism, according to him), signifies "releasing history from the hold of teleology" (*soustraire l'histoire à l'emprise de la téléologie*) both "from its religious forms" (Providence, the notion of the meaning of history, origins and final ends), and from its philosophical forms: the periodization in accordance with the manifestation of the principle of the "Progress of Humanity. . . . In short, any identification of a subject of history" (ibid., pp. 7–8). This Marxist critique, says Balibar, also denounces making man, "a universal abstraction," into the illusory subject of the historical process. However, upon my reading, Marx did not free himself of a teleological illusion. If so, then his own materialistic critique should apply to the residual deep structure of Marx himself. Marx had chased God from being but, to paraphrase Nietzsche's language, he did not overcome the *shadows* of the dead God. Or, in terms of this book— Marx did not go back from Hegel to Spinoza's objective naturalism, free of any teleological patterns—as Balibar and the disciples of Althusser would perhaps have him do.

Specifically, I agree with Balibar that in Marx there is no universal "subject of history," as in Hegel's idealism; nor is there utopia in the Kantian sense of the human moral will imposing itself upon an alien nature. Marx, as I have stressed all along, is Spinozistic in seeking all historical changes within the inner forces and pregnancy of immanent reality. But this leads him to expect, or presuppose, that reality in and of itself will lead to a state where the deepest aspirations of humanity and its true need (alleviation of alienation and restoration of humanity) will be fulfilled. The problem, or the paradox, arises in Marx's broader sense of Spinozism: his combining a vision of universal liberation with the inner natural laws of reality. The teleology lies in the presupposed harmony between the two realms, and is closer in type to that of Leibniz's harmony or Kant's postulate of "God" (i.e., to what Nietzsche criticized as a "moral world-order") than to Hegel. In a word, it is a natural harmony without a direct subject of history. But in this sense it is a momentous departure from Spinozism. (I concede that the old Marx became more sober and somewhat pessimistic; his predictions were less strong and high-flown, but this is perhaps a personal more than a systematic fact.)

39. Its main danger is the total politicization of values. There can be no normative authority other than the state by which to judge the deeds of the state. In his (still Hobbesian) concern to avoid a "realm within a realm," Spinoza did not provide a higher ethical viewpoint from which to judge the polity. The rational philosopher can advise, but can set no real norms.

40. Recall the story of Spinoza advising his good landlady to go to church as planned: he respected her in her very stage of *imaginatio*.

41. At the other extreme, the multitude cannot be completely brainwashed according to Spinoza, and this provides a natural barrier to the possibility of totalitarianism. As Balibar put it ("Spinoza: la crainte des masses" in *Proceedings of the First Italian International Congress on Spinoza*, ed. E. Giancotti [Naples: Bibliopolis, 1985], pp. 293–320), "Spinoza is the anti-Orwell." Whether this is realism or the naiveté of the pre-Enlightenment is another question.

CHAPTER 5

1. See William S. Wurzer, "Nietzsche und Spinoza" (doctoral dissertation, University of Freiburg, 1974), p. 84. This study seems to contain all the quotations in Nietzsche where Spinoza is mentioned or alluded to, as well as many helpful insights. Wurzer reports having failed to find a precedent to *amor fati* in all the philosophical handbooks and encyclopedias he perused.

2. Nietzsche mentions "Heraclitus, Empedocles, Spinoza, Goethe" (*Gesammelte Werke* [Munich: Musarion, 1920–1929], 23 vols., 14: 109); "Plato, Pascal, Spinoza, and Goethe" (21: 98); in *Human, All-Too-Human*, §408 he mentions three pairs as follows: "Epicurus and Montaigne, Goethe and Spinoza, Plato and Rousseau."

3. *Twilight of the Idols*, "Skirmishes of an Untimely Man," 49, in *The Portable Nietzsche*, ed. Walter Kaufmann (New York: Viking, 1965). In all refs. to Nietzsche's works, numbers refer to sections, not pages.

4. Postcard to Franz Overbeck from Sils Maria, July 30, 1881; I used Kaufmann's translation (*Portable Nietzsche*, p. 92) but rendered *Einsamkeit* as "solitude" (not "lonesomeness") and the pun *Zweisamkeit* as "dualitude" (not "twosomeness").

5. I render this term according to its philosophical meaning, not its literal translation, which is, of course, "gay science."

6. In Spinoza, the alleged eternity of the soul, discussed in the last part of

his *Ethics* (5) is impersonal; it is the eternal idea of myself in the "infinite intellect" which exists without the body. The mind-body parallelism is not broken but the problem is shifted to another duality, that of eternity and duration.

7. They were collected and analyzed by Wurzer (see note 1 above).

8. *The Will to Power* 688, tr. Walter Kaufmann and R. J. Hollingdale (New York: Viking, 1965).

9. *Beyond Good and Evil* 13, in *Basic Writings of Nietzsche*, tr. and ed. Walter Kaufmann (New York: Random House, 1968).

10. *Gay Science* 349 (New York: Random House, 1974).

11. For example, in *Ethics*, pt. 3, prop. 13, Spinoza shifts from the original *conatus* to the concept of "the power of activity" of the body and/or the mind.

12. In the preface to *Ethics* 4, Spinoza rejects the usual concept of perfection and imperfection, then gives them a new use: greater perfection means that the power of activity has increased (meaning self-originating activity or freedom). This is independent of duration; one cannot say that a thing is more perfect because it has persisted longer in existence. Hence, the goal of increasing the power of activity of the individual is dissociated from self-preservation and linked directly to freedom.

13. This contrast remains significant even if we choose to read Nietzsche's words metaphorically rather than literally. Such a reading is invited because the crude physicalistic translation of will to power runs into grave difficulties, not the least of which results from Nietzsche's own critique of the concepts of "matter," "body," and "quantifiable space" as "fictions."

14. *Will to Power* 636. This corresponds roughly to what non-Cartesian philosophers (such as Locke and his followers) called "impenetrability," namely, the ontic quality that constitutes materiality. (In Spinoza and Descartes, extension alone is sufficient for this purpose, but Spinoza, in the physical side of the *conatus*, implies a form of impenetrability as well.)

15. Karl Jaspers, "Man as His Own Creator," reprinted in *Nietzsche, A Collection of Essays*, ed. R. C. Solomon (Notre Dame: University of Notre Dame Press, 1980), p. 153. Recall also Nietzsche's comment on Goethe: "he created himself."

16. *Gay Science* 333.

17. Richard Rorty, *Philosophy and the Mirror of Nature* (Princeton: Princeton University Press, 1980). The "mirror" in this case is the objective order and connection of ideas, which Spinoza also calls (metaphorically) "the infinite intellect of God," namely, all the true ideas with their true connections. This set exists in itself in nature, as part of the attribute of thought that does not depend upon our actual subjective thinking. Hence nature, so to speak, has its own "mirror" within it; the "mirror" is its inner self-reflection.

18. *Gay Science* 108.

19. Neither in the realist sense, nor in the Kantian sense of a necessary universal structure of self-consciousness.

20. *Gay Science* 110. By "appearance," Nietzsche seems to mean the scientific picture of a phenomenon, not its bare sensual face. Scientific "explana-

tions" are phenomenal, but taken to express some "true being" of what they stand for.

21. *Gay Science* 110.

22. *Will to Power* 512. By "logic" we should understand beside formal logic also rationalist thinking in general which uses it as a basis.

23. *Will to Power* 511.

24. *Twilight of the Idols*, "The Four Great Errors," 3.

25. *Gay Science* 127.

26. Ibid. 112.

27. *Will to Power* 488.

28. That immanence is Nietzsche's main theme and the meaning of his claim that "God is dead" was recognized by Heidegger. God, says Heidegger, stands for the supersensible world in general, which since Plato (or more precisely, his late Greek and Christian interpreters) has been "considered the true and genuinely real world" in contrast to the sensible and changeable world down here, which therefore is unreal. "The world down here is the vale of tears in contrast to the mountain of everlasting bliss in the beyond." Therefore, Heidegger concludes, Nietzsche's word that God is dead means the denial of this transcendent world, the "supersensible world is without effective power." Transcendence is negated; immanence is all there is. (M. Heidegger, "Nietzsches Wort: 'Gott ist Tot,' " in *Holzwege* [Frankfurt a. M.: Klostermann, 1963], p. 200; English tr. "The Word of Nietzsche: 'God is Dead,' " in *The Question Concerning Technology and Other Essays* [New York: Harper & Row, 1977], p. 61). Heidegger, incidentally, comes close to Heine at this point (see chap. 3).

29. *Will to Power* 1067.

30. Ibid. 1066, 796.

31. This suggests, as Schacht holds (see *Nietzsche* [London: Routledge and Kegan Paul, 1983], that Nietzsche does recognize causation, but objects to the duality of cause and effect as separate items. The world process is a continuum and a totality, where both simultaneously and consecutively innumerable features take shape and flow into each other; it is flux in the ancient sense of Heraclitus, or rather Cratylus, where one cannot enter the same river even once, yet the river flows on.

32. For a detailed study of Nietzsche from this perspective, see Alexander Nehamas, *Nietzsche: Life as Literature* (Cambridge: Harvard University Press, 1985).

33. Nietzsche would agree with Cratylus, who radicalized Heraclitus in saying that one cannot enter the same river even once, since flux undermines self-identity and there is no such thing as the same river. But even Cratylus did not deny—as Nietzsche does—the eternal logical order of the universe which the flux constitutes and reproduces.

34. I share Schacht's view that eternal recurrence appears primarily as a test for the Dionysian life; only later did Nietzsche also try to see "whether it might as well be true" (Schacht, *Nietzsche*, p. 260). This attempt powerfully

tempted Nietzsche but is overridden with problems, both within the theory proper and in its status as metaphysical "truth." On this last issue it ties in with the general problem of truth I sketched above. But even as a perspectival hypothesis it has its problems of coherence, both within the rest of science and concerning its postulates. How can identical states recur if there is nothing identical in the world? This in itself should have undermined all efforts by Nietzsche to canonize his existential fable of recurrence into a semiscientific theory. Fortunately, however, the existential and ethical function (and meaning) of this fable does not depend on its being also a full-fledged cosmological theory; hence I may ignore this question when trying to use eternal recurrence to explicate the experience of immanence in *amor fati*. B. Magnus calls it a "countermyth" (*Nietzsche's Existential Imperative* [Indiana U.P., 1978], chap. 6).

35. I am using Magnus's slight corrections.

36. But Nietzsche is less naive than the young Heine. Nietzschean man is no stranger to suffering and the temptation of pessimism and there is a Sisyphean element in the fable of eternal recurrence.

37. "Duration" is Spinoza's term for the temporal process as a *real* mode of being, before its continuity is broken by limits and measurements. The latter is called *tempus* and is considered unreal, a mere (though necessary) "auxiliary of the imagination."

38. Hegel, incidentally, unites them both in the same *telos*. The goal of historical progress in Hegel is the suprahistorical (or eternalistic) standpoint which is to emerge from it. After this occurs, there will be a kind of eternal recurrence of the same in Hegel's world too—namely, the same rational and timeless principle maintaining itself as actualized throughout the empirical varieties in time. Time will again lose its qualitative nature; there will be only chronological time, but not a strictly historical one.

39. *Will to Power* 1059, 1060.

40. One can, however, argue whether this overcoming of Christianity is essential to the Dionysian posture or only a necessary historical condition; but Nietzsche writes for his contemporaries. Even if the future *Übermensch* will celebrate immanence immediately, Zarathustra can only do so as an overcoming of Christianity.

41. *Will to Power* 1038, 1037, 1038.

42. Ibid. 1062.

43. Ibid. 1038.

44. Perhaps there is some doubtful room for a kind of left-Nietzscheanism as tried in America since the 1960s, to which Nietzsche himself would almost certainly have objected. For another objection, see Allan Bloom, *The Closing of the American Mind* (New York: Simon and Schuster, 1987), pp. 225–26.

45. *Thus Spoke Zarathustra*, "On The New Idol" (*Portable Nietzsche*, p. 160).

46. *Twilight of the Idols*, "What the Germans Lack," pp. 1, 4.

47. On this and related issues, see also Zvi Rosen, "Friedrich Nietzsches politische Welt," *Jahrbuch des Instituts für Deutsche Geschichte* 14 (1985): 221;

Raymond Polin, "Nietzsche und der Staat," in Hans Steffen (ed.), *Nietzsche, Werk und Wirkung* (Göttingen, 1974).

48. *Genealogy of Morals* 3, in *Basic Writings*, p. 543.

49. *Gay Science* 349.

50. *Beyond Good and Evil* 25.

CHAPTER 6

1. See chapter 5.

2. From "The Resistance to Psycho-Analysis," in S. Freud, *Standard Edition* tr. from the German under the general editorship of James Strachey in collaboration with Anna Freud (London: Hogarth, 1953) 19: 222; see also "An Autobiographical Study," 1, *Standard Edition* 20: 9.

3. From "New Introductory Lectures on Psycho-Analysis," Lecture 32, *Standard Edition* 22: 107; emphasis added.

4. On Freud's problematic relation to philosophy, see P.-L. Assoun, *Freud, La Philosophie et les Philosophes* (Paris: Presses Universitaires de France, 1976).

5. Letter to Lothar Bickel of June 28, 1931; English translation in H. Z. Winnik, "A Long-Lost and Recently Recovered Letter of Freud," *Israel Annals of Psychiatry* 13 (1975): 1–5. Original German (with facsimile) recently reproduced in *Spinoza in neuer Sicht*, ed. Leo Sonntag and Heinz Stolte (Meisenheim: Anton Hain, 1977), pp. 169–71.

6. From a letter to S. Hessing, in S. Hessing (ed.), *Spinoza-Festschrift* (Heidelberg: Karl Winter, 1932), p. 221; see also Hessing's paper, "Freud's Relation with Spinoza," in his *Speculum Spinozanum 1677–1977* (London: Routledge & Kegan Paul, 1977), pp. 224–39. See also J. Golomb, "Freud's Spinoza: A Reconstruction," *Israel Annals of Psychiatry* 16 (1978): 275–88.

7. His *Unglaubensgenossen*, a pun used by Heine with reference to Spinoza, and quoted by Freud ("The Future of an Illusion," 9, *Standard Edition* 21: 50) who thereby joins them both.

8. "Leonardo," 1, *Standard Edition* 11: 73.

9. Ibid., 11: 75–76.

10. Ibid., 11: 74.

11. I mean "science" as the metatheory of psychoanalysis (or other natural sciences). Freud saw his theory as a *Naturwissenschaft*, not as particular knowledge gained by the individual about himself or herself through psychoanalytic hermeneutics.

12. See chapter 5.

13. Freud's idiom is in part hermeneutical and in part semimechanistic; the latter, roughly speaking, obtains in his description of mental processes in general, and the former in the investigation of individual case histories. But the ambivalence of the two affected psychoanalysis for a long time and marred its scientific standing. For a recent discussion of this ambivalence, see Carlo Strenger, *Between Hermeneutics and Science* (New York: International Universities Press, in press).

14. Sartre, *Les Mots* (Paris: Gallimard, 1964), pp. 210–11.

15. Stuart Hampshire, in his stimulating discussion linking *libido* and *conatus*, has not, however, taken some of the major differences into consideration. See his *Spinoza* (Penguin, 1962), pp. 141–44. On some other differences see Véronique M. Fóti, "Thought, Affect, Drive and Pathogenesis in Spinoza and Freud," *History of European Ideas* 3 (1982): 221–36.

16. "New Introductory Lectures," Lecture 32, *Standard Edition* 22: 94.

17. Ibid., pp. 102–3. See also "Instincts and Their Vicissitudes," *Standard Edition* 14: 124ff., where the definition of the ego-instincts as "self-preservative instincts" and their distinction from and rivalry with the sexual instincts are restated.

18. This does not contradict my previous statement, that *libido* is presupposed by all affective phenomena; yet it is not their *unique* presupposition. Sexual instincts are active in opposing the ego-instincts from which they are to be distinguished; but as such they still are psychologically ubiquitous.

19. This has similarities with Nietzsche's account of the origins of conscience, guilt, and interiorized moral norms.

20. In his famous letter to Einstein, Freud calls this "a theoretical clarification of the universally familiar opposition between Love and Hate" ("Why War," *Standard Edition* 22: 209).

21. For a clear restatement of this dualism (including its definition) in "Ego and Id," see *Standard Edition* 19: 40–41.

22. *Ethics*, pt. 3, prop. 6 dem. and pt. 3, prop. 4, respectively. Cf. the exact opposite in Freud: "Everything living dies for *internal* reasons . . . the aim of all life is death" ("Beyond the Pleasure Principle," *Standard Edition* 18: 36).

23. *Ethics*, pt. 4, prop. 68.

24. See "New Introductory Lectures," Lecture 31, *Standard Edition* 22: 73–74; on Schopenhauer's role as a link between Spinoza and Freud—and also between Nietzsche and Spinoza—many interesting comments can be made (e.g., that Schopenhauer, as another "irrationalist," attempts to combine Spinoza and Kant, understanding the *Ding an sich* in terms of an irrational, immanent monism).

25. Hampshire, *Spinoza*, p. 141.

26. Even on the fundamental level, a pertinent difference will be noted later: *conatus*, not *libido*, is ultimately a striving for infinity, or salvation.

27. This account of the third kind of knowledge is not the standard one, but includes my own interpretation. I have elaborated it in vol. 1, chap. 6.

28. Preface to *Ethics*, pt. 3.

29. "On the History of the Psycho-Analytical Movement," *Standard Edition* 14: 16.

30. "Autobiographical Study," *Standard Edition* 20: 30.

31. Ibid.

32. "On the History of the Psycho-Analytical Movement," *Standard Edition* 14: 16; "Autobiographical Study," *Standard Edition* 20: 27–30. See also note 33.

33. "Introductory Lectures on Psycho-Analysis," Lecture 28, *Standard Edition* 16: 450. "Hypnosis had screened from view an interplay of forces which

now came in sight and the understanding of which gave a solid foundation to my theory" ("Autobiographical Study," *Standard Edition* 20: 29).

34. "Introductory Lectures on Psycho-Analysis," Lecture 28, *Standard Edition* 16: 454.

35. Spinoza seems to attribute some degree of mental life to any individual in nature, even without attaching consciousness to it.

36. Cf., e.g., "Unconscious," or "Ego and Id."

37. "New Introductory Lectures," Lecture 31, *Standard Edition* 22: 80.

38. Eternity in Spinoza is the mode of existence specific to things whose existence follows from their essence of definition, as a timeless truth. Thus defined, eternity has no relation to time or duration, not even to endless duration (*Ethics*, pt. 1, def. 8). As for duration, it is the other mode of existence, the one pertaining to finite things whose existence does not follow from their essence but from external causes. Time is distinguished from duration; it is the external device by which duration is quantified and measured. Time is thereby, according to Spinoza, only an "auxiliary of the imagination"; in providing relative and comparative values, it renders no specific knowledge of a real entity. Duration (the object which time measures), however, is considered real by Spinoza; it is the mode of being specific to finite things, whose essence does not entail existence.

39. Herein lies a crucial difference between Spinoza and the Aristotelian tradition (by which he is certainly inspired): the cognitive act by which my mind is identified with a universal kind of *logos* is an act of *self*-knowledge, not the knowledge of God or the universe as such. In Aristotle we attain this stage by knowledge of an object, here by knowledge of ourselves. In Aristotle God has self-intellection (God knows himself eternally); in Spinoza only man does. This is an important modern feature of Spinoza's doctrine.

40. An interesting return to the metaphysical tradition occurs in Sartre. Sartre combines Freud and Spinoza. He, too, defines man as desire—the metaphysical desire to become a *causa sui*, which is impossible and therefore doomed to failure; and even the "libidinal" and other concretely erotic manifestations of life, on which Sartre, following Freud, insists in great detail in his existential psychoanalysis, is fundamentally a metaphysical desire to overcome our contingent existence. While the substance of Sartre's analysis is heavily influenced by Freud, the fundamental structure of desire is Spinozistic, only the salvation is in principle impossible and man is therefore by nature doomed to metaphysical frustration.

41. Though this topic falls outside our present concern, I may venture a speculation based upon Spinoza's "complementarity" principle, which may be of some assistance to Freud. Spinoza saw the study of the body and the study of the mind as two parallel approaches to describe a single entity, using different language and methods which cannot be mixed or reduced to each other without committing a fallacy, but which have the same ontological reference. Similarly—with certain adjustments—a Freudian might say that mental phenomena are to be investigated on three different levels, each subject to a differ-

ent methodological paradigm: (1) biophysical analysis of the somatic substrate; (2) analysis of the corresponding "psychic energy" and its structural vicissitudes; (3) analysis of meaning-relations and the work of interpretation that constitute and move the same mental system. Spinoza's body-mind parallelism is here adapted and expanded into a body-mind-meaning parallelism based on three complementary approaches to the same ontic system—namely, the integral organism.

If this speculation holds for Freud (even in part), then we have found another link to Spinoza, this time on the level of epistemology. But the actual similarity resides in the integral view of man as a psychosomatic system; the methodological *rapprochement* only follows from here.

42. On this see P. Ricoeur, *Freud and Philosophy* (New Haven: Yale University Press, 1970), p. 474.

43. Ibid. Ricoeur even sees "a remarkable structural homology" between the patient-analyst situation and Hegel's dialectic of master and slave. Cf. also Jean Hyppolite, "Phénoménologie de Hegel et la Psychanalyse," in *La Psychanalyse* 3 (1957): 17ff.

44. "New Introductory Lectures," Lecture 31, *Standard Edition* 22: 75, 76–77.

45. Paul Ricoeur has tried to ascribe a "subject" to Freud, but he does so, admittedly, as part of his own philosophy, which is imbued with Husserl's phenomenology and accepts the *I think, I am* as primary. Ricoeur, however, points out "the absence in Freudianism of any radical questioning about the existential and thinking subject" (*Freud and Philosophy*, p. 420) and goes on to illustrate the impossibility of locating the subject in any of the mental structures and typologies offered by the literal theory of Freud (p. 421). Ricoeur's own "archaeology of the subject" avowedly puts Freud's ideas "in a different philosophical dimension" (p. 422).

46. "Spinoza et Freud: La problématique du savoir dans ses rapports avec l'éntendu," in *Spinoza, science et religion*, ed. R. Bouveresse, Actes du Colloque, Cerisy-la-Salle, 1982 (Paris: Vrin, 1988), pp. 77–87; see also "Le fini, l'autre et le savoir chez Spinoza et Freud," *Cahiers Spinoza* 1 (1977): 267–319.

47. "Ego and Id," *Standard Edition* 19: 26.

48. Freud seems to have in mind a literal meaning of "surface" and "depth": the surface of the body, the parts spatially closer to the environment, serve the function of the ego more specifically than the hidden and protected parts. At the same time, Freud insists that the ego-id-superego distinction is not rigid, for their limits merge in various degrees ("New Introductory Lectures," end of Lecture 31, *Standard Edition* 22: 79).

49. "Future of an Illusion," *Standard Edition* 21: 53–54, and note 1. About the private information I learned from P.-L. Assoun.

50. Ricoeur, *Freud and Philosophy*, p. 262.

51. Herbert Marcuse, in *Eros and Civilization* (New York: Vintage Books, 1955), p. 16 identifies *ananke* with the struggle for existence and economic scarcity (*Lebensnot*); but this is a Marxian bias far from faithful to the concept.

52. Ricoeur (*Freud and Philosophy*, p. 328) suggests that it may have elements of both.

53. By the second kind of knowledge, we perceive things from the standpoint of necessity and acquire in ethics the foundations for new and correct understanding. But this kind of knowledge is still general and abstract; therefore, its emotional resonance cannot supply sufficient power to overcome the affects and provoke an overall transformation of the person. One of the results is the notorious gap, of which moralists have always complained, between understanding and motivation: what we know to be better for us we are unable to realize in fact. This gap is typical of the level of mere *ratio*, or abstract rational understanding in Spinoza.

54. "Beyond the Pleasure Principle," *Standard Edition* 18: 45.

55. "Future of an Illusion," *Standard Edition* 21: 56. For Freud's defense of scientific objectivism and his attack on "anarchist" epistemology, see "New Introductory Lectures," Lecture 35, *Standard Edition* 22: 175–76; also the end of "Future of an Illusion," where science is, by implication, deified as part of the feeble God, *logos*. ("Our God Λόγος is perhaps not a very almighty one" but, by it, "it is impossible for scientific work to gain some knowledge of the reality of the world by means of which we can increase our power and in accordance with which we can arrange our life.")

56. See P.-L. Assoun, *Freud, la Philosophie et les Philosophes* (Paris: Presses Universitaires de France, 1976), pp. 99–105.

57. "New Introductory Lectures," Lecture 35, *Standard Edition* 22: 168; also "Future of an Illusion," *Standard Edition* 21: 43, 53–55.

58. "Future of an Illusion," *Standard Edition* 21: 53–55.

59. Would Freud suggest that a collective form of transference is needed here, spun about the figure of a new spiritual leader, an antireligious prophet, a modern Moses, Jesus, Spinoza or *Freud*? Is that one of the reasons why psychoanalysis, ostensibly a science, was also called a movement (*Bewegung*), and organized like one, with dissenters seen as heretics?

60. It is indeed in the "Leonardo" that *ananke* makes its first appearance in Freud. See "Leonardo," *Standard Edition* 11: 124–25.

61. See, e.g., "Autobiographical Study," *Standard Edition* 20: 51–53.

62. On Freud's Jewish affiliation see Ernst Simon, "Sigmund Freud the Jew," *Are We Still Jews* (Hebrew) (Tel-Aviv: Sifriat Poalim, 1982), pp. 173–213; see also "Freud und Moses," in his *Entscheidung zum Judentum* (Frankfurt a. M.: Suhrkamp, 1980), pp. 196–211. See also the concluding chapter in Peter Gay's biography of Freud: *Freud, A Life for Our Times* (New York-London: Norton, 1988).

63. For Freud's statements mentioned in this paragraph, see Peter Gay's chapter cited in note 62; and also his *A Godless Jew: Freud, Atheism, and the Making of Psychoanalysis* (New Haven: Yale University Press, 1987).

64. On Freud's hesitation to publish *Moses and Monotheism* while the Nazis reigned, see *Standard Edition* 23: 55–56. See also Marthe Robert, *From Oedipus to Moses* (New York: Anchor, 1976).

CHAPTER 7

1. This cosmic and moral order is pictured as having been planted in the world as specific events in time; hence the King is also Creator, Lawgiver, and the Maker of a covenant. (Creation in the Bible is not *ex nihilo*, but order from disorder, cosmos from chaos.)

2. Under another interpretation (however hard to sustain), by the recurring patterns of "eternal return"; but (as explained in chap. 5), eternal return as an objective cosmological truth is incompatible with the rest of Nietzsche's teaching. The idea should be accepted as he intended it at first—as a Dionysian myth, symbolizing the "burden" and inescapability of immanence.

3. I refrain, however, from Wittgenstein's term *the mystical*, because it suggests filling the void with arbitrary mystical experiences, cults, and the like, much against Wittgenstein's own intention. In Wittgenstein there is something "about which" (*worüber*) one keeps silent, though it can be given no positive being or content. Beyond the paradoxes of discourse, Wittgenstein tended to think of this as a kind of thing in itself. So did Kant and Schopenhauer; but Kant had no valid claim to his view. Critically, he could not affirm the existence of "things in themselves."

4. Here I refer to a horizon which (unlike transcendence) can in principle be filled with positive content but never be completed.

5. I use the word *deficient* as a *façon de parler* only; actually, Spinoza was right in claiming that nothing can be missing in a world for which no transcendent paradigm exists. On the other hand, if we admit even an empty horizon of transcendence, and see the *causa sui* as ontologically impossible yet inevitable as an ideal, then we do attribute some shortcoming to this world even while refusing to admit another world beyond it.

6. Of course, the transcendental element is said to inhere in man himself, who is seen as autonomous and the founder of his own moral world. But the actual agent is not the "empirical" man enmeshed in nature and history but his "noumenal" will, which Kant conceives as a transcendent power foreign to nature and empirical history and projecting itself against them as an Ought.

7. Grasping the immanent world as related to some form of human experience is indeed a critical requirement. To this extent idealism (in a very general sense) is related to an immanent approach. But whatever man's role in this relation, he can fulfill it only as a finite being, not as a substitute God. Kant's critical revolution should apply not only to the "thing in itself" but also to the other great dogma of rationalism as well, that of reason as a unique, immutable system. Yet for Kant this was unthinkable; indeed, it was to save the belief in an immutable truth that Kant sacrificed (and thus happily overcame) the other rationalist dogma about the thing in itself.

8. Marx sees this, though he imprisons this idea within a rigid concept of material production. In chapter 4, when analyzing Marx's tacit ontology in terms of "man-in-nature," I tried to extract a broader structure from underneath the narrow Marxian doctrine. This structure recurs in a different form in Heidegger's concept of "being-in-the-world"; both owe something to

Feuerbach and, especially, translate Kant's Copernican revolution into onto-logical (and practical) terms.

9. In analyzing Marx I attribute to him a kind of "practical idealism," a ma-terial variety of the Copernican revolution. This may indicate the way in which idealism should be transformed: making the human role in being inner-worldly, practical, and carried out by the preconscious process of life itself. And, like life itself, this process also has a historical dimension: no interpreta-tion or life-form which embodies it is produced by a single individual or iso-lated Cartesian *ego cogito*, nor does it emerge *ex nihilo*. In this sense humans and their histories are ontologically related to whatever shape and meaning the immanent world has.

Index